D0912412

HOW TO STAGE A
MILITARY COUP

HOW TO STAGE A
MILITARY COUP

From Planning to Execution

DAVID HEBDITCH AND KEN CONNOR

Skyhorse Publishing

Copyright © 2009, 2017 by David Hebditch and Ken Connor
Introduction copyright © 2017 David Hebditch

All rights reserved. No part of this book may be reproduced in any manner without the express written consent of the publisher, except in the case of brief excerpts in critical reviews or articles. All inquiries should be addressed to Skyhorse Publishing, 307 West 36th Street, 11th Floor, New York, NY 10018.

Skyhorse Publishing books may be purchased in bulk at special discounts for sales promotion, corporate gifts, fund-raising, or educational purposes. Special editions can also be created to specifications. For details, contact the Special Sales Department, Skyhorse Publishing, 307 West 36th Street, 11th Floor, New York, NY 10018 or info@skyhorsepublishing.com.

Skyhorse® and Skyhorse Publishing® are registered trademarks of Skyhorse Publishing, Inc.®, a Delaware corporation.

Visit our website at www.skyhorsepublishing.com.

10 9 8 7 6 5 4 3 2 1

Library of Congress Cataloging-in-Publication Data is available on file.

Cover design by Rain Saukas

Print ISBN: 978-1-5107-2969-8
Ebook ISBN: 978-1-5107-2971-1

Printed in the United States of America

Contents

Illustrations

Map

Text Figures

Introduction to the 2017 Edition

Democracy might not be all that elected politicians crack it up to be. In the eight years since the first edition of this book appeared on shelves, much has happened on both sides of the Atlantic to prove that the law of unintended consequences looms over all attempts to anticipate the behavior of the human race. Yet the concept remains central to the modern study of "political science" (an oxymoron in the same league as "military intelligence").

The *in situ* government being targeted by a military coup could be based on a freely elected parliament, a long-standing dictatorship, an unelected monarchy, a theocracy, or nothing more than the junta put into power by last year's coup d'état. The motivation will always be power, greed, or patriotism. It is usually a combination of power and greed disguised as patriotism. But cynics might observe that this is the real motivation of anyone seeking political office, by whatever means.

This book provides what it promises on the cover: a practical guide to the planning of government takeovers using limited resources backed by the power of arms. But it is not a guarantee of success . . .

Before dawn on New Year's Day 2015, FBI special agents executed warrants in synchronised strikes at locations near Austin, Texas, in Lexington, Kentucky, in the suburbs of Minneapolis, Minnesota, and in the brown-collar town of Jonesboro, Georgia. Among the items recorded in chain-of-evidence paperwork were a plan of operations, gun-store receipts for assault rifles and a well-thumbed copy of this book, *How to Stage a Military Coup*.[1]

The coup-plotters included a recently fired lieutenant-colonel, a former captain in the Kentucky National Guard, and a US Army veteran. Their financial backer was an entrepreneur from Texas. But the target of their takeover was the government of the Republic of the Gambia, not the "swamp" in Washington DC.

That country lies on the banks of the River Gambia, surrounded by Senegal, in West Africa. Its population of 1.8 million comprises nine ethnic groups who share five tribal languages plus English. Soon after gaining independence from Britain in 1965, its people voted in a referendum to become a republic, and a new constitution introduced civil rights and free and fair elections. The first coup attempt in The Gambia took place on July 29th, 1981, when President Sir Dawda Jawara was visiting London. It was a reaction to a failing economy and allegations of widespread corruption in government.

Seven days later, the coup was defeated by a force of 2,700 Senegalese troops, who seeped through the porous border at the invitation of President Jawara. A team of three British SAS soldiers was already conducting spoiler operations on the ground in the capital of Banjul after reaching the country on commercial flights; they carried their weapons through a Paris airport in duffle bags. One of the hostages they rescued from a Red Cross hospital was the president's wife.

Remarkably, Sir Dawda survived in power another thirteen years. In 1994, he was overthrown by a group calling itself the Armed Forces Provisional Ruling Council. The coup's leader, twenty-nine-year-old Lieutenant Yahya AJJ Jammeh, appointed himself president and announced a ban on opposition political activity but promised an early return to civilian government.

That sounded fine, but, after winning elections in 2001, Jammeh turned out to be what one western leader might call "a nut job." The former lieutenant tore a page from the Idi Amin playbook and was now, "His Excellency Sheikh Professor Alhaji Dr Yahya AJJ Jammeh Babili Mansa." This "conqueror of rivers" would "rule for a billion years" like a member of the SeaOrg. More seriously, he claimed to be able to cure AIDS and diabetes, demolished human rights groups, and threatened to behead gays. Protesters were gunned down in the streets and political opponents "disappeared." All this made Jammeh vulnerable to the same kind of military action that brought him to power.

And so it was, at the end of 2014, that a small group of middle-aged Gambian-American ex-patriots with some military experience (one had seen action in Iraq) crossed into their former homeland from Senegal (it had to be from Senegal; there are no other frontiers). The so-called Gambia Freedom League was undermanned, under-equipped, and under the illusion they would be welcomed with open arms by the guards protecting the presidential mansion. At least four were cut down in a hail of bullets; the fatalities included coup leader Colonel Lamin Sanneh.

President Yahya Jammeh survived unscathed—he was out of the country, apparently tipped off about the imminent power grab. The US State Department declared disinterest in regime change in The

Gambia, and the Justice Department indicted the co-conspirators under the 1794 Neutrality Act along with conspiracy and weapons charges.

And what of Jammeh? In the December 2016 presidential elections he was defeated by Adama Barrow. At first, Jammeh locked himself in his room and refused to accept reality. Only after Barrow was sworn in in neighbouring Senegal did the deposed president throw in the towel and go into exile.

Taking a global perspective, it's easy to dismiss the Gambia Freedom League coup attempt as inconsequential. But what happened in Egypt in 2013 was of far greater significance.

As the "Arab Spring" swept across North Africa, western pundits looked on as people took to the streets and to social media to demand greater democracy, human rights, and economic renewal. They were beaten and shot at for their pains; some degree of success was achieved in Tunisia, but in Libya the basket-case dictator who took power in a 1969 coup was swapped for a basket-case battleground of warring factions. Many observers confidently predicted this wasn't going to happen in Egypt, a country whose military was backed by the US to the tune of billions of dollars.

Those observers were wrong.

Inspired by what was happening across the region—especially the uprising against Muammar Gaddafi—Egyptians decided they'd had enough of the thirty-year autocratic rule of President Hosni Mubarak. Night after night, television stations throughout the world broadcast scenes of mass protest from Cairo's Tahrir Square. The response was brutal and deadly but not even the best-equipped military and police can supress a popular uprising of hundreds of thousands. By the time Mubarak finally quit in February 2011, 846 civilians had been killed and more than 6,000 injured.

Then the law of unintended consequences kicked in. When a group called the Supreme Council of the Armed Forces took power they announced parliamentary and presidential elections. At the end of 2011, the Muslim Brotherhood–backed Freedom and Justice Party took 44 percent of the seats and the Al-Noor Party took 25 percent. This gave an Islamist alliance 69 percent of parliamentary seats.

It got worse in June 2012 when Mohamed Morsi of the Muslim Brotherhood was elected president with 51.7 percent of the vote. It was too much for many in the West that Egypt could fall into the

11

hands of a Sunni Islamist group condemned as a sponsor of terrorism—even if it had been fairly elected. On July 3rd, 2013, the Egyptian Armed Forces, headed by General Abdul Fatah al-Sisi issued a forty-eight-hour ultimatum and then intervened "on behalf of the people." After the constitution was suspended and Morsi detained, a call was made for early elections.[2]

Brotherhood supporters protested about the imposition of military rule. That resulted in more than 600 of them being killed, 539 being sentenced to death, and anywhere between 16,000 and 40,000 being imprisoned—depending on whose numbers you believe. When General el-Sisi stood for the presidency in the 2014 elections, he was officially declared the winner with 96.9 percent of the vote, the kind of support the discredited Hosni Mubarak used to get when he was in power. Western governments breathed a collective sigh of relief.

If the events in Egypt rattled the West, the July 2016 coup attempt in Turkey was both baffling and worrying. Turkey was a controversial candidate for membership of the European Union. Even for many enthusiasts for expansion of the union, the idea of "Europe" having borders with Iran, Iraq, and Syria was a step too far. Although EU-membership might have been a pipe-dream, Turkey's membership of NATO was both real and long-standing. That signed-up status has nothing to do with the country's proximity to the North Atlantic and everything to do with the Cold War reality of its propinquity to the former Soviet Union.

But when it comes to military coups, Turkey is a serial offender. The 2016 coup attempt—if that's what it was—was the fifth since 1922. The first resulted in the overthrow of the monarchy; those of 1960, 1971, and 1980 are described in Chapter 1.

Without question, the July 15th attempted putsch was bloody and indiscriminate; the air force bombed parliament and the Presidential Palace. Although the plotters claimed resistance to the undermining of secularism, increasing disregard for human rights, and the elimination of democracy as the stimuli, it didn't look like they were riding on an upsurge in popular opposition to hard-line Islamist President Recep Tayyip Erdoğan. In fact, many loyal to his government turned out to support the police in their street battles with the insurgents.[3] The coup was so swiftly overthrown that there were allegations the whole thing had been faked.

While the Gambian coup plotters learned the hard way the cost of trying to overthrow a government shorthanded, it's also possible to have too many people in the loop. Indeed, there has to be a direct, maybe exponential, relationship between the number of co-conspirators and the likelihood of that conspiracy failing.

What happened in Turkey when the fighting died down was astonishing. The detention of 10,000 soldiers may have been unsurprising. But if the mass arrest of 2,745 judges seemed weird, so was the dismissal of 15,000 education ministry staff and 21,000 private school teachers. When the dust settled, over 100,000 people were in jail or out of work. That number of conspirators has all the credibility of a 96.9 percent approval rating.

The 2016 coup in Turkey was either faked, its players deceived into walking into a cleverly laid trap, or Erdoğan seized the moment and carried out a brutal and senseless purge of perceived adversaries.

Prefacing each chapter in this book is an episodic account of the planning and execution of a military coup aimed at usurping the elected government of the United Kingdom. This is for illustration purposes only; don't try this at home.

David Hebditch
May 2017

Notes

1 Andrew Rice, "The reckless plot to overthrow Africa's most absurd dictator," *Guardian*, London, July 21, 2015.
2 Patrick Kingsley, "Army's role in the fall of Mohamed Morsi stirs fears among Egyptian protesters," *Observer*, London, July 14, 2013.
3 "Turkey's failed coup attempt: All you need to know," *Al Jazeera*, December 30, 2016: www.aljazeera.com/news/2016/12/turkey-failed-coup-attempt-161217032345594.html.

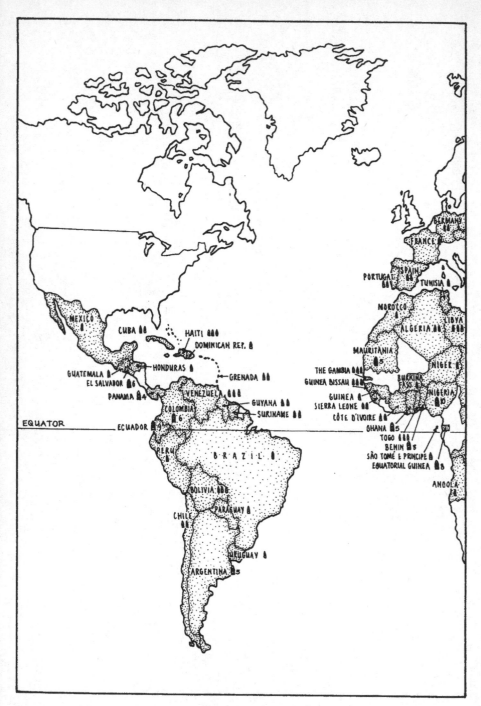

The World Map of Military *Coups d'État*

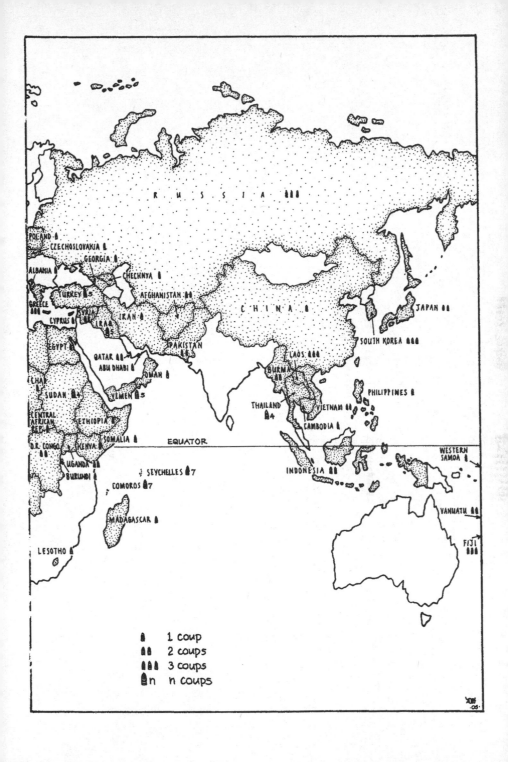

RUSSIA ▮▮▮

POLAND ▮
CZECHOSLOVAKIA ▮
GEORGIA ▮
ALBANIA ▮
CHECHNYA ▮
TURKEY ▮5
AFGHANISTAN ▮▮
CHINA ▮
GREECE ▮▮▮
CYPRUS ▮
SYRIA
IRAN ▮
IRAQ
EGYPT ▮
PAKISTAN
JAPAN ▮▮
SOUTH KOREA ▮▮▮
LAOS ▮▮▮
QATAR ▮▮
ABU DHABI ▮
OMAN ▮
BURMA ▮▮
CHAD
SUDAN ▮+
YEMEN ▮5
PHILIPPINES ▮
CENTRAL AFRICAN REP. ▮
ETHIOPIA ▮
THAILAND ▮4
VIETNAM ▮▮
CAMBODIA ▮
D.R. CONGO ▮
KENYA ▮
SOMALIA ▮
EQUATOR
WESTERN SAMOA ▮
UGANDA ▮▮
BURUNDI ▮
SEYCHELLES ▮7
INDONESIA ▮▮
COMOROS ▮7
VANUATU ▮▮
MADAGASCAR ▮
FIJI ▮▮▮
LESOTHO ▮

▮ 1 coup
▮▮ 2 coups
▮▮▮ 3 coups
▮n n coups

Chapter 1
The Military in Politics

The Merlin HC.3 assault helicopter banked steeply to the right over the Thames Estuary. A loadmaster stood braced in the mid-side starboard door, his body almost horizontal as he looked down at the dark water a hundred feet below. The helicopter completed its turn and levelled out, revealing the lights of Southend in the distance. The 'loadie', a vastly experienced master aircrewman, leaned out into the battering slipstream to watch the three trailing Merlins make the same turn onto the new leg.

It was not, he thought, a routine day for the Merlins of 28 Squadron. The aircrews of RAF Joint Helicopter Command had been up since well before dawn and, over at RAF Odiham, there were more helicopters on the apron being prepared for flight than the old-stagers had seen for many years. Since the withdrawal from Iraq the new government had continually squeezed the military's budgets, so both flying hours and maintenance had been cut back to a minimum.

The triple-engined high-tech Merlins were the vanguard for the support helicopters. A crack unit, 28 Squadron is trained in special-forces insertions and combat search-and-rescue missions. They'd collected their 'chalks' of heavily equipped paratroopers from a heli-landing site on the sportsfields of Colchester garrison in the county of Essex. Through their night-vision goggles it seemed that the whole of 16 Air Assault Brigade was gathered in chalks waiting patiently for the helis to come in and lift them to their target.

With the lead Merlin now flying straight and level as it raced up the Thames, the loadie checked back inside the airframe. There were twenty-two paratroopers wedged into the crash-proof seats, crushed in by their bulky webbing and with weapons held tightly between their legs. Jump helmets topped with scrim were strapped tightly onto their heads over the headsets of their personal radios. The loadie could just make out the 'suicidal budgie' patch of 16 Air Assault, but in the darkness could not discern what colour flash they were wearing; that would have told him which battalion they were from. Not that it mattered, 16 Air Assault was probably the best the army had. And they still had a backbone of experienced NCOs from operations in Sierra Leone, Afghanistan, Iraq and other deployments from before Britain's second big pullback from 'East of Suez'.

The two pilots were chattering away up front, identifying landmarks and potential hazards. The loadie turned back to his door, smiling. An exercise of this size was just like the good old days.

Freight traffic was already heavy on the decaying M25 motorway as it crossed the Dartford River Crossing heading for the docks at Folkestone and Dover. A truck driver, crawling along in the nearside lane singing tunelessly along to The Clash's 'London Calling', gawped as four large helicopters flashed underneath the 160-foot-high span of the bridge. He tried to follow their passage up-river but soon lost sight of them. Yet, in what seemed only a minute later, another four, distinctive twin-rotored Chinooks, came clattering up the same route. In the gathering dawn he could see the flashing of light on the blades of yet more machines approaching at speed.

The lead pilot, a nerveless squadron leader seemingly younger than the truck driver's own daughter, pushed the west-bound Merlin faster and lower. He pivoted the night-vision goggles upwards and away from his eyes as he looked out for landmarks and hazards, calling them into the intercom. The Merlin had a top-of-the-line navigation system but you could never have too many 'Mark 1 Eyeballs' backing them up.

The night editor of a 'red-top' tabloid newspaper stood on the balcony of the company's executive suite looking out over the Isle of Dogs. He liked to watch the sun come up at the end of the graveyard shift. He shivered slightly as he lit a cigarette, gazing dully out at the river from his 600-foot-high perch.

He heard them first; the sound of helicopter blades slapping the air and bouncing off the walls of converted warehouses and high-rise apartments. It was a noise familiar from too much time spent in war zones. Then he saw them, beyond the Thames Barrier, flying fast and perilously low, the rotor-wash of big helicopters churning the surface of the river. Pumas? No, they were

Merlins, but what the hell were they doing flying up the Thames at this ungodly hour?

He watched as they looped tightly around the Millennium Dome following the bending course of the river. He was admiring the menacing display of power when the noise of more helicopters reached his ears and he strained to catch sight of the next package of aircraft coming from the east. These were Chinooks, lumbering heavy lifters. The military were sometimes involved in counter-terrorist exercises, but this seemed over the top.

As the first Chinook clawed its way around the loop in the river, its blade tips dangerously close to the water, he flicked his unsmoked cigarette off the balcony. 'Good morning, Vietnam,' he muttered, and headed back to the newsroom.

The squadron leader at the controls of the lead Merlin led the snake of war machines up the river. The landmarks came thick and fast now: Millwall Outer Dock, Canary Wharf Pier at Limehouse Reach, Shadwell Basin, Wapping Underground Station and then the gradual turn at Wapping that brought Tower Bridge into view. So far, so good, he thought. The lead Merlin pitched rapidly up to clear the famous landmark then surged back down again, creating negative G-force. The loadie's feet came off the floor with the motion but he was already braced with his hands on the doorframe. HMS *Belfast*, a war machine from a different era, flashed by as the helicopter levelled out and his feet slammed onto the deck again.

'Three minutes,' the pilot called, as the familiar sights of central London rushed by his side window. The loadmaster held up three fingers to the troops inside and each one aped the gesture ensuring the whole chalk knew how long they had left to go. They made their own preparations, straightening up as best they could, most feeling for the quick-release buckles of their harnesses.

The tabloid night editor was back at his desk. He opened the contact book on his computer and scrolled to the entry for the Ministry of Defence duty press officer. The cellphone was answered in seconds.

'Eight military helicopters just flew past my office.'

'Heading where?'

'Up-river, very low and fast. Chinooks and Merlins, I think.'

'Probably an exercise. I'll call you back.'

He replaced the receiver, thought for a moment, and then found a number for the London Air Traffic Control Centre at Swanwick.

The Merlin pilot thumbed the press-to-talk button on his control stick: 'Two minutes,' he told the loadmaster in the back. As he passed over Waterloo Bridge he throttled back, quickly bringing the speed below a hundred miles per hour. There were only a few hundred metres to go. The huge London Eye Ferris wheel loomed ahead and to his left; that was the final turning point. Now the Hungerford rail bridge. He thumbed the button again.

'One minute.'

The observer looked over his shoulder to see the troops checking their equipment as the doors slid open and the tail-ramp lowered.

Glancing quickly right and left the pilot tilted the rotor, gently pressing on the pedals to swing the tail through ninety degrees. It was a tight profile but they'd practised it in the simulators several times. As he levelled off, he was already over the Embankment and creeping low over the roof of the Ministry of Defence building. A few black taxi-cabs and delivery vans were already moving sleepily along Whitehall. In the distance he could now see St James's Park and, beyond that, Buckingham Palace.

'Ten seconds.'

As the four Merlins descended onto Horse Guard's Parade, the loadies called the distances until their wheels touched the crushed pebbles.

'Go, go, go!'

Only then did the troops snap open their safety belts, most of them struggling to stand, some with their harnesses caught on webbing, others dragging their heavy Bergens from the floor of the Merlin. But they were clear in a minute, fast but maybe not fast enough. The loadie watched them lumber away, securing the perimeter as the chalk commander made one last check of the aircraft before giving the thumbs up and doubling away.

The night editor clicked the mouse-button and switched the screen to an Internet telephone directory. He keyed in 'London

Eye' and the number appeared in a fraction of a second.

'London Eye,' a wary voice answered.

'Good morning. Are you at the London Eye itself?'

'Sorry, mate, we don't open until eight.'

'Fine. Have you seen a load of helicopters fly past in the last few minutes?' The line went quiet for a moment. Then the voice returned at almost a whisper.

'They didn't fly past – they turned and flew across to Whitehall. I saw them hovering over Downing Street.'

'Really?' asked the journalist. 'Did they land?'

'I suppose so. They disappeared and I couldn't hear them any more. Now the ones from the boats are here. I'm just the security guard – I don't know what's going on.'

'Tell me about the boats.'

'Black boats over at Westminster Pier,' his voice quickened, revealing near-panic, 'Soldiers in green berets, blacked-up faces, guns...' Then the line went dead.

The lead Merlin surged away from the ground, clearing the Queen Elizabeth II Conference Centre by a few feet. The loadie, and a small but growing crowd of curious onlookers, watched the other three Merlins lift off from the landing site. The first of the Chinooks was edging in to land under the control of a newly land-ed marshaller. Then the scene was gone, the Merlin turning past the Houses of Parliament and accelerating along the river on a reciprocal course.

'Did my eyes deceive me?' the pilot eventually asked the load-ie, 'I didn't see any yellow Blank Firing Adapters on their weapons.'

'Roger that, no BFAs.' came the reply, 'They must be carrying live ammunition.'

Get Your Tanks off My Lawn

'A sudden decisive exercise of force in politics; especially: the violent overthrow or alteration of an existing government by a small group'[4] is a well-crafted description of the common expression '*coup d'état*'. However, the standard book on coups (until now) defines coups slightly different-ly: 'A coup consists of the infiltration of a small but critical segment of the state apparatus, which is then used to displace the government from its

23

control of the remainder.'[5] This both adds something and takes something away from the previous, more familiar definition; it adds the need to identify (and seize) the key control centres of government. At the same time it takes away the dimension of violence and opens up the possibility for its author, Edward Luttwak, to consider the so-called non-military coup. As civilian coups (men in suits armed with cellphones storming the radio station?) are rare indeed, this book will focus on more common military incursions into politics.

There are, however, variations on the theme. Perhaps the most important general distinction to make is between internally instigated coups and those initiated in smaller foreign states by powerful nations. Who's picking up the bill? Or, at least, who's looking the other way? Who stands to gain? Who's got an interest to protect, whether it's oil or bananas? Externally backed coups can be considered the alternative to all-out invasion. They are more cost-effective, produce fewer dead young soldiers for the sponsor's army (in turn less upsetting for the voters back home) and there is no need to get involved in the messy aftermath. The United States, the Soviet Union, France and Britain have all promoted coups aimed at getting a regime change that served their own interests. Vary from this strategic policy and you end up in... Iraq? (A coup was indeed being planned for Iraq and training was under way in 2002 when the US chose the war option. See Chapter 8.)

Regardless of whether a coup has a sugar daddy or is a home-brewed concoction, the basic mechanism remains the same: small and nimble against big and sluggish.

Edward Luttwak identified three main types of military *coup d'état*. No one has really demurred from his classifications, so we will fall in line too. There are Breakthrough Coups, Guardian Coups and Veto Coups plus a few variations on those themes.

Breakthrough Coups: China 1911, Egypt 1952, Cuba 1959

When a guerrilla army or a rebellious part of regular forces overthrows a traditional, established government you have a 'breakthrough coup' An essential feature of this is that the overthrow is a 'one-off' and not just the round of 'musical chairs' one finds with 'guardian coups' (see page 27).

The breakthrough coup that had the greatest impact on world history was the Wuchang Uprising of 1911, which ended the Manchu (Qing) Dynasty in China. The emperor had already planted the seeds of his own destruction when he decided the country needed a New Army, one trained in Western strategies and tactics and armed with the latest weapons. But the New Army also picked up some dangerous new ideas – like 'Who needs an emperor?'

A group of officers based at the Wuchang garrison on the south bank of the Yangtze River formed a Triad-like secret society and started to plot. A front organisation called the Literary Association was established. Supporters were recruited and listed, elaborate seals were carved and fancy membership certificates designed. And, in the same lock-up near their secret headquarters, they also assembled some 'improvised explosive devices'; this was their *second* big mistake. On 9 October 1911 one of the home-made bombs went off in what British soldiers in Northern Ireland would have called an 'own goal'. The huge bomb blasted the membership lists, banners, minutes of meetings and secret insignia all over the neighbourhood. The police arrived in short order and picked up all the evidence they needed to mount an instant raid against the group's headquarters a few blocks away. Big mistake number one? Never put anything incriminating in writing!

The cops moved with impressive speed, closing the city gates, surrounding the garrison and arresting hundreds of rebels and anyone who even looked a bit rebellious.

The coup plotters now faced an interesting dillema. Should they surrender to the police or make a fight of it? Instant public beheading or, given the poor state of their planning and leadership, public beheading a little later? While their officers were contemplating that issue, the garrison mutinied and its four battalions (four thousand men) got on with the job and seized the city. On the following day, 10 October – the 'Double Tenth' as it is still known – the civil governor panicked and made his escape on a gunboat down the Yangtze; China's third-largest industrial centre was in rebel hands. By the 12th a provincial republican government had been declared and the region's army commander Li Yuan-hong was named revolutionary military governor.

The country was ripe for fundamental change and one by one other provinces backed the uprising and declared themselves for a republic. One careless explosion, the speedy capture of a city and, a few weeks later, the two-thousand-year imperial rule of China was over. (The Wuchang Uprising is also an example of an 'accidental coup'. See page 33.)

Playboy King Farouk of Egypt was a gossip-page regular in the tabloids of the pre- and post-war decades. Made monarch at the age of sixteen, he had a Saddam-like passion for palaces and collected luxury cars by the six-pack. His shopping trips were legendary in the hallowed halls of Harrods. During World War II the Italians found it easy to bomb the northern port of Alexandria. The lights of the royal palace stood beacon-like in the blacked-out city. Farouk may have been bombed but the palace never was – his servants were all Italian. When British ambassador Sir Miles Lampson suggested they might be a security risk, the king replied, 'I'll get rid of my Italians if you get rid of yours!' The ambassador's wife was Italian.

After the war Farouk gained the nickname 'The Thief of Cairo' for his annoying habit of stealing things while on official overseas visits. Where most people would be happy with a teaspoon or towel from the Ritz, Egypt's monarch was more ambitious. He stole a ceremonial sword from the Shah of Iran. And after Winston Churchill had waved him farewell from the steps of 10 Downing Street, the old war-leader noticed that a priceless fob-watch had gone with him.

The kleptomaniac king was much more famous for his red fez than for his sense of humour; but he did say this in 1948: 'The whole world is in revolt. Soon there will be only five Kings left – the King of England, the King of Spades, The King of Clubs, the King of Hearts, and the King of Diamonds.' This was not only witty, but prescient; four years later he was out of a job and in the stateroom of his mega-yacht, course set for the fleshpots of Europe.

Farouk neglected the needs of his people, but it was his neglect of the army that led to his downfall. In July 1952, the military were still licking their wounds after being trounced in the 1948 war with Israel in the Negev Desert. They complained of being badly trained and poorly equipped. A number of soldiers including a young colonel called Gamal Abdel Nasser formed a clandestine group, known as the Free Officers, which easily toppled the top-heavy king. As in 1911 China, the coup was popular among the ordinary people of Egypt but Nasser's banner proclaimed Arab nationalism rather than 'democracy and liberty'. The monarchy was scrapped and by 1954 the colonel had become installed as president and prime minister; having had enough of Israel, he turned his attention to ending British influence. The Suez Canal was nation-alised and in 1956 the British invaded in an ill-starred attempt to get it back.

And what of King Farouk? He died in Rome in 1965, aged forty-five and weighing 136 kilos (300 lb). He had just eaten a meal of oysters, lob-ster thermidor and roast lamb when his heart finally gave in and his head slumped into the English trifle. From desert to dessert in only thirteen years.

The 1959 takeover of Cuba by Fidel Alejandro Castro Ruz and his supporters could also be classified as a breakthrough coup. When Castro's force of nine thousand armed irregulars marched on Havana, they overthrew the US-backed dictatorship of Fulgencio Batista. Pro-Washington politicians had ruled Cuba since Spain's 1898 withdrawal from the colony. Under various enforced treaties these had allowed nearly 75 per cent of agricultural land to fall into the hands of American sugar-producers and for Havana to become a kind of offshore Las Vegas providing booze, prostitution and gambling to tourists during Prohibition. So, in nationalising the land and closing the casinos, Castro managed to annoy both organised crime *and* Washington DC, which was backing the Batista military to the tune of sixteen million dollars a year; a lot of money at the time, but clearly not quite enough.

The outcome was the establishment of the only East European-style government still remaining in the twenty-first century and one that has proved impossible for a long succession of US presidents to dislodge. The Cubans themselves describe these events as '*la Revolución*', implying that it happened on the wave of a massive popular uprising. However, most successful breakthrough coups get called 'the revolution' sooner or later.

Guardian Coups: Turkey 1960, 1971 and 1980

Guardian coups are better described as 'musical-chairs coups'. Unlike the breakthrough version, there is no fundamental change in socio-economic structure; just the usual suspects on rotation. The three coups that took place in Turkey between 1960 and 1980 are good examples.

- *27 May 1960*. A military coup led by General Cemal Gürsel removes President Celâl Bayar and the cabinet from power and dissolves parliament. Martial law is declared but, seven days later, General Gürsel is given a non-optional opportunity to spend more time with his family. Then Gürsel announces – without apparent irony – that 'the purpose... of the coup is to bring the country with all speed to a fair, clean and solid democracy'. It takes years to achieve anything close to that, but in 1965 Süleyman Demirel is victorious in a free election.

- *12 March 1971.* The government of Süleyman Demirel is forced to resign after the military high command threatens the president with a coup. Armed-forces leaders demand a new, strong government which will tackle the anarchical situation in Turkey. The military obliges the leaders of the main political parties to form a coalition government. Violence is suppressed by force.

- *12 September 1980.* A military coup led by Chief of Staff General Kenan Evren overthrows newly elected government of Süleyman Demirel proclaiming that the *army* will tackle the anarchical situation in Turkey.

...which is, more or less, where we came in. There is certainly no doubt that Turkey super-sizes on anarchical situations. The country's border with the Soviet Union and membership of NATO throughout the Cold War gave the Turkish army a certain immunity and its long-term interference in politics never attracted criticism from the United States and Britain. This is how it was in 1980 after two decades of alternating coups and free elections.

> Within Turkey, the political situation was deteriorating. Locked in a mortal rivalry, [President] Demirel and [Prime Minister] Ecevit were unable to cope with rising political violence from the extreme right – the ultra-nationalist party led by Alparslan Türkes – and the extreme left. The Kurdish provinces of the southeast were restive, and all were governed under martial law by late 1979... Political killings, bombings, and threats were commonplace; by summer, thirty fatalities a day were attributed to extremists of left and right.[6]

Well, apart from that, how was the state of the nation? And were the *coups d'état* the solution to the anarchy? Or were they just another ineffective part of the chaos? In recent years, since Turkey decided it was a perfect candidate for membership of the European Union, the military has faded into the background somewhat.

Guardian coups like these, where the same familiar faces in the military and political hierarchies take turns to run the country, are most common in Latin American countries. In Bolivia you may have to check page nine of a local newspaper to find out there had been a coup the previous day; little if any violence, and no perceptible change to one's daily routine. But not all coups are like that.

Veto Coups: Argentina 1943, 1955 and 1976

When a coup is targeted at overthrowing a popularly elected government, it is known as a 'veto coup'. These are the kind of coups that get coups a bad name; repression and bloodshed are the usual outcome.

In 1943 Juan Domingo Perón was a colonel in the army of Argentina. He joined a clique of military plotters and overthrew the civilian government, his participation being rewarded with his first political appointments: minister of war and vice-president. In 1946 he was elected president. During his time in power he oversaw the industrialisation of the country and kept the workers onside with regular pay increases and benefit packages. However, he also took away their constitutional rights and civil liberties. But, in spite of his being commander-in-chief of the military, the army and navy took against him and removed him from office in 1955. With his personal secretary, Isabelita, he went to live in Paraguay (his popular wife Eva – 'Evita' – had died in 1952), but the social life wasn't up to much and they soon moved on to Madrid. They married in 1961.

In 1973 the Peróns returned to Argentina, where they were elected president and vice-president. A proponent of a variation of the Third Way, Perón had cultivated the left wing and the trade-union leaders while in exile; on his return he nurtured right-wing opposition groups but suppressed the left while managing to keep the military sweet. It's unknown whether anything would have come of this juggling act because, on 1 July 1974, Perón died. When power automatically ceded to Isabelita, it became clear that much of the support her husband had attracted was personal – and non-transferable. Terror groups became more active and political violence generally increased until, on 24 March 1976, the military stepped in.

Under the junta, the violence didn't stop, it just became different. The people might not have taken to Isabelita, but they liked the junta even less. What started then has been called 'The Dirty War', years of thuggish repression in which an estimated thirty thousand people were 'disappeared' by military and police death squads. The word 'disappeared', *desaparecidos*, was invented, not because the victims were exiled to Tierra del Fuego, but because, unlike in Guatemala, the psychopaths doing this to their own people made sure the bodies were not found in the ditches alongside the airport road. In many cases, navy aircraft were used to dump them, still alive, into the Atlantic. Even children were abducted.[7]

In 1982, the economy was once more in a severe crisis. As a solution to this, General Leopoldo Galtieri's junta ordered the invasion of the Malvinas, the Falkland Islands. With Margaret Thatcher in power in London, this bid for domestic popularity was hardly a brilliant idea. The reckless venture resulted in the deaths of hundreds of British servicemen and thousands of poorly trained and poorly motivated young Argentinian soldiers, airmen and seamen. Three days after the unconditional surrender of 14 June, Galtieri resigned from the presidency. Another junta took over.

The 1973 veto coup in Chile was almost as bad in its outcome, but we will describe that in more detail in Chapter 6.

Operation *Valkyrie*: The July Putsch, Germany 1944

In this book we use the German word 'putsch' interchangeably with the French *coup d'état* for variety and because there doesn't seem to be a single English word which does the job. Merriam-Webster's *Collegiate Dictionary* says that a putsch is 'a secretly plotted and suddenly executed attempt to overthrow a government'. Luttwak, on the other hand, insists that refers specifically to a coup that takes place during or in the immediate aftermath of war.[8]

The best example of this is the July Putsch – Operation *Valkyrie* – against Hitler in 1944. It started – and ended – with an assassination attempt. A group of senior army officers were unhappy with the Führer's conduct of the war and, seeing the end coming, wanted to begin peace talks with the Allies. On 20 July 1944, Lieutenant-Colonel Claus Phillip Schenk, Graf (Count) von Stauffenberg, planted a bomb during a planning meeting at Hitler's *Wolfsschanze* (Wolf's Lair) field headquarters at Rastenburg, East Prussia. The bomb was in a briefcase which von Stauffenberg placed under the table before stepping outside, supposedly to make a telephone call. Such was the force of the explosion that the officer was convinced Hitler must have been killed.

Von Stauffenberg flew back to Berlin to meet up with the other plotters – including Colonel-General Ludwig Beck (ex-Chief of the General Staff), Major-General Henning von Tresckow and Colonel-General Friedrich Olbricht. The next stage of the plot was to seize key government buildings including the Supreme Command HQ.

But Hitler was not dead; the massive oak conference table was so heavy that it had shielded him from the worst of the blast. It took the plotters three hours to get back to the German capital, by which time word of Hitler's survival had already reached General Friedrich Fromm. Previously a supporter of the putsch, Fromm decided that a counter-coup was the best course of action and promptly rounded up the leading plotters. Many historians put the failure of what is sometimes called the 'Rastenburg Assassination Plot' down to inadequate planning and a string of errors in its execution. But the instigators did not live to learn the lessons; the ones who were not shot out of hand were given a Nazi show-trial before being hung from meat hooks, a procedure which was filmed for Hitler's viewing pleasure.

Ken Connor: Thoughts on Prussian Thinking

It is difficult to imagine that even if the 1944 attempt on Hitler's life had been successful that this would have led to the collapse of the German war effort. The German military machine was extremely conventional and would obey orders to the letter. Any study of the German army during World War II will confirm this. The crucial difference between the German and British military at this time was that the Germans, because of their success in the early part of the war, were able to concentrate on their very successful conventional units whereas the British, whose every action had been a disaster, were forced to give their special forces free rein to get the victories that were so important psychologically. There is also a fundamental difference in the German and British psyches. The British function best when they are at the edge of a cliff and the rocks are crumbling under their feet, when there is only one thing to do – get your act together and go forward or perish. The Germans, by contrast, operate best when everything is functioning correctly and in the order which is pre-planned and organised.

The German difficulty is with *improvisation* due to a very conventional thought process.

This was best illustrated to me when I was working in East

Germany at the time of the Cold War. I was with a tour in a town called Ludwigslust waiting for the Russian rocket unit to leave its barracks so that I could photograph them. I inadvertently parked my vehicle outside the house of a member of the Volkspolitzei. The VOPOs were the uniformed armed police of the East German State. When I looked through his window the VOPO was staring at us with eyes bulging. He quickly donned his uniform and rushed out, incandescent with rage. He told us that we were under arrest and not to move. He then had the dilemma of leaving us in the car while he reported us to higher authorities and making sure we did not drive off. He very firmly said, 'Do not forget you are under arrest – do not move.' and strode back into his house. I watched him pick up the phone and dial before I nodded to my driver to move off slowly.

The VOPO came storming out of his house, trying to catch up with us, literally leaping up and down with rage like a character from a Laurel and Hardy movie. Such is the German attitude to authority he could not comprehend that we would not obey his orders. I can't imagine the same scene occurring in the UK or the US.

The Bloodless Coup and the Less-Blood Coup

In rare cases both breakthrough coups and guardian coups may also be 'bloodless'. Egypt 1952, Ghana 1972, Pakistan 1999, São Tomé e Príncipe 2003, Guinea-Bissau 2003 and Georgia 2003 have all been portrayed in this way. Even the reference coup of France 1799 (usually called the 'Coup of 18 Brumaire') in which Napoleon gained power was 'bloodless', but all of them involved the use of force and the threat of violence.

Here is an account of how close a Fijian coup came to bloodshed. On 14 May 1987, a group of soldiers led by Lieutenant-Colonel Sitiveni Rabuka took over Parliament House in the capital of Suva and arrested the newly elected government.

There was only [one] true, temporary, hitch. [Member of Parliament] Tupeni Baba declined to board military transport waiting outside the Parliament. 'No, no,' he protested, 'we are not getting into the trucks.' That is, until Lieutenant-Colonel Sitiveni Ligamamada Rabuka, OBE (Mil.), took a loaded M16 rifle from a soldier, cocked it, and pointed it at Baba's head. It was an electrifying moment, Rabuka recalls. He simply could not allow any challenge to the Army's authority to survive. 'I don't like pointing a gun at anyone, believe it or not. But in these circumstances, I would have fired and deliberately missed had that been necessary to make my authority stick,' Rabuka says. His point was promptly understood by others; and a Coalition colleague urged Baba to do what the military wanted. Baba boarded the truck.[9]

As Rabuka found, it is not always possible to predict what people will do when confronted with such a situation. Will it be acquiescence? Or anger and counter-attack? During Portugal's relatively peaceful 'Carnation Revolution' of 1974 a group of soldiers decided to resist; four of them were shot and killed. Supporters of the 'revolution' are, of course, likely to suggest that the coup itself was bloodless – it was the attempted counter-coup that cost lives.

In some cases, the mere threat of military involvement is enough to initiate a change of civilian regime. This has happened twice in the Philippines.

The Accidental Coup: Sierra Leone 1992 and 1996

The accidental coup of 1911 in China was unusual, but certainly not a one-off incident.

Captain Valentine Strasser has two main claims to fame: he is, supposedly, the winner of innumerable disco-dancing awards; he is also the youngest-ever head of state, other than those born to the title. Sierra Leone on the west coast of Africa is a dirt-poor but diamond-rich ex-client of the British Empire. In 1992 the country was under the military dictatorship of Major-General Joseph Momoh. At the time, Momoh was breaking one of the fundamental rules of regime security; he was failing to pay his own troops.

In April that year, 25-year-old Strasser was fresh back from a course at the Royal Military College Sandhurst. Good news and bad news were waiting for him. The good news was that he was being given a company to command; the bad news was that it had been posted up-country to Kenema in the diamond mining region and far distant from the night-life of the capital, Freetown. Nonetheless, Strasser hopped into his Land

Rover and headed off to inspect his men. His reception was understandably guarded but, his head full of the stuff they taught him at Sandhurst, he asked the assembled troops if they had any problems they wanted to tell him about. As one they complained they hadn't been paid for three months and in the circumstances it was difficult to get motivated about chasing Foday Sankoh's vicious RUF irregulars around the bush. Sierra Leone was in the middle of a protracted civil war and the Revolutionary United Front, many of whom were children, was making a bid for the hearts and minds of the people by chopping the arms off anyone they didn't like the look of. (Some years later, in a live television interview, the Joint Taskforce Commander of British Forces in the country, Brigadier David Richards, said, 'I'm not the sort of man who would wish anyone dead, but in the case of Foday Sankoh I'm prepared to make an exception.')

The fact that Captain Strasser's troops were making a little on the side by smuggling diamonds over the border into nearby Liberia was the part they didn't want to talk about. However, eager to please, he told them he was going straight back to Freetown to 'sort the problem out' and disappeared down the road in a cloud of red African dust. Now, for the average, unpaid Sierra Leonean soldier 'the problem' was Major-General Joseph Momoh. The telephone and radio messages that reached the capital ahead of Strasser said that he was going to overthrow the government. That was probably the last thing on the mind of the young career officer but, as he drove up to the door of Momoh's headquarters, a disgruntled army not far behind, he was greeted with... surrender. Unable to think of a way of reversing out of this embarrassing communications problem, Strasser shrugged and assumed responsibility as head of government – in the form of a junta of fellow army officers.

With the support of the South African mercenary firm Executive Outcomes, his accidental coup made considerable inroads into the RUF's regional power bases. Throughout this, Strasser complained that he was unable to become legitimate head of state because the constitution specified that he was too young. This problem was solved on 6 January 1996 by Brigadier Julius Maada Bio, who seized power from Strasser in a relatively painless coup of his own making. Young Valentine was helicoptered off to check out the discos in Guinea-Conakry (where Major-General Momoh had been cooling his heels) and lived off a stipend from the British Government. Elections followed and Ahmad Tejan Kabbah became prime minister... only to be overthrown by another coup.

The situation in Sierra Leone did not improve with any of these new regimes and by 1997 the RUF had entered Freetown. This came as something of a shock to Will Scully. Scully, a former member of a British SAS territorial regiment, was working up-country on mine security and taking a break at the Mammy Yoko Hotel. What started as a quiet break with a few beers by the swimming pool soon went 'pear-shaped'. The hotel was packed with over a thousand civilian men, women and children, journalists, local police and a platoon of UN-bereted Nigerian troops when the RUF attacked, firing RPGs at the high-rise building.

Fearful that the situation was going to turn into a blood-bath, the young Brit ran up onto the roof to see if he could help the Nigerians. But they were doing nothing to stop the rebel encroachment into the grounds of the hotel. Scully took matters into his own hands and opened fire with a 7.62-mm GPMG (General Purpose Machine Gun) from behind a low wall. Any hope he had of leading the UN soldiers by example disappeared when he looked round and saw they had left him to it. Before long he came under fierce incoming fire and was running out of ammunition; fortunately, the Nigerian platoon was using the same calibre in their personal weapons. Scully found them sheltering in a storeroom: if they were not going to fight they might as well hand over their magazines, he told them. A couple of them helped him by 'linking' the rounds.

After hours of this one-sided firefight, the British ex-soldier was beginning to feel the strain, especially when an RPG round just missed the wall and exploded on the lift housing behind him. Then, suddenly, he had company. A man with cut-glass British accent introduced himself as Major Lincoln Jopp of the Scots Guards. Sadly, he didn't have the rest of the Scots Guards with him but he worked in support of Scully, feeding him link to keep the hot GMPG firing into the rebels. The ex-SAS trooper found time to ask his new companion what he was doing in Sierra Leone and Jopp told him he had been training cadets at the officer school: 'I was teaching them about civic responsibilities and why they should not get involved in *coups d'état*. When they didn't turn up for class this morning I assumed they had gone off to organise their own coup.'[10]

Major Jopp was later awarded the Military Cross after being wounded in an engagement in Sierra Leone. However, it was later alleged that the engagement involved a number of mercenaries fighting in support of a West African 'peace-keeping' force to overthrow the military government and reinstate Kabbah.[11] Coincidentally, Jopp had served in the

Scots Guards with Colonel Tim Spicer, the founder of the controversial private military company Sandline, a firm associated with Executive Outcomes (see Chapter 9). Will Scully was awarded the Queen's Gallantry Medal for his single-handed defence of the Mammy Yoko Hotel.

Valentine Strasser was allowed to return to Freetown, where he now lives with his mum in a quiet suburb.

The Faux *Coup d' État*

A *faux* or 'fake' coup is one staged by the incumbent government with the objective of discrediting the legitimate opposition. It has all the packaging of a real coup and may even be violent, but basically it is a frame-up. Bombs may be heard going off at night and troops may drive through the main square at dawn, but the *faux* coup will only last as long as it will take to arrest the opposition politicians and their supporters and to plant 'evidence' of a conspiracy in their homes and offices.

President Teodoro Obiang Nguema Mbasogo of Equatorial Guinea is a master of the black art of the *faux* coup and has used it in a number of pre-emptive strikes against anyone threatening his considerable power-base. (See Chapter 9.)

Military Intervention

Once upon a time a president of the United States came up with a pretext that enabled him to invade a foreign country which he claimed was a threat to America. The country concerned was immensely rich in mineral resources. The former governor of a southern state, he had been elected on the narrowest majority of the popular vote in US history.

But the comparison with George W. Bush ends there. President James K. Polk was a Democrat, an award-winning scholar in mathematics and the classics, a lawyer and a consummate orator. On 25 April 1846 Mexican soldiers crossed the Rio Grande into Texas and attacked American troops, killing sixteen of them. At that time Mexico didn't recognise the Rio Grande as the border and, although Texas had been 'annexed' by the USA the previous year, it still considered the territory as part of Mexico. However, President Polk packaged the incident as a foreign invasion and secured the backing of Congress for outright hostilities. What followed was the two-year Mexican War or, as the

Mexicans call it, *Guerra de Estados Unidos a Mexico* (The War of the United States against Mexico). The outcome was an overwhelming victory for the US and the eventual addition of eight stars to Old Glory: Texas, Arizona, Nevada, New Mexico, Colorado, Utah, Wyoming and California.

As with the Iraq 2003 regime change, this was not a *coup d'état*, nor even an action in support of a coup. It was a war. However, politicians these days do not like to use the word 'war' because it carries all kinds of national and international legal baggage. Britain's war with Argentina over the Falkland Islands (or Las Malvinas) was always described as the 'Falklands *Conflict*'. For Britain to have a war, 'war' must be declared against someone and that is a political–legal process that was never followed. Another possibility is the use of the word 'invasion', but the PR people do not like that at all; it sounds like something Hitler used to do a lot of.

So that brings us to the current parlance: 'military intervention'. A military intervention is not a coup, but a coup may involve military intervention, either in support or in opposition.

Chapter 2
Motivation and Massage

When the colonel left the London Underground train at Knightsbridge Station, he knew he was going to the most important meeting of his life; it was imperative to him and the others in the conspiracy that he was not followed.

He had started his journey several hours before, driving down the motorway towards London, keeping a particular look-out for helicopter surveillance. He had eventually parked at Hatton Cross near to Heathrow Airport before taking the tube to Hammersmith, where he had left the station and taken a stroll around the unfashionable shops close to the tube. He then took the underground again, travelling to the high-rent areas close to the centre of the city. He had practised the route several times in the last month. Ahead of him his anti-surveillance teams were spread along the circuitous route that was going to take.

Emerging from the station, he paused to light a cigarette. He was a forty-a-day addict who also liked to drink, but only in company he enjoyed and respected. Physically he was a small, dark-skinned man who, except for his piercing blue eyes, could have been mistaken for Asian. As he moved off, he checked his watch.

It was important that he didn't keep looking back, no matter how tense he was. Even if he knew he was being followed, he must give no indication of being aware of it. He knew from his own experience that the finest surveillance teams in the world were all British and run by offshoots of MI5 and Defence Intelligence. His own anti-surveillance teams were equally skilled. Their job was to lie in wait, to see who was close to him, and to photograph them using covert digital cameras. They would then transmit the results among the watchers to compare who was still near him at various points further along his route. They had all agreed on an itinerary which would make it difficult for the followers to use cars and other vehicles. All the teams had enough experience to know that, when on a surveillance job, a car was very useful to allow you to rotate your teams and provide a mobile repository for the camera bags and radios which make the task easier.

He had carefully rehearsed his own cover story for that day; he was shopping for shirts and a new pair of shoes for his upcoming birthday party. He rode up the escalators at the tube station and quickly crossed Knightsbridge into Hyde Park. He knew that any surveillance people could be very close to him on the train; wherever there were crowds they had to be almost within touching distance. In open spaces like Hyde Park where there were fewer people, they had to keep further away. His job that day was to get them close and stretch them out and, by using his counter-surveillance skills, pick out anyone who may be watching him. He walked at a leisurely pace across Hyde Park and used one of the underpasses to reach the east side of Park Lane. This was a natural surveillance trap. Anyone following him had to be close and if they followed him into the underpass they would really stand out. He paused to drop a few coins in the tin cup of a beggar who had set up home under one of the richest thoroughfares in the world. He guessed from the cleanliness and neatness of the guy's meagre belongings that he was probably one of the many ex-servicemen living rough on the streets of London. He was aware too, without seeing them, that his anti-surveillance crew was somewhere close.

The colonel exited the underpass, turned left and headed north past the luxurious hotels towards Oxford Street. He turned into the busiest shopping street in Britain and was immediately surrounded by hordes of people intent on finding a bargain. He took advantage of a demonstration of video camcorders; cameras were photographing passers-by and showing the results on a TV screen in the window of an electronics retailer. This was an added bonus. He could see who was around him without actually moving his head. He then crossed Oxford Street towards Marks & Spencer, giving him the opportunity as he was doing so, checking the traffic, to look left and right. As he reached the other pavement he glanced back, again totally naturally, and used the large expanse of glass in Marks & Spencer's windows to check who was behind him. He walked into the store, strolled leisurely to the menswear department and pretended to check the quality and price of the shirts.

He exited from another doorway into a side street and then strode quickly into Wigmore Street where the density of shoppers was much lower. He walked along Wigmore Street for a couple of hundred metres and then turned right back into a side street towards Oxford Street. He took the opportunity, as he went round the corner, to check quickly who was behind him. Again it looked clear. He continued like this for a couple of hours, walking in and out of shops and, as he entered each one, he very politely held the door open for people entering behind him. This gave him an opportunity to make eye contact with anyone who was close to him. He knew it was a fact that if you make eye contact with any other person, you will subconsciously remember that face for the rest of your life. If you see it again, even ten years later, you may not recognise the circumstances but you will know that you have seen that face before.

He used escalators as much as he could because on every escalator there is usually a mirror for shoppers to check their appearance. But the colonel used the mirrors to check if anyone was behind him. He knew that the great skill of British followers is that they will always try to get an operative in front of you. *You* are always looking for followers behind you; very seldom will you look for a follower in front of you. Eventually, he bought a couple of shirts and tried on many pairs of shoes. He knew that for surveillance people, killing time was hard work and he made a lot of time for them to kill.

Glancing at his watch he realised that now was the time to get serious. He crossed quickly into Mayfair walking swiftly and purposefully, made his way down to Piccadilly, crossed Piccadilly into Green Park and then turned swiftly into St James's. He was now close to his destination. As he turned into the street, which was his final destination, he passed one of his anti-surveillance teams, who briefly gave him a covert signal that everything was okay. The colonel smiled to himself; he and his guests had been brought safely and securely to the rendezvous. Now the real work could begin.

Reasons to be Cheerful: Nigeria 1990

No coup plotter ever has one single reason for wanting to overthrow the *ancien régime*. If he did, and you asked him what it was, the answer would either be a lie or meaningless rubbish.

'We did it to defend the Constitution!' A coup victory speech is incomplete without this one. We guarantee that no one will challenge it by asking which specific clause in the constitution legitimises the overthrow of an elected government by a group of soldiers. And, therefore, the irony of committing an unconstitutional act in support of the constitution will be totally lost.

'Someone had to put an end to corruption!' This does not mean that the coup leader is against kick-backs and pay-offs. What it means is that he is against getting 10 per cent when he could be getting 20 per cent – not at all the same thing. Corruption is endemic in the world of politics. A businessman supports a candidate's election campaign and expects an ambassadorial appointment if he or she is successful. A million-dollar party contribution can get an advertising ban on cigarettes suspended. Even the most humble parliamentarian will expect a fistful of non-executive directorships when he is finally voted out.

'Power had to be restored to the people!' What this actually means is 'Power had to be taken away from the present regime!', but that's not quite so snappy. It is, of course a huge leap of faith, if you are one of 'the people', to believe you are going to win power as a consequence of *any* regime change. After all, it doesn't happen with an election, so why should it happen with a *coup d'état*? It is the new incumbents or wannabe leaders who get the power and the pay-offs.

Or, a favourite of ours: 'There was no other way!' This is an excellent one-size-fits-all slogan. It also works as a street-slogan for use in demonstrations: 'No other way! No other way!' It sounds even better in Spanish: '*Ninguna otra manera!*'

On 22 April 1990 there was the following unusual addition to the Federal Radio Corporation of Nigeria's breakfast show:

> Fellow Nigerian citizens; on behalf of the patriotic and well-meaning peoples of the Middle Belt and the southern parts of this country, I , Major Gideon Orkar, wish to happily inform you of the successful ousting of the dictatorial, corrupt, drug baronish, evil man, deceitful, homosexually centred, prodigal-istic, un-patriotic administration of General Ibrahim Badamasi Babangida. We have equally commenced their trials for unabated corruption, mismanagement of national economy, the murders of Dele Giwa, Major-General Mamman Vatsa, with other officers as there was no attempted coup but mere intentions that were yet to materialise and other human rights violations...

41

> We wish to emphasise that this is not just another coup but a well-conceived, planned and executed revolution for the marginalized, oppressed and enslaved peoples of the Middle Belt and the south with a view to freeing ourselves and children yet unborn from eternal slavery and colonisation by a clique of this country.[12]

This victory speech wins Major Orkar a very commendable eight out of ten; he covers all the bases ('dictatorial', 'corrupt', 'revolution for the oppressed') but tosses in a sexual slur ('homosexually centred') and a few murders. We liked the bit about freeing 'children yet unborn' but had to look up 'prodigalistic' in the dictionary. A reference to protecting the constitution could have got him a rare nine out of ten.

The truth of the matter is that there are two sets of motives for any one political action. The first set includes the justifications you are going to mention to potential sponsors and supporters, and these will feature in your victory speech from the balcony of the presidential palace. The second set includes the real reasons you are leading your troops into the political arena, and these you want to share as much as you want to share your wife with a corporal. Of course, do not fool yourself into believing that none of your co-conspirators really knows what is going on. Equally, do not fool yourself into thinking that you are aiming at some higher ideal; such as 'saving the integrity of the Nation'. You are in it for the power and the money, just like everyone else.

The Cuba Card: Venezuela 2002

During the Cold War it was essential to claim that the prime coup objective was to block a communist takeover of your country if you were to gain the support of the US State Department and the CIA. Today, after the downfall of the Soviet Bloc, such a proposition would not be taken seriously. But there are two exceptions. The first is North Korea, but we have never heard of anyone, anywhere wanting to be sponsored by a mad-cap regime that couldn't organise a drinking session in a brewery. The suggestion that the Democratic People's Republic of Korea is a threat to anyone except its own people is not even taken seriously by its neighbours to the south. (The 650,000 local and 25,000 US troops in South Korea would not be expected to have much trouble dealing with the poorly motivated 1.2 million North Korean soldiers, most of whom would offer up their AK-47s in return for an iPod as they crossed the Demilitarised Zone.)

If, however, your country is in the Caribbean or Latin America, playing the 'Cuba Card' is bound the get Washington's attention. The decision of the Grenadian government of 1979-83 to allow the Cubans to build them an airport big enough for the long-haul tourist trade precipitated an all-out invasion by the US. (At least the Americans had the decency to finish the construction work and, by all accounts, made a better job of that than they did of the invasion.) From this perspective, President Hugo Chávez of Venezuela would seem to be playing with fire; he has no fewer than ten thousand Cuban doctors in the country. They are not armed and are not building an airport, but extending free healthcare to the people of the barrios is seen by some people to be a threat to democracy and freedom.

Here are some key facts about Venezuela. It produces more than three million barrels of oil a day – nearly half that of Saudi Arabia – making it one of the richest countries in the region. Unlike Saudi Arabia, Venezuela has universal suffrage and that is how Chávez, then *Colonel* Chávez, got himself elected in 1998. Although he won convincingly he did not go down well with the wealthy élite, who disliked being in opposition. The new president wanted to see the introduction of social reforms to enable the predominantly poor population to benefit from the oil revenues. That was bad enough, but the chap was clearly not of Spanish extraction; in fact he is of Amerindian descent. Worst of all, he was a friend of Fidel Castro, which is how Chávez gets his doctors and Castro gets his oil.

Venezuela's new leader was smart enough to know that if you do not behave yourself in America's 'backyard', you can expect trouble. And sure enough, trouble came in 2002 with a coup-attempt. For the plotters, the 'Cuba Card' didn't have to come out of someone's sleeve; it was for real. The coup was led by some twenty generals close to the wealthy opposition. This highlighted one of Venezuela's more serious problems – the army has a total of a hundred generals. For a country that is not at war, and has not been at war for some time, why does it need a hundred generals? They cannot possibly have much to do, other than to sit around drinking Jack Daniels and plotting government takeovers; idle hands... (It has to be noted, however, that the likelihood of success is *inversely* proportional to the number of generals leading the coup.) On the up-side, only twenty of them took part and there was a reason for that. Remember that Chávez had been an officer himself and cultivated a good deal of support for his policies among the junior officers and NCOs. Indeed, there were rumours of a pre-emptive coup during his

1998 election and his backers in the military had managed to pre-empt that.

The April 2002 attempt went much further and Chávez later described the people behind the plot.

> Almost all of the conspirators are men of privilege, with political contacts with the previous government... or officers who had become wealthy, sometimes through dubious businesses in association with 'dogs of war'. There were 'dogs of war' involved in the coup: [for example] Mr Pérez Recao, dealer of weapons and military equipment.
>
> I continue thinking, despite what happened that the majority, even among the generals... was not participating in the coup.[13]

After the second putsch failed, Chávez met individually with the rebellious generals and reasoned with them. He won some of them around, and even promoted a leader to head up the defence ministry. This policy of keeping the military sweet seems to have paid off; it has averted two almost-inevitable coups.

Evidence of the extent to which he had won the army over to his social-democratic outlook came on 9 May 2004 when the police and army launched an assault on the Rancho El Hatillo near the capital of Caracas. Acting on a tip-off, the Venezuelan security forces detained eighty-eight fit young Colombians – who initially insisted they were agricultural workers. Much of the subsequent investigation was leaked to the media. It seemed that the country's disgruntled élite was no longer able to recruit a whole domestic army unit to its cause and had decided to import a private army of three thousand mercenaries. The Colombians were being paid 250 US dollars a week but were short of weapons.

The switch in tactics from direct involvement to routing through Colombia makes a lot of sense from the point of view of the CIA and the State Department. In 2004 the US pumped 600 million dollars into counter-terrorism and anti-drug operations in what the rest of South America calls 'Locombia'. This is not done by dropping a cheque in the mail; Bogotá is crawling with American soldiers, private military contractors and federal agents. Such is the control exercised by the US that the decision to give the nod (and funding) to an assisted coup in neighbouring Venezuela could have taken place around the embassy coffee machine.

Rancho El Hatillo was owned by Robert Alonso, a Cuban exile and prominent member of Venezuela's right-wing opposition; as brother of the television actor Maria Conchita Alonso, he was a B-list celebrity who featured in the gossip columns of the Caracas tabloids. Rather than have three thousand idle young Colombians forever escaping to the waterfront fleshpots of the capital the plan was for the advance party (130 were eventually rounded up) to carry out a raid on a local army munitions store. The target was thought to be the underground bunkers of the National Guard's Urban Security Command. The stolen cache would then be used to arm and train the full mercenary force, due to arrive in Venezuela some eight days later.

In a nice twist the local newspapers described the mercenary force as 'terrorists' and questioned the origin of the one million US dollars per week of funding. Later in 2003 the opposition invoked a constitutional provision for a national referendum to 'recall' the president, California-style. The result was announced in August 2004 and President Hugo Chávez won a landslide victory. That is unlikely to be an end to the affair, with alarmist talk of an all-out invasion by US-backed Colombian forces.

Ken Connor: Mutiny!

There is an oft-quoted assertion that there has not been a mutiny in the British Army for several hundred years. In my own experience I have actually seen three occasions when troops of the parachute battalion in which I was serving refused to obey orders.

The difference between not obeying orders and a full-blown mutiny lies in the reaction of the ranking officer unfortunate enough to be present at the time. On all three occasions the senior officer present, the commanding officer of the battalion, decided that he would give in to all the demands of the 'mutinous other' ranks. As soon as things returned to normal, the iron fist descended from above and mass punishments were meted out. No knowledge of these events percolated up the chain of command. The reason for this was simple; it would have meant certain death for the career of any commanding officer that finds himself in such a position.

The most vivid recollection I have of this type of situation was when I was serving in Bahrain with 1 Para; it was Christmas, 1962. The battalion officers' mess, which was built on a slight rise, was decked out with fairy lights. The commanding officer had brought out the regimental band to entertain the officers over the festive season, but the biggest mistake was that he had also flown out some of the officers' wives, including his own.

Meanwhile, the 'trogs' had been left to their own devices. At around midnight on Christmas night, the whole battalion – who had been drinking heavily – stole across the desert under the bright moon, collecting rocks as they went. When they got within fifty metres of the officers' mess, and without a word being said, everyone in the battalion hurled a barrage of rocks. There must have been twenty tonnes of real estate in the air at the same time. This descended on the tin roof of the officers' bar. The lights went out, the roof buckled and collapsed and dishevelled officers and their ladies came staggering out into the desert to hear the sound of six hundred giggling soldiers staggering back to their lines.

The RSM went to one of the rifle companies to investigate and was promptly taken hostage. A note was sent to the sergeants' mess demanding ten crates of beer as ransom. The sergeants sent twenty crates with a note telling the guys to 'keep the bastard'. The other ranks couldn't believe their luck – they thought they'd won! They had, until dawn the next morning. When the battalion woke with hangovers, the officers, RSM and Provo staff were waiting. The circumference of Bahrain Island is about twenty-four miles and the whole of the battalion walked it continuously for fourteen days. In the end, the exercise was deemed a draw. The commanding officer realised he'd made a mistake, and the troops realised that when you take on the army you can win the battle but not the war. Afterwards a new feeling of mutual respect permeated the battalion.

Going Native: Ecuador 1963 and 2000

Ecuador, on the Pacific coast of South America, is most famous for owning the Galapagos Islands. It is also renowned for being the stomping ground of CIA officer Phillip Agee during the first three years of the 'Swinging Sixties'. There would be nothing remarkable in that if Agee hadn't incurred the wrath of Washington insiders by writing a book about it.[14] In spite of his being hounded for breaking the intelligence community's code of silence, no one has ever challenged the veracity of his account of the CIA's activities in Latin America; even after thirty years, it remains a remarkable book.

What Agee describes is a systematic campaign of interference in the internal politics of Ecuador. Far from working to establish 'liberty and democracy' he worked from his office in the Quito embassy to infiltrate the whole spectrum of the country's body politic. Left-wing groups were penetrated to undermine support for Cuba; right-wing groups to recruit people and resources to the CIA cause. If a suitable group didn't exist, they would invent one. One station officer created a group called the 'Ecuadorean Anti-Communist Front' only to discover that it already existed. He shrugged, crossed out 'Front' and replaced the word with 'Action'.[15]

The *yanqui dollar* played a big part in the scheme of things. Ecuador's vice-president was on the payroll for 1,000 dollars a month. Trade union leaders were provided with all-expenses-paid trips to the United States, where they were wined and dined, lectured on the evils of communism and groomed for future work as paid agents. Feature articles were ghosted for political figures, publication guaranteed by the expediency of having editors on the payroll too. The postmaster-general was also slipped bulky unstamped plain brown envelopes in return for ensuring that any mail to and from Cuba and Eastern Bloc countries was checked and copied at the US embassy. Customs officials were bribed to plant incriminating documents in the baggage of travellers returning from Havana. In spite of the meticulous attention to detail, mistakes were made. The agency ordered two of its agents, both senior police colonels, to go in hard against a leftist demonstration. Quito station officer Bob Weatherwax went along too, just to ensure that the job was done properly. He was recognised and exposed as an embassy official and had to be ordered back to Washington.[16]

By 1963 small groups of ill-trained and poorly equipped supposedly pro-Cuba insurgents began to attack government targets. It was the excuse needed to bring back the military and on 11 July the army had taken over the capital and installed a junta. And so it goes in Ecuador.

Fast forward now to the year 2000 for a coup that offered much more than the plain vanilla variety. Eighty-five per cent of Ecuadoreans claim full or partial Amerindian descent; only some 20 per cent lead an indigenous lifestyle and follow traditional cultures. This significant part of the population had never previously participated in national politics, failing to see that it would make any difference to their lives of gruelling poverty, malnutrition and high infant mortality. Then all that changed. On 21 January Colonel Lucio Gutiérrez overthrew the government of President Jamil Mahuad in a military putsch; so far, so familiar. But standing next to him was Miguel Lluco, a leader of the Pachakutik indigenous political movement. This coup was being billed as a *levantamiento popular*, a popular uprising. The Gutiérrez victory address was a classic of its kind. Not only did he include all the right buzzwords, but he managed to combine it with his resignation speech.

> Our objective was not to take power. Our objective was firstly to defend the constitution which had been systematically violated by the government of Dr Mahuad. Secondly it was a persuasive protest against corruption in order to get the people to react, so that they would stop being passive, so that they would stop being witnesses to the debacle of our country. We did it to raise the people's self-esteem, to make them the protagonists of their own destiny. That was what we were attempting, to bring about a change of attitude in the population. It wasn't our objective to take power. And for that reason, once we arrived at the presidential palace we handed over power. If our ambition had been to stay in power we wouldn't have handed it over just like that. The idea was to pressurize the democratic institutions of our country into strengthening themselves, allowing the participation of all citizens. In Ecuador democracy has been reduced to elections, the candidates deceive the people with all manner of promises that they never fulfil. Once the candidates get into power they forget about the people, and they use their power for their own personal benefit. That's not democracy. So that is what we were fighting against, against that pseudo-democracy – because corruption is the main enemy of democracy, not us, not the people.

Miguel Lluco's speech was even more interesting:

> We are fighting for life, not only for the lives of humans, of people, but for the lives of all living beings: animals, plants, rivers, the environment, so we have a global vision. That means we can't use the same arms that they use. They use them with the police, the armed forces; they use arms to put a gag on hunger. Instead of arming ourselves we would rather carry out, with the majority of Ecuadoreans, peaceful and democratic actions and from there we can get rid of the

wrong people who are in our institutions so that we can get on with the political administration of the state, which we can do honourably. So our aspiration is to keep moving on. We will fight to the death against wrong. It is a fight of life against death. That is our fight; those are our aspirations, dreams, and efforts.

Was this short-lived political event the world's first *green coup d'état*? A coup for the trees and the rivers? It was certainly a coup which gained huge support for Lucio Gutiérrez among the ordinary people of Ecuador; in November 2002 he told them, 'The only path left to we Latin Americans is unity, as Simon Bolivar the Liberator brilliantly predicted.' And they elected him president.

One month later Gutiérrez was in the White House shaking hands with his new best friend George W. Bush. They announced to the media that they had spoken about 'friendship, cooperation in the war on terrorism, and the financial assistance that the United States could give to Ecuador.'[17] There was no mention of trees and rivers. On his return to Quito, the new president turned sharply to the right, dumping his Pachakutik coalition partners along the way.

In 1999, the US Department of State said this about the situation of the indigenous people of Ecuador:

> Despite their growing political influence... and the efforts of grassroots community groups, which were increasingly successful in pressuring the central Government to assist them, Indians continue to suffer discrimination at many levels of society. With few exceptions, the indigenous people are at the lowest end of the socio-economic scale.[18]

Other than getting himself elected president, Colonel Lucio Gutiérrez achieved nothing; it was business as usual.

The al-Qaeda Franchise and the War on Terror

In the twenty-first century 'terrorism' has become the new 'communism' and Osama bin Laden has become the new Fidel Castro. You now need to claim that your coup is targeted at dealing with some terrorist threat, domestic or international; in other words, the *in situ* government is soft on 'terror'. From a practical point of view this may mean you have to turn an indigenous people's rights group, or a troublesome neighbour giving you some grief over a border issue, into a bunch of terrorists.

Al-Qaeda is usually described as an 'international terrorist organisation'. That implies a degree of unity and a level of integration which do not exist: there is no clearly defined management structure, no constitution, no elections of the leadership, no corporate logo, no membership card, no Office of Public Affairs. Anyone can be in al-Qaeda; set up a group with a name, open a web-site claiming affiliation to bin Laden and proclaim a *jihad* against the US, Britain and the rest of the infidels. But if the campaign of terror has nothing to do with al-Qaeda the enemy will stick the label on the group anyway.

This can be done easily (and harmlessly) with a few well-placed bombs. If you are a military unit you should have no real trouble getting hold of some C4 plastic explosives, detonators and timers. This is not rocket science – unless you have a premature detonation and see a member of your team going into low orbit. (See Chapter 1, China 1911.) You could start by taking out an electricity sub-station, remembering to call a broadcaster or newspaper claiming to be from the group you are trying to discredit. This will considerably irritate some people for a while, but that is what you are trying to achieve. If that is successful you can graduate onto other low-casualty targets; a statue in a park at night, a McDonald's at midnight, maybe even a bridge. Try not to kill too many innocent members of the population; they are the ones whose support you are trying to win over with your forthcoming coup.

'Bomb' equals 'terrorist'. But there are other things you can do. The opposition group might have a political wing, and if it has a political wing it will have an office. Arrange a break-in and plant fake planning documents for a far more serious bombing campaign. Make sure the documents are left lying around on desks and in filing trays. Then light a small fire at the front door and call the fire fighters and the police... Of course, all this is very much easier if you are in a Muslim country or, at least, a country with a minority Islamic population. Then you can claim that there is an al-Qaeda franchise setting up business. This can be made convincing by finding a really remote shack in the hinterland; plant a matchbox-full of C4, a handful of AK-47 'Short' rounds, a few copies of the Koran and a bin Laden video tape.

Once you have everyone worked up to a certain level of hysteria and it is clear that the government seems unable to do anything about it, that is the time to make contact with the CIA's Head of Station at the US embassy. (He is the guy who seems to be a member of all the right clubs and has been in post far longer than the ambassador.) The neat thing about this approach is that when you take over power, all the 'acts of terrorism' stop immediately.

Getting the Message Across: Media Ops

It has become something of a running joke that the first thing a coup team does is seize the radio station. But there are good reasons for the state broadcaster to be a primary target; for as long as it in the hands of the government, the incumbents will use it to systematically misrepresent the motivation and objectives of your coup. That, of course, will jeopardise your chances of winning popular support.

We must stress, however, that taking over the station and forcing the presenters to play non-stop martial music is an opportunity missed and is likely to have a negative effect if what they normally air is the kind of stuff played in the cafés and kitchens and taxi-cabs of the country. Insist that they stick to their normal programming but add regular bulletins on the progress of the coup as well as a *short* statement of objectives issued by your leader. (We will give you some suggestions for this later.) Even in developed countries, radio broadcasts reach a wider audience than television during the early hours and throughout the day; when people arrive home from work in their factories, offices or the fields, the situation reverses and television dominates. If your coup is going to strike at dawn and you take the radio station first, that gives you the rest of the day to deal with the TV broadcasters. (Another factor to bear in mind is that bad television is always a lot worse than bad radio. So keep things simple.)

Before we go into more detail, a word about newspapers and news magazines might be appropriate. You will already know which publications stand where in the political spectrum. While it makes sense to close down any government-controlled papers, do not try to close them all down – you are unlikely to have the resources. But do try to get at least one paper on side; even if they will not back the objectives of the coup, try to persuade them to report what is happening in a fair and balanced way.

The best strategy for dealing with the media at large is to identify two or three high-profile journalists known to be critical of the government. Then use a subaltern and a driver to get them out of bed just as the coup is about to start and offer them the scoop of their lives. Tell them to bring along stills- and video-cameras and take them into the heart of the action. They will be a pain in the arse, they always are, but if you do not get a grip on the situation from the start, they will cause even more rectal discomfort later. Give them specific things to do: record the coup leader's preliminary statement on objectives; give them situation reports as the takeover progresses; get them to call their buddies when you are ready for a press conference. But whatever you do, don't tip them off in advance – you cannot trust any of them, not even the one who is the coup leader's nephew – and try to prevent them being shot because only *you* will get the blame.

The first global coverage of the coup will probably show your teams manning vehicle checkpoints (VCPs), guarding the parliament building (if you've got one) and shooting at the local electorate trying to loot your cousin's television shop. How did the tapes get out so quickly? The most common way film crews do this is to take the material to either the state broadcaster or to the headquarters of the state telecommunications authority. Both of these will have big fat satellite dishes on their roofs or in the car park. When the news producer or reporter walks in he or she will ask for time on a link to their newsroom back in Europe, the US, Japan or wherever. While they are waiting for the satellite slot to come through, financial matters will be dealt with. A company American Express card might be flashed but, although that might do nicely for the accountants, an additional cash disbursement might be needed to ensure the booking is expedited.

You may have decided to close down these facilities but it is important not to underestimate the resourcefulness of foreign correspondents and their local 'stringers'. A common fall-back used to be the commercial airlines. A member of an aircrew (usually a female flight attendant) would be approached in the hotel where they were enjoying a stop-over. Cocktails would be bought, money would change hands, arrangements made for a hand-over at the destination airport and the tape secreted in checked baggage. With increased security since 11 September 2001, this is no longer a reliable option. In any case, you may have had to close the airport.

Film crews are now a lot more self-sufficient. Those from the big players like CNN, the BBC and Reuters TV come equipped with suitcase-sized satellite antennas powered from twelve-volt car batteries through which they can set up high-quality links to their home broadcasting services from somewhere out in the bush. More recently the even-smaller satellite videophone has become a common way of setting up live feeds into news programmes; the quality is not too good but the system is relatively cheap and cheerful. You are going to have to decide in advance how you will tackle this problem, if problem it is. As your coup progresses, it's going to become increasingly hard to keep track of these media people; closing them down is going to demand resources that you will probably need for more urgent tasks – like containing the presidential guard.

Rather than trying to suppress the media, use them to get your mission statement across at home and abroad; this job is important, so you need to give it to someone as a specific task. That means finding a camera-friendly junior officer who can string more than a few sentences of English together. French or Spanish will not help much and Mbajja will do more harm than good, even if it is the language of your tribe. If you cannot find such an individual in the officers' mess, consider using a civilian; maybe someone has a relative who just did a media studies course in Europe. And, if the relative is an attractive female, that's even better.

Base your newly appointed PR at the hotel where the foreign media congregate and provide her with a couple of serious-looking NCOs; some of these correspondents are animals. Give her a cellphone so you can keep her briefed on what's happening. The trick is to convince the media that they can only get the truth about the coup by keeping close to the PR, in other words, staying in the hotel bar out of harm's way. Make sure she has plenty of copies of the 'mission statement' to hand out. This can say pretty much anything in the first instance, but if you are short of ideas, here is a pro-forma that can be modified as appropriate.

A NEW BEGINNING!

Fellow citizens of [INSERT NAME OF COUNTRY]! We, a concerned group of officers of the National Defence Force, declare an end to the evil and corrupt regime of [INSERT NAME OF HEAD OF STATE].

We have taken this action not to seize power ourselves but to defend the constitution and restore honour to the sacred flag of our nation. There was no other way! No longer will the unelected cronies of [INSERT NAME OF HEAD OF STATE] and his family exploit the poor people in the fields and the workers in the factories. No longer will multinational corporations be permitted to exploit the nation's natural resources of [INSERT APPROPRIATE COMMODITY: COPRA, OIL, GUANO ETC.].

Law and order will be restored to the streets of our towns and cities! The terrorist gangs will be captured or killed! We will close down the opposition parties in the pay of [INSERT NAME OF HATED FOREIGN STATE]!

In the interests of public safety, martial law has been declared and a curfew will be in effect from 7 pm to 7 am until further notice. All soldiers should remain in their barracks until they receive new orders. A general election will be declared to take place before [INSERT SOME DISTANT DATE], subject to the ongoing security situation.

We salute [INSERT NAME OF FOUNDING FATHER OF NATION, POPULAR HERO]! Long live [INSERT NAME OF COUNTRY]!

At some stage the media are going to demand a press conference. This should be presided over by one or more of the coup leaders but don't agree to this until you are certain that it is the right time to 'go public'. Also ensure that the perimeter of the hotel is secure; it would be embarrassing for your first appearance on CNN to show your dramatic arrest by an angry-looking platoon of presidential guards who sneaked in through the kitchens.

Decide in advance who is going to do the talking. Keep the whole thing short but take questions. Give out free pens and, more importantly, free drinks. Look like the good guys.

Chapter 3
Planning the Perfect Putsch

The sharp bows of the 42-foot yacht sliced through the oily swell of the English Channel. The helmsman gazed forward through narrowed eyes. In the distance, off his starboard bow, he could see the white rocks of the Needles at the western tip of the Isle of Wight. The yacht was sailing on a broad reach and making nine knots in a slight wind. The other two members of the crew were below, tidying up, bagging refuse and folding sleeping bags, making everything shipshape before they handed the yacht back to its owners. It would save time once they'd tied up at the marina on the River Hamble near the south-coast port of Southampton.

On its white GRP hull the yacht was showing signs of their hard sail from Gibraltar north across the Bay of Biscay and then through the busy shipping lanes of the Channel. The voyage had started five days ago, the working crew contracted to bring the boat back home for a refit.

The whole story, in fact, was a cover; the three crew members were members of Force S, the Executive Arm of MI6, Britain's Secret Intelligence Service. The men had joined Force S having finished long and illustrious careers in Special Forces. On operations, the three of them were usually travelling the other way, out of the UK. Their life since leaving the military had consisted of being paid in brown envelopes, having clandestine meetings with their handlers and getting involved in the deniable dirty business of their political masters. If any of the three had been inclined to be indiscreet they would tell you of trips into Bosnia to snatch war criminals, and other trips to Israel and the occupied territories where terrorists were puzzlingly assassinated or arrested. And then there were the trips to various parts of the African continent when political leaders and despots mysteriously disappeared or were deposed. All this was done with the use of deep cover, false passports, fake documentation and intricate legends learned and memorised.

This job, however, was going to be a cakewalk. On a difficulty scale of one to ten, it was close to zero. The surveillance was already being done by the MI6 equivalent of 14 Intelligence Company. All the three had to do was get the yacht to the Hamble, tie it up, hand it over to the owners and then link up with the recce team. After a final briefing they would be taken to the target and place charges in the power links into the Air Traffic Control centre at Swanwick just outside of Southampton. This was all part of an extensive exercise to test how ready the UK was for a terrorist attack. If that is what they were told, that is what they believed. They had often been fed cock-and-bull stories only to find out later that the truth was totally different. But if the 'powers that be' said it was an exercise, it was an exercise and as long as the brown paper envelopes kept coming in with the necessary amount of money, then it was still an exercise.

Secrets of Success

Coups d'état are the most effective device for regime change in modern history. But why should that be the case? What makes a coup a coup is the concept of political action by *a small group* using force of arms. When faced with larger armed groups (the rest of the army, the police, paramilitary forces, armed irregulars and foreign military, for example) the coup plotters should in theory fail. And, if the government being targeted is a democratically elected one, wouldn't the sheer numerical superiority of a hostile population make it impossible for the instigators to gain a grip on the day-to-day running of the country?

Of course, many coups do fail for these very reasons. But the successful putsch succeeds because it relies on much more than raw firepower. Here are some of the factors that might contribute to a positive prognosis for a plot:

- GOOD PLANNING! (See Iran 1953, later in this chapter.) *If you fail to plan, you plan to fail.*
- A government structure that lends itself to takeover by a small, disciplined and armed group.
- Declared objectives aimed at gaining overwhelming popular support. (See Chapter 2 and Iran 1953, this chapter.)
- Subsidiary objectives that will attract the support of any possible 'loyalist' groups (e.g. the promise of immediate payment of any back wages for the army and civil service). (See Chapter 2.)
- Swift and total seizure of all broadcast media in order to get

those two messages across. (See Chapter 2 and Iran 1953, this chapter.)

- The pre-empting of any international support for the incumbents by securing it for the plotters first. For example, get US backing by claiming that the incoming regime will deal with the terrorist problem once and for all. If you haven't got a terrorist problem, invent one. (See Chapter 2.)

The factors that will influence, if not absolutely guarantee, failure will include:

- POOR PLANNING AND EXECUTION. For example, the unfocussed concentration of resources and bad timing.
- Lack of training, especially in the specialist skills needed for a coup. (See Chapter 4.)
- Underestimating the power of the incumbent regime and the strength of opposition to the coup. (See Algeria 1961, this chapter.)
- Misreading the popular mood. (See Algeria 1961, this chapter.)
- Failure to take account of international support for the established regime.
- One or more double-agents within the ranks of the plotters. (See Chapter 5.)
- Sloppy operational security (OpSec) causing the plot to be revealed to the *in situ* government. (See Chapter 5 and Algeria 1961, this chapter.)
- Lack of courage and commitment. (See Algeria 1961, this chapter.)

This chapter includes case studies in the rewards of good planning, and the consequences of bad, or non-existent planning. These are the successful CIA/MI6-sponsored veto coup in Iran 1953 and the failed coup by parts of the French army in 1961 Algeria. The latter eventually brought the Revolutionary War to a successful conclusion for the opponents of French rule; in other words, the opposite of the stated objective.

Positive Prognosis: Iran 1953

In 1953 a popular uprising in Iran overthrew the communist-leaning government of Prime Minister Mohammed Mossadeq and restored the heroic figure of the beloved young shah to the throne.

That was common perception of the events that, eventually, led to the 1979 replacement of the monarchy with a theocracy headed by Ayatollah Khomeini. However, what really happened was a carefully staged military coup sponsored by Britain's Secret Intelligence Service (SIS, or MI6) and the CIA. The objective was to protect the UK's extensive oil interests and to block an imagined attempt by the USSR to extend its sphere of influence south into the Middle East. But Mossadeq (sometimes spelled Mossadegh) was a liberal democrat, an ardent nationalist and not a communist; he was a popular politician heading a democratically elected government and even had the support of President Harry Truman. This, then, was an ill-considered veto coup, the consequences of which remain with us more than fifty years on.

A 1954 report on the planning and execution of the putsch, written by a participating CIA officer, Dr Donald M. Wilber, was recently declassified under the Freedom of Information Act. Titled 'Overthrow of Premier Mossadeq of Iran: November 1952–August 1953', it can be read in full at the National Security Archive.[19]

In the last two months of 1952, three senior SIS officers were attending a series of meetings with the CIA in Washington DC. The purpose of the conferences was to discuss 'joint war and staybehind plans' for Iran. The MI6 representatives were Christopher Montague Woodhouse (formerly Chief of Station for the SIS in Tehran), Samuel Falle (then of the Tehran station) and John Bruce Lockhart (SIS representative in Washington). The American side included Kermit Roosevelt (Chief of the CIA's Near East and Africa Division), John H. Leavitt (Chief of Iran Branch) and James A. Darling (Chief of NEA Paramilitary Staff). What the Americans didn't know was that the Brits wanted to add something to the agenda; would the Agency like to join the SIS in staging a military coup in Iran? The Anglo-Iranian Oil Company had been nationalised and Prime Minister Mossadeq was too close to the Russians for comfort.

Attempts by the British to negotiate a resolution had failed. As historian Laurence Elwell-Sutton wrote, 'Really, it seemed hardly fair that dignified and correct Western statesmanship should be defeated by the antics of incomprehensible orientals.' On his part, Premier Mossadeq confided to US Special Envoy W. Averell Harriman, 'You do not know how crafty [the British] are. You do not know how evil they are. You do not know how they sully everything they touch.'[20] Little prospect for an amicable outcome there, it would seem. (But it has to be said that

Professor Elwell-Sutton probably had his tongue wedged firmly in his cheek. He became a renowned scholar of Middle East language and culture and his books on Farsi are still available via Amazon.com. His irony may well have been lost on the author of the CIA report which quoted him.) In any event, Kermit Roosevelt said the Americans would consider the British proposal and get back to them on the matter.

There could have been a specific reason for the CIA's hesitancy about a CIA–SIS joint venture. Bruce Lockhart's predecessor as SIS liaison officer in Washington was Kim Philby, a long-term KGB double-agent. That little embarrassment would not be exposed for some time, but the Americans had been working with MI6 through Philby since 1949 on an expensive covert operation to undermine the pro-Soviet government of Albania. Émigrés living in Italy and Greece were being trained in guerrilla warfare tactics in Malta, West Germany and the UK before being returned to Albania to undertake a campaign of recruitment, propaganda and sabotage. But the motley crew of monarchists and World War II fascists had been singularly ineffective; most of them had been intercepted and arrested. Philby was clearly unimpressed with the material he had to work with: 'Even in our more serious moments,' he observed, 'we Anglo-Saxons never forgot that our agents were just down from the trees.'[21] Moscow never responded to the provocation and even when Enver Hoxha dumped the USSR in favour of China, the Russians merely yawned.

So, the expected response never came but, a few months later, the Americans received a similar offer from a different quarter. The Wilber Report describes the incident.

> In March 1953 a telegram was received from the Tehran Station [of the CIA] stating that General [NAME REDACTED] had contacted the assistant military attaché and had requested Ambassador Henderson's views as to whether or not the US Government was interested in covertly supporting an Iranian military effort to oust Premier Mossadeq.[22]

The CIA's 'cautiously worded reply' was 'mildly encouraging and revealed some US interest in the idea'. That interest resulted in a change of State Department policy towards Iran and the agency was 'authorized to consider operations which would contribute to the fall of the Mossadeq government'. Project *TP-Ajax* (the SIS called it Operation *Boot*) was on and the Director of Central Intelligence authorised a preliminary budget of one million dollars. The Tehran station soon decided that it would back a takeover headed by Shah Reza Pahlavi and General Fazlollah Zahedi, a member of Mossadeq's cabinet, 'especially if this combination should be able to get the largest mobs on the streets and if a sizeable proportion of the Tehran garrison refused to carry out Mossadeq's orders'. The US Naval Attaché, Commander Eric Pollard, was given the job of opening a channel to Zahedi via the general's son Ardeshir, who was later to be rewarded with ambassadorships to Washington and the Court of St James's.

During the Albanian affair Kim Philby proposed to Frank Wisner, the CIA's chief of covert operations, the use of Malta as a training ground for the guerrillas. Wisner concurred, observing that: 'Whenever we want to subvert any place, we find that the British own an island within easy reach.'[23] And so it was that, in May 1953, 'covert consultant' Dr Donald N. Wilber found himself in Cyprus poring over maps and plans with MI6's Norman Darbyshire. Darbyshire headed SIS's Iran desk and was a fluent Farsi speaker. Two weeks later, the plot was complete and their report was on its way to Washington and London.

At this stage no one was discussing the motivation for the coup; in fact it is doubtful that any of the spooks considered it much of an issue. The Anglo-Iranian Oil Company (AIOC) had been set up in 1909 to exploit Persian resources that had been exclusively granted to Britain by the shah's father in 1901. When the Mossadeq regime nationalised the company in 1951, Whitehall protested that this action was unfair and unnecessary – the company had already been nationalised by the British during the First World War. This anti-nationalisation stance was a bit rich coming from a government that since World War II had taken its own coal, steel and rail industries under state control. Offers by Iran of massive compensation were to no avail and Royal Navy warships were sent in intimidating numbers (when it still had intimidating numbers of warships) to blockade The Gulf.

The Iranians could do nothing and the Russians, who could have done something, chose not to; it would have been the perfect excuse for the Soviet army to cross the 1,600-kilometre (1,000-mile) border. As far as internal politics were concerned, there was no love lost between Mossadeq and the Iranian communists, the Tudeh Party. President Truman's Secretary of State, Dean Acheson, once characterised the veteran politician as 'essentially a rich, reactionary, feudal-minded Persian.'[24] As if to prove those right-wing credentials, Mossadeq had in 1951 ordered the dispersal of a Tudeh-backed demonstration in Tehran, an action that resulted in a hundred fatalities and some five hundred injured. The CIA officers knew the claims that Mossadeq was pro-communist were untrue. The operational plan appended to the Wilber Report included this checklist item: 'Just prior to movement [coup] CIA would give widest publicity to all fabricated documents proving secret agreement between Mossadeq and Tudeh.'[25] Exactly how a 'fabricated document' could prove anything will have to remain a mystery. The other 'black' items the CIA fabricated included wall posters, leaflets and political cartoons as well as ghosted articles to be placed with sympathetic journalists.

The second potential problem concerned their choice of General Fazlollah Zahedi as premier-in-waiting. During World War II, the British had imprisoned Zahedi for attempting to set up a pro-Nazi government. But never mind, the Brits wanted their oil back and, in the context of the burgeoning Cold War, that was good enough for the CIA.

Two specific matters needed to be addressed if the coup was to be successful. In addition to predictable opposition from any loyal units of the army and police, there was concern that popular resistance to intervention by infidels might be stirred up by the mullahs. And a worst-case possibility was that the Soviet Union would invade the country in support of Mossadeq. The strategy team decided that the best way to deal with opposition from the religious hierarchy was to stage public unrest during which supposed supporters of the government would attack mosques and other Muslim institutions.

The problem of dealing with the Russians was put into the hands of an MI6 officer stationed at the British embassy in Tehran. Unlike so many of his colleagues, Beverly Gayer Barnard was no soldier but he had the title of 'Civil Air Attaché' and had a roaming brief which covered Iran, Iraq and the Gulf States. He even had his own aircraft to facilitate this. ('Military, air and naval attaché' jobs are standard cover for intelligence agents.) The Iranian side of the border with the USSR was the real estate of a number of warlike tribes. It was known that they would resist any Russian incursion and certainly had enough guns, but a little incentive was considered appropriate. Barnard was to make a number of flights up-country, his little plane loaded down with the currency of empire – gold sovereigns.[26] (Beverly Barnard went on to plan an MI6-backed coup in West Africa: see Uganda 1971, Chapter 6.)

From the Wilber Report it is clear that *TP-Ajax* team members thought even less of the Iranians than Kim Philby thought of the Albanians: 'It was felt that every effort should be made to bring the rather long-winded and often illogical Persians into a position where each one of them knew exactly what specific action was required of him.'[27] This concern manifested itself in a detailed checklist, the first page of which is included as Appendix A of the report and shown in Figure 1. Every page of this remarkable document is revealing. For example, the CIA and SIS paid former Nazi-supporter General Zahedi a total of sixty thousand dollars; a remarkable sum in those days. So much for patriotic motivation. The CIA was prepared to pay further 'subsidies' to 'key military figures if… necessary'. It is also clear that, by June 1953 when this plan was written, the shah himself was not yet committed to supporting the coup.

Without question, this was a meticulously planned coup, well funded and with some interesting innovations. But the first attempt on 15 August 1953 stalled for reasons that were unclear. As the report said, almost poetically, 'The early accounts of various participants differed widely enough to make it impossible to follow the slender thread of truth through the dark night.' It seems that the plan was exposed by the indiscretion of an Iranian army officer, but that might not have been terminal 'had not most of the participants been inept or lacking in decision at the critical juncture.' In other words, the officers who didn't lose heart lost their nerve. However, the operational plan survived contact with the incumbent government – but only just.

By the early hours of 16 August Radio Tehran was announcing a failed military attempt to overthrow the government. A desperate and sleepless Kermit Roosevelt got into his car and headed north from the US embassy to meet up with General Zahedi's son Ardeshir. Ardeshir told the American that his father was still optimistic that the coup could be pulled off – but a subterfuge was needed: spread the lie that the shah had sacked Mossadeq, who had initiated the coup as a countermeasure. That would stir a popular uprising – especially among the army – and calls for the prime minister to be physically ejected from office. The real coup plotters would then follow the original plan.

Roosevelt raced back to the CIA station and within hours had leaked the story to the Associated Press wire service. The CIA graphics team rushed out a broadsheet newspaper which nicely embellished the story by adding that the coup plotters were targeting the shah. The head of the US military mission was sent off to double-check that the shah had indeed completed and signed all the necessary firmans (imperial edicts) but the supreme head of the Pahlavi Dynasty had, not to put too fine a point on it, run away and the Americans could not find him.

S E C R E T

SUMMARY OF PRELIMINARY PLAN PREPARED BY
<u>SIS AND CIA REPRESENTATIVES IN CYPRUS</u>

I. <u>Preliminary Action</u>

    A. <u>Interim Financing of Opposition</u>

        1. CIA will supply $35,000 to Zahedi.

        2. SIS will supply $25,000 to Zahedi.

        3. SIS indigenous channels Iran will be used to supply above funds to Zahedi.

        4. CIA will attempt subsidize key military leaders if this necessary.

    B. <u>Acquisition Shah Cooperation</u>

        1. <u>Stage 1</u>: Convince the Shah that UK and US have joint aim and remove pathological fear of British intrigues against him.

            a. Ambassador Henderson call on the Shah to assure him of US-UK common aid and British supporting him not Mossadeq.

            b. Henderson to say to the Shah that special US representative will soon be introduced to him for presentation joint US-UK plan.

        2. <u>Stage 2</u>: Special US representative will visit the Shah and present following:

S E C R E T

Figure 1: The Wilber Report, Appendix A, page 2

Meanwhile, Mossadeq (who knew very well that the coup was not of his making) decided it would be prudent to deploy loyal troops around the city and to reinforce the guard at key buildings and installations. Knowing who the real coup leader was, he also sent a company of soldiers to arrest Zahedi, but Roosevelt had the general secure in a safehouse. Once the newspapers hit the streets (there was a free press at the time) even more rumours gained currency. One said that the plot had been hatched by the shah and General Schwarzkopf (Stormin' Norman's father) during a meeting they'd had on 9 August. Another rumour said that the Imperial Guards had been planning a coup and that the coup of 15 March was actually a counter-coup to forestall that plan. Remarkably, another newspaper got it dead right when it claimed that the coup leader was General Fazlollah Zahedi and he was being backed by Mr Kermit Roosevelt of the CIA in an attempt to depose Premier Mossadeq. Someone in the know was talking.

Later, on 16 August, a large crowd rallied to listen to speeches by government ministers and Mossadeq supporters. As the gathering was broadcast live by Radio Tehran, they launched vehement attacks on the shah. It was through this that the Americans and British learned that the shah was holed up in Baghdad. But Mossadeq's decision to turn on the imperial leader was misguided; too many of the ordinary people still revered him.

Seeking to capitalise on this, the station proposed that someone should fly to Iraq and persuade the windy shah to make a radio broadcast backing Zahedi. CIA headquarters vetoed the idea, suggesting they ask the British to do it. So Roosevelt proposed that Darbyshire and Leavitt be flown from Cyprus to Baghdad in an 'RAF fighter jet'.[28] London vetoed that idea, which was probably fortunate; the RAF has never had a fighter jet that could carry two passengers and it would have been necessary to strap the spies to the wings. At the start of the second day of this disastrous sequence of events, the CIA station was able to cheer up a little:

> As the station personnel entered on another day after a second sleepless night, some real encouragement came from word that, in breaking up Tudeh [communist] groups late the night before, the soldiers had beaten them with rifle butts and made them shout, 'Long live the shah.' The station continued to feel that the 'project was not quite dead'[29]

Well, that's all right then; increased support for the shah must be counted as some kind of progress. Much more significant was that fact that the Mossadeq government dropped its guard far too soon and ordered its troops return to barracks. Another coup attempt was scheduled for 18 August. Before then an attempt was to be made to persuade the supreme cleric to issue a fatwa declaring a holy war against communism.

But 18 August started with bad news; the shah had flown to Rome, putting himself at an even greater distance from the turmoil in Tehran. What happened when he reached the Excelsior Hotel could have brought the coup to an unseemly premature end. By coincidence, Director of Central Intelligence Allen Dulles was there on vacation. When the shah checked into the hotel, Dulles was standing next to him trying to do the same thing. The incident is recorded in a transatlantic telephone conversation between CIA officers Frank Wisner and John Waller. The frantic call took place between 0200 and 0300.

> Wisner was agitated. 'He's gone to Rome,' Wisner told Waller. 'A terrible, terrible coincidence occurred. Can you guess what it is?' Waller could not.
>
> 'Well,' Wisner continued, '[the shah] went to the Excelsior Hotel to book a room with his bride, and the pilot, there were only three of them, and he was crossing the street on his way into the hotel. Guess... can you tell me, I don't want to say it over the phone, can you imagine what may have happened? Think of the worst thing you can think of that happened.'
>
> Waller said, 'He was hit by a cab and killed.'
>
> 'No, no, no, no,' Wisner responded impatiently, by this time almost wild with excitement. 'Well, John, maybe you don't know, that Dulles had decided to extend his vacation by going to Rome. Now can you imagine what happened?'
>
> Waller answered, 'Dulles hit him with his car and killed him.'
>
> Wisner did not think it was funny. 'They both showed up at the reception desk at the Excelsior at the very same moment. And Dulles had to say, 'After you, Your Majesty.'[30]

The following day, the shah made a few non-committal remarks to the press. Internationally, the Associated Press wire service ran a statement by General Zahedi which summed up the situation. It was addressed to the officer corps of the Iranian army: 'Be ready for sacrifice and loss of your lives for the maintenance of independence and of the monarchy of Iran and of the holy religion of Islam which is now being threatened by the infidel communists.'

Operation *TP-Ajax*, the on-again, off-again coup was back on again. The evening of the 18th was one of rioting and looting by both pro- and anti-Mossadeq activists. Security forces were ordered to clear the streets, the result being inevitable bloodshed. The situation was so dire that the CIA once more decided to call off the operation. But on the morning of the 19th the newspapers carried a copy of the shah's firman appointing Zahedi prime minister. Large groups of pro-monarchists took to the streets; all they needed now was leadership. The Americans told their contacts to get the security forces on the side of the demonstrators and to make plans for the capture of the radio station. By mid-morning tanks and truckloads of anti-Mossadeq soldiers had rolled into the city and occupied all the main squares. Most of the army had changed sides and loyalist support was reduced to one battalion.

The coup leaders were working to the CIA/SIS checklist again and, one by one, key targets were taken; the telegraph office, the Ministry of Foreign Affairs and Radio Tehran. After some fierce fighting, Police Headquarters surrendered at 4 p.m. that afternoon. A non-stop stream of telegrams was sent to the provinces urging them to declare for the shah. The release of the officers arrested on the 16th was quickly secured and the Imperial Guard (not apparently loyal to His Imperial Majesty) were locked up in the newly available cells. As the day progressed each of the designated military targets was taken and names ticked off the 'arrest list'. Radio Tehran announced the appointment of new government ministers. The day had been a success after all and, as darkness fell, a curfew was imposed to prevent any counter-demonstrations. A few days later the situation was considered safe enough for the shah to return from Rome and to be greeted as the saviour of the Iranian people.

For the next twenty-five years those same people suffered a reign of repression. Zahedi became prime minister and made some interesting appointments to his government. Sharif-Emami, who had been a fellow-inmate in a British jail in the 1940s, became Secretary General of the Oil Industry and, later, prime minister. Another Nazi-supporter, Bahram Shahrokh, had been a trainee of Joseph Goebbels and was Radio Berlin's first Farsi programme announcer; he got the obvious job of Director of Propaganda. Ardeshir Zahedi preferred life in the West and after a short time as chamberlain to the shah became ambassador to the United States (twice) and once to the UK. The Zahedis have their photo album on the Web for 'friends and family'.[31] Don't miss it.

Britain got its oil back and, whenever you see a roadside gas station showing a 'BP' sign, remember that the company used to be called the Anglo-Iranian Oil Company. But also remember that BP's good fortune was not achieved without bringing a considerable amount of grief down on the heads of the people of Iran, a country that now has two governments, one secular, one religious. In his 2005 State of the Union Address President George W. Bush accused Iran of developing weapons of mass destruction and of being the world's worst sponsor of 'terror'. Watch this space.

Risible Results: Algeria 1961

Good planning is the essence of any successful military operation. That is what officer cadets learn in their training and, if they get to Staff College, they learn even more. If the planning fails, you might be able to fall back on chance – but luck can only be relied on if you own the casino.

Now, if you have a *general* leading your coup, you would expect the planning to be impeccable in the extreme. Even if the rest of the plot goes pear-shaped, the planning is going to be case-book stuff, rock solid. Well, the 'Generals' Putsch' in Algeria, 1961 had no fewer than *four* generals behind it, plus more colonels than you could shake a swagger stick at. But, in the words of one historian, it was 'an ill-conceived and hurriedly prepared attempt to seize power'. The plan for the coup was 'hazy' and the outcome 'disastrously divisive for the army'.[32] For weeks after the coup French military units chased around Algiers arresting each other's leaders; a staff officer was good but, failing that, your own platoon commander would do fine.

It wasn't the beginning of the end; that really got started during World War II. French rule over this huge Muslim area of North Africa had always been fractious and bloody to varying degrees. But, when metropolitan France became occupied, the Algerians stood by their colonial masters and 200,000 of them fought for the Free French against the Germans and Italians. Wartime leader Charles de Gaulle conceded that the nation owed something to the Muslims. 'Something' turned out to be citizenship for a handful and nothing towards the political independence being sought. In May 1945, a pro-independence demonstration took place in the garrison town of Sétif. Nationalist flags were flown and the troops opened fire on the crowd. That sparked off a disorganised retaliation in which eighty-four French settlers were killed. The result of the French retaliation to that was, by most accounts, eight thousand dead Algerians. *That* was the beginning of the end, and nine years later the country was in the throes of a bloody civil war.

At dawn on 1 November 1954, guerrillas of the National Liberation Front (*Front de Libération Nationale* – FLN) attacked military garrisons, police stations, telephone exchanges and electricity power stations throughout Algeria. The FLN had widespread support throughout North Africa, including Egypt, Libya and neighbouring Morocco. What developed was essentially a three-cornered fight. The Muslims wanted independence for what they saw as their country. The *colons*, or *pieds noirs* ('black feet'), were the economic and political power in the land; for them Algeria had to stay as a province of France. The French Government began with firm opposition to any suggestion of independence: 'the only possible negotiation is war,' declared Interior Minister François Mitterrand. A few days after the outbreak of hostilities, Prime Minister Pierre Mendès-France added, 'One does not compromise when it comes to defending the internal peace of the nation, the unity and integrity of the Republic. The Algerian departments are part of the French Republic. They have been French for a long time, and they are irrevocably French. Between them and metropolitan France there can be no conceivable secession.' From that point onwards, the war escalated and the position of the Paris government softened; for all but the most *dogmatique*, independence was inevitable and it was just a question of how many people would die before it happened.

As the *well-planned* FLN campaign stepped up, the *colons* sold their farms and businesses and moved to the relative safety of Algiers. There they took a leaf from (or maybe wrote the preface for) the Guatemalan book and set up 'death squads'. Every night, while the police looked the other way, they would conduct *ratonnades* – 'rat hunts' – in which they would murder Arabs they suspected of being FLN activists. As most of the population supported the liberation movement, this kept them quite busy. The security forces did their bit by systematically torturing anyone they considered to be a terrorist. Far from resolving any issues, this sparked off even further escalation, especially the bombing of Western cafés and other targets.[33] This is not the sort of mistake an occupying power would make in the twenty-first century, of course.

As the civilian body-count climbed, the position of the French Government inevitably shifted and in December 1960 President de Gaulle was characterising the shift as being 'not towards an Algeria governed from France, but towards an Algerian Algeria'. This caused huge problems for an already-troubled army. Its leadership was instinctively inclined to support the *pieds noirs*, but those same generals had also fought under de Gaulle for a free France throughout World War II. Their loyalty was being stretched to breaking-point and, for some, it went beyond that.

De Gaulle's 1960 visit to Algeria was a disaster and had to be curtailed. As the president's motorcade changed routes to avoid an Arab nationalist demonstration, it would come across another organised by the *colons*. During the same few days there were no fewer that four serious attempts on his life. This, however, was only slightly above average; it is generally agreed that, between 1958 and 1965, there was a remarkable total of thirty assassination attempts against a man who was either the best protected or luckiest head of state ever. (De Gaulle died aged eighty watching a soap opera on television.) A referendum was held in January 1961. The result in metropolitan France was predictably in support of withdrawal; in Algeria the *pieds noirs* boycotted the ballot but, if they had voted, they would not have overturned a 69-per-cent 'yes' vote.

The fiasco of the failed visit seemed to be the final straw and by November 1960 the undercurrents of a coup were beginning to stir. The conspiracy was being pondered by General Raoul Salan, who at that time was sitting out a semi-exile in Madrid. Franco's Spain was a haven for right-wing extremists and the five-star Hotel Princesa was their favourite watering hole. Juan Perón and Isabelita were in town, as was former SS Colonel Otto Skorzeny (who had rescued Mussolini from the US Army) and a motley crew of quasi-fascists from across Europe.

Mainly as a result of service in France's many overseas possessions in the 1920s and 1930s, Salan was to become his country's most decorated soldier; he had been awarded the *Croix de Guerre* as a young man in World War I. In 1958 he was one of a right-wing group of movers and shakers who had pressed for Charles de Gaulle to be brought to power. Three years later, he sat in the Hotel Princesa feeling aggrieved about de Gaulle's declared intention to ease France out of Algeria.

General Salan was courted by various bit players in the coup, but few impressed him. Then, in March 1961, came news that three other senior generals were already making plans of their own and wanted Salan on board. The others were André Zeller, Edmond Jouhaud and, to Salan's amazement, General Maurice Challe, supposedly a staunch supporter of de Gaulle. Until recently, Challe had been NATO's Commander-in-Chief, Allied Forces, Central Europe; as such, he should have known a thing or two about planning. But, whatever the four of them knew, they failed to apply it to a coup which would not just cause a shift of power in Algeria, but had the potential to bring down the French Government itself. At one stage, tanks were lined up outside the National Assembly building in Paris.

It may have been that the generals believed they only had to issue the order for the whole of the French military to leap into action. It was never going to be like that. The conscripts from metropolitan France, like all conscripts, never wanted to be in the army. They certainly never wanted to be in Algeria and they definitely didn't want to get involved in a crazy attempt to overthrow the government. This was particularly true of some 150,000 North African Muslim soldiers; engagement in anti-terrorist operations was one thing, but attempting to overthrow a government that was then on the brink of giving your homeland independence was not a sensible option for them. Further up the chain of command, the younger and smarter career officers would have realised that a lot of senior ranks were about to become vacated, thus opening up their own prospects for promotion.

The only solid, guaranteed support for the coup was going to be from the 1er REP ('*Premier Rep*'), or *Premier Regiment Étranger de Parachutists*, the airborne unit of the French Foreign Legion. Its acting CO was Major Élie Denoix de Saint-Marc. Many of 1er REP's soldiers were German; at the end of World War II, France recruited twenty thousand Wehrmacht troops, mostly from POW camps. They were hardened shock troops, veterans of France's colonial war in Vietnam. More importantly, they had more loyalty to the Foreign Legion than they ever had to the French Government. (The concept of using foreign soldiers was later employed during the UK-sponsored coup in Uganda in 1971.) The commanding officer of 1er REP was one of the plotters and two more airborne regiments were solidly in support; that was only enough for them to take the city of Algiers.

The *coup d'état* kicked off on the evening of 20 April 1961 and twenty-four hours later it became clear that the generals had spent far more time plotting than planning. They took the radio stations and made impassioned pleas for support from the rest of the army. De Gaulle did the same and spoke the military keywords of honour, country, duty, ending with '*Française, français, aidez-moi!*' It worked; the generals failed to extend their support beyond the fourteen thousand troops they started with and the putsch collapsed after four days.

Very elementary mistakes were made. For example, General Lhermitte, deputy commander of the garrison in the western province of Oranie, had pledged support. But, come the day of the coup, he had his feet up at home in France. It probably would not have made any difference in the event, but was it beyond the wit of these four military masterminds to have a junior officer keep track of where the key players were likely to be on the start-dates being considered? Most of the commanders who had originally agreed to take part just no-showed. The psychology of this is important for all coup planners. A junior or middle-ranking officer standing in front of a general will tend to agree with any proposition put to him, in spite of what is going through his head. 'If I say no, how will it affect my career?' 'Is this coup plot for real? Or is it a test of my loyalty?' 'Do I really want to lead my battalion against the rest of the army?' The natural reaction is to say 'yes' and hope the problem will go away and that is exactly how support for the Generals' Putsch vaporised into thin air. The delusion that France's armed forces would rise in support became apparent when the air force and the navy sat back and watched events unfold without the slightest intention of taking any part. All but one of the army sector commanders had promised support but, as Challe later admitted, 'Unhappily this was only true in theory, while nothing had been fixed in practice. We were going to have a sad experience here.'[34]

Operational security was as bad as the planning. It seems the generals never thought much about what their wives got up to once they had set off for divisional headquarters in the morning. Well, with little risk of being politically incorrect, we can quote the intercept of part of a telephone conversation that took place on the evening of the coup between Madame de Saint-Hillier (whose husband commanded the 10th Division) and Madame de Saint-Marc (wife of the acting commander of the 1er REP):

MADAME DE SAINT-HILLIER: '*Dîtes-moi, Madame,* is your husband up to some dirty trick tonight?'

MADAME DE SAINT-MARC: 'Yes, I fear so…!'[35]

But to be fair, there had been gossip about the coup in military circles for many months and de Gaulle was well-informed about the intentions of the plotters. Nonetheless, there was serious concern about an airborne assault on the capital, and the threat of paras landing in the Bois de Boulogne brought tanks and infantry onto the streets of Paris. The officers who didn't surrender were arrested and the ill-planned and ill-fated coup failed.

This was a veto coup which, although it had no chance of succeeding, still had a bloody aftermath. General Raoul Salan had gone into hiding and set up a terrorist organisation to continue the fight. Pro-coup soldiers left the military in droves and joined his OAS (*Organisation de l'Armée Secrète*) and set to in a murderous campaign against the civilian Arab population of Algeria. No pretext was needed to make someone a target and doctors, waiters, accountants and bus drivers were gunned down without distinction.

The group was even more determined to assassinate President de Gaulle and this set the background for the classic 1973 movie *The Day of the Jackal*, based on the thriller of the same name by former BBC correspondent Frederick Forsyth.[36] According to media reports, the year before the film was made Forsyth was allegedly involved in a little coup of his own making. It is said that he raised two hundred thousand dollars to back a plot to overthrow the government of Equatorial Guinea by kidnapping President Francisco Macias Nguema. The coup foundered because the ammunition no-showed, but the subsequent book, *The Dogs of War*, was a best-seller.[37] The 2004 coup in Equatorial Guinea foundered because the mercenary *team* no-showed, having been arrested in Zimbabwe *en route* (see Chapter 9).

Salan was eventually arrested, tried on treason charges and in May 1962 jailed for life. Finally, for any French staff officers reading this, 'Prior planning and preparation prevent piss-poor performance' translates as '*La planification et la préparation antérieures empêchent l'exécution pisser-pauvre*'.

Pro-Formas for Perfect Planning

So how should a coup be planned? Well, it should be planned as you'd plan any other military campaign that you seriously want to win. Orders should be specific, detailed and appropriate to the units available for deployment.

Nothing should be taken for granted. Don't assume that your troops will take ration packs with them, especially if they are in short supply and especially if there are plenty of McDonald's and Pizza Express joints in town. Don't even assume that they will take more than the usual three magazines of ammunition with them. Will they have sleeping bags? What happens if an armoured fighting vehicle breaks down? Spell it all out and make sure everyone knows what role they are to play in the grand scheme of things. Even though it would be unwise to state this explicitly in the kind of pro-forma 'Planning Instruction' shown below, make the objective clear. After all, if they don't know the objective, how will they know when they have won?

Figure 2, which follows on the next few pages is an outline 'Planning Instruction' for a coup attempt by a (very ambitious) Motor Rifle Battalion. Mechanised infantry are interesting units to use because of the mix of capability they have available to them. They have mobility in the form of troop-carrying armoured fighting vehicles (such as the American Bradley and the British Warrior) as well as a useful range of support-weapons capability. These include anti-tank and mortar platoons as well as vehicle maintenance and medical sections. Clearly, if you can draw on resources up to brigade level that would be even better, especially if it includes additional transport and a few attack helicopters.

This kind of detailed planning is best done by junior staff officers. Give the job to your most competent and most trusted, specify the objectives and let them get on with the rest.

There is a stark saying which supposedly originates from American seafarers: 'Shit happens'. Now more common in military circles, it is a close relation to Murphy's Law: 'If anything can go wrong, it will go wrong.' Less well-known is McGonagall's Law: 'Murphy is an incurable optimist!' Anticipating the unanticipated is fundamental to good planning of all kinds, but it is interesting that Iran 1953 stuttered because key unit leaders 'lost heart' and returned to barracks without undertaking their objectives. And in Algeria 1961, commanders who had previously promised support for the coup failed to turn up on the day. In both cases this should have been anticipated and contingencies put in place.

The British Army calls the process of contingency planning, 'actions on'. It would comprise a list: 'Action on the presidential palace being protected by more than the night guard', 'Action on the armoured battalion being deployed towards the capital before the anti-tank company is in defensive positions on the ring road', and 'Action on the joint chief of staff being in his office at dawn.' The appropriate action or actions can then be written next to each of the events as on page 79.

Date: June 2006

**PLANNING INSTRUCTION
EXERCISE BLUE GARDENIA JULY 2006**

INTRODUCTION

1. 2 Motor Rifle Battalion will deploy on
Exercise Blue Gardenia from 7-11 July 06.

AIM

2. The aim of Exercise Blue Gardenia is to:
'Test in the most realistic way possible the response effectiveness
of the Presidential Guard, the Police, the Emergency Services and
the General Public in dealing with a terrorist attack on the
Nation's Capital.'

EXECUTION

3. Exercise Format

a. **Phase 1 - Muster.** All personnel fit for active duty parade at
garrison at 0300 hours on 07 July 2005. All leave has been
cancelled as per earlier order. Equipment and vehicles to be
inspected and checked.

b. **Phase 2 - Deployment.** All companies will depart garrison
promptly at 0400 hours and move expediently to forward staging
positions as per the attached Movements Order. ETA all units 0500.

c. **Phase 3 - Positioning.** On command from Battalion HQ, company
commanders will deploy their platoons to their designated targets.
Platoon commanders to report in position to their Company
commanders, Company commanders to report to Battalion HQ.
Platoon commanders must immediately report any contact with the
enemy.

d. **Phase 4 - Engagement.** On command from Company
commanders, platoons will move into final positions or attack
designated targets as detailed below (Annex A). Platoon
commanders to report attainment of objectives.

e. **Phase 5 - Holding.** Following the seizure of objectives, units will
establish hasty defence and VCPs until further notice. Platoon

Figure 2: Planning Instruction

commanders will make sitreps on an hourly basis. Contact with the enemy will be reported immediately to Company commanders.

f. **Phase 7 - Recovery.** At 1500 11 July 06 all platoons to recover to Company forward staging positions prior to return in convoy to home garrison following routes specified in the Battalion movement order.

SERVICE SUPPORT

4. **Dress and Equipment**

a. 1 x Fatigues, Camouflage with Cap, Camouflage, Helmet.

b. Webbing.

c. Body Armour.   ~ check

d. Blue armbands (to be issued by CQMS) to be worn at all times.

e. Field sleeping kit.

f. Field rations for 2 days. Field kitchens to be established.

5. **Weapons.** All units to deploy with personal and support weapons. Civil disorder equipment to be available from vehicles.

6. **Ammunition.** Battalion is to deploy with 2 DOS (Days of Supplies) of SAA natures, Echelon is to carry a further 1 DOS.

Ser	Nature	Amount	Notes
1	Rd 7.62-mm	SHORT	210,000
2	Rd 7.62-mm	N 4B1T	90,000
3	Rkt 1.5-in	HH illum	300
4	Gren Smk Scr	White	300
5	Rkt	RPG-7	600
6	Gren	HE	1400
7	Gren	WP	350

— short of these

— none of these

7. Feeding Plan:

Supply of fresh food cannot be guaranteed. All personnel will therefore carry field rations sufficient for 2 days.

8. **Transport.** Battalion is to deploy with all A and B Vehicles.

9. **Medical.** Battalion will deploy with normal scales of medical support, Battalion Aid Post will be located at GR 147872.

10. **Discipline.** All soldiers will exercise strictest discipline during exercise. The battalion will be on show in the capital and Officers and NCOs will be responsible for ensuring the highest standards of personal conduct, especially in relation to dealings with civilians.

11. **Logistic Support.** A Echelon to be established at GR 149871 National Football Stadium. B Echelon to remain in barracks.

COMMAND AND SIGNAL

12. Battalion Command post at GR 138865.   — HQ

13. Alternative command: A Coy Commander is designated as alternative commander until Battalion 2i/c can take over.

14. Passwords: As per CEI.

15. EMCON: Use of unsecured Combat Radio Net to be kept to an absolute minimum.

(SIGNED)

BATTALION CO

Annexes:

A – Targets and Objectives

B – Orbat

ANNEX A
TO 2 MOTOR RIFLE BATTALION
DATED JUNE 06

TARGETS AND OBJECTIVES 07–11 JULY 2006

COY	PL	ACTION	OBJECTIVE
A	1	CONTAIN	REPUBLICAN GUARD BARRACKS
	2	PERIMETER	PRESIDENTIAL PALACE
	3	SEIZE	NATIONAL ASSEMBLY
B	4	SEIZE	POLICE HEADQUARTERS
	5	SEIZE	RADIO/TV STATION
	6	SEIZE	DEFENCE MINISTRY
C	7	SEIZE	AIRPORT TERMINAL
	8	SEIZE	AIR TRAFFIC CONTROL CENTRE
	9	CONTAIN	VCPs CITY CENTRE ROADS
SW	AIR DEF 1	DEFEND	AIRPORT
	AIR DEF 2	DEFEND	BATTALION HQ
	AT 1	DEFEND	MAIN ROAD NORTH
	AT 2	DEFEND	MAIN ROAD EAST
	AT 3	DEFEND	AIRPORT ACCESS ROAD
	AT 4	DEFEND	BATTALION HQ
	MORTAR	CONTAIN	REPUBLICAN GUARD BARRACKS
	GRENADE	CONTAIN	REPUBLICAN GUARD BARRACKS
HQ	ARTLY 1	DEFEND	MAIN ROAD NORTH
	ARTLY 2	CONTAIN	REPUBLICAN GUARD BARRACKS
	RECCE	COMMS	AS REQUIRED
	MAINT.		AS REQUIRED
	SUPPLY		AS REQUIRED
	MEDICAL		AS REQUIRED
SF	SF 1	SEIZE	PRESIDENTIAL PALACE
	SF 2	SEIZE	NATIONAL ASSEMBLY

(handwritten annotations: "OC not reliable?" beside B company; "Short" beside MEDICAL)

AT:	ANTI-TANK	
ARTY:	ARTILLERY	
SF:	SPECIAL FORCES	

ANNEX B
TO 2 MOTOR RIFLE BATTALION
DATED JUNE 06

2 MOTOR RIFLE BATTALION
OUTLINE ORBAT

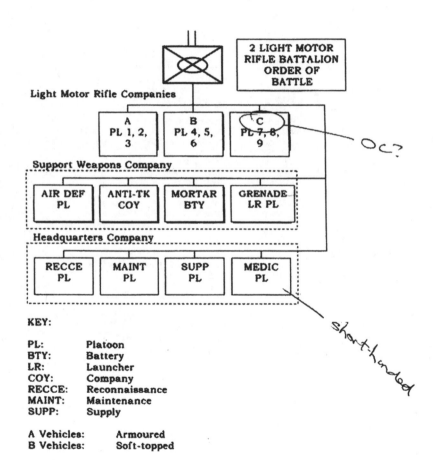

KEY:

PL:	Platoon
BTY:	Battery
LR:	Launcher
COY:	Company
RECCE:	Reconnaissance
MAINT:	Maintenance
SUPP:	Supply

A Vehicles:	Armoured
B Vehicles:	Soft-topped

EVENT	ACTION
Presidential palace protected by more than the night guard.	1. Divert resources from Presidential Guard barracks perimeter and try again.
	2. Divert resources from National Assembly (if already taken) and try again.
	3. Change tactics from seizure to containment and await orders.
The armoured battalion is deployed towards the capital before the anti-tank company is in defensive positions on the ring road.	1. Establish defensive position within ring road on Main Road North closer to presidential palace.
	2. Request activation of recce platoon for observation and artillery targeting.
	3. Request activation of Artillery Battery to fire on prearranged targets.
Joint chief of staff is still in his office at dawn.	1. Arrest him.
	2. Arrange his immediate transportation to Battalion HQ.

It should be clear from this limited example that more work can be invested in 'actions on' than in the basic planning of the coup itself. But don't skimp on the effort; it is a discipline demanding that all assumptions be challenged.

'Of course the damned Republican Guard will stay in its barracks!' insists the general.

'Yes, sir, of course, sir,' says the major charged with planning, 'but we thought it might be prudent to let the platoon commander know what he should do if they start to defend aggressively.'

Unlike the somewhat sanitised 'Planning Instruction', these 'actions on' might be difficult to explain away if challenged. In the interests of 'OpSec' it might be preferable to brief platoon commanders and expect them to memorise the contingency arrangements that apply to them.

Finally, do not confuse 'planning' with 'plotting'; they are two quite distinct activities.

Chapter 4
Recruitment, Training and Tactics

The section of eight soldiers from 4 Platoon, B Company of the 2nd Battalion of the Parachute Regiment strode purposefully up Whitehall towards Trafalgar Square. As tradition dictated, they had switched from the uncomfortable Kevlar jump helmets to their red berets, each one individually moulded to its owner's close-cropped scalp. The rest of the British Army disparagingly calledthese 'conquering-hero red berets'. The Paras couldn't care less, the rest of the army were 'Crap Hats'. The section moved tactically, in two columns, well spaced, personal weapons ready with index fingers alongside the trigger-guards. They covered their arcs, one man always scanning behind them; when deployed they never moved any other way, a lesson learned the hard way in countless small wars. Always alert to their surroundings, each one made a mental note of a small Victorian pub on the east side of the wide road, not far up from the Cenotaph.

Once at the traffic lights the section commander, a corporal, ordered two of his men to take up covering positions while the others pulled folding signs from a hold-all. These variously read 'STOP' and 'CHECKPOINT'. The NCO pointed to a heavy-set Para carrying a Minimi machine gun which looked small in his massive hands.

'Bob! Stand in the middle of the road and stop the traffic. This so-called high-visibility jacket comes courtesy of the Health & Safety at Work geniuses. It will make you immortal to everything but red double-decker buses and short-sighted terrorist gunmen on top of Nelson's column.'

Bull-necked Bob stepped out into the road and held up a hand, causing a black taxi to screech to a halt inches from the soldier's knees. After the cabbie had expressed a profane opinion on Bull-necked Bob's intellectual capabilities, he swung the taxi into a U-turn and drove off to find an alternative route to Victoria Station. The corporal ordered the rest of the section to wave off other approaching vehicles.

'If they ask what's going on, tell them there's a security alert.'

Then he thumbed the remote pressel on the forestock of his rifle and talked to the platoon commander over the personal radio network: 'One Zero, this is One One Charlie. VCP at Point Alpha is in position. Out.'

In a London Eye capsule over four hundred feet above the Thames, three Royal Marines scanned the scene through powerful binoculars.

'Point Alpha and Point Bravo vehicle checkpoints now in place,' one of them said. 'Whitehall now looks clear of traffic.' Point Bravo, at the Parliament Square end of the road was manned by another section from 4 Platoon of 2 Para.

'They should be able to manage that,' said another marine, hinting at the rivalry between the units. According to the marines, the Paras had to hand over their brains in exchange for the red beret; according to the Paras, the marines were gay sailors to a man.

'Four more Merlins... correction... four Lynx approaching along the river,' said the marine on the other side of the glass capsule. The light battlefield helicopters of the Army Air Corps had flown a circuitous route from their base at Middle Wallop in Hampshire to collect their passengers from Colchester garrison but were still arriving exactly on schedule. The marines manning the observation post watched as they split from their formation and flew unhesitatingly to hover low over key buildings. The first hung low-enough above 10 Downing Street for two soldiers to climb out, the second man standing on the skid and passing down two Bergens and what looked like a long sports bag before stepping off himself. The Lynx tilted forward and lifted before moving to deliver two more men to the roof of the Old Admiralty Building on the north side of Horse Guards Parade. The other helicopters delivered their passengers to the rooftops of the Ministry of Defence, the Queen Elizabeth II Conference Centre overlooking Parliament Square and Portcullis House, the annex of MPs' offices opposite Big Ben.

Each sniper team of two men was equipped with a .338 Long Range Large Calibre Rifle – or LRR – and the Light Support Weapon variant of the standard .556-mm SA80 assault rifle. The LRR has a range of 1100 m and had become the key weapon in the British Army's renewed commitment to the use of snipers. The teams also had binoculars, night-vision kit and radios, providing enough eyes for 360-degree coverage of the areas around London's political heartland.

As the snipers were being deployed, the VCP at the north end of Whitehall was having its own flurry of excitement. Across the square, three army vehicles emerged from the far side of the National Gallery; a Land Rover Defender followed by two 4-tonne trucks. Even at that distance the Paras could see the red and white boards reading 'BOMB DISPOSAL'. With blue lights flashing and horns blaring, the vehicles bullied their way through the traffic and screeched to a stop at the checkpoint. The Para corporal was there to meet them.

'Good morning, gentlemen,' he snapped, failing to spot any indication of rank on the camouflage fatigues of the driver and front-seat passenger. They were both wearing dark blue berets sporting Royal Engineers cap badges. The Para's neatly trimmed moustache twitched at the sight of the driver's hair curling over the nape of his neck.

'Good morning, Corporal,' replied the passenger, in the clipped accent of a Sandhurst graduate, 'Thirty-three Engineer Regiment EOD.' The corporal gave him the benefit of a salute and waved for the 'STOP' signs to be moved away. As he watched the vehicles race off down Whitehall, behind him in Trafalgar Square all the traffic lights changed to red at the same instant. The same happened at major intersections across the city; King's Cross, Marble Arch, Cambridge Circus, Oxford Circus, Hyde Park Corner. Gridlock spread like a virus.

The sniper team high on the MoD building watched as the gates to Downing Street swung open and the sturdy steel barrier folded into the ground. The three bomb-disposal vehicles drove in and stopped outside the much-photographed door to the prime minister's office and official residence.

'Did you remember to bring the plastic Pepsi bottles?' asked the sniper.

'Yep,' said his number two.

'And the bog roll and the snappy bags?'

'Aye. It's all right for those buggers up there,' he added, gesturing toward the OP in the London Eye Ferris wheel.

The shooter glanced sideways at him: 'How do you mean?'

'Every few hours they'll get rotated.'

The armed policeman who normally has the job of standing outside No. 10 was actually inside having breakfast and watching the surveillance monitors when he saw the army drive into his domain. He was still chewing a mouthful of bacon sandwich when he stepped out to greet the tall young officer from the Land Rover. A former soldier, the constable forced himself not to salute.

'Royal Engineers, 33 Regiment Explosive Ordnance Disposal. You'll need to evacuate the building – and the Cabinet Office,' said the officer, glancing at his watch, 'I'd say you've got no more than five minutes. I suggest you use the rest of the security team. Then get well clear yourselves.'

'But nobody told us anything about...'

The officer checked his watch again and raised an eyebrow. The policeman swallowed hard and spoke into his radio as he re-entered the building.

The men of B Company's 5 Platoon were not manning checkpoints but were instead running down Whitehall and storming through the main doors of each government office.

'Security alert!' they announced. 'Evacuate the building and get everyone down to the QE Conference Centre.' Few of the underpaid contract security guards put up any argument and immediately pressed the manual-override buttons of their fire alarm systems. The MoD Police guarding the monolithic Ministry of Defence building were a different matter. Armed with Heckler & Koch MP-5 machine pistols, Glock 9-mm sidearms and wearing body-armour, the four officers in the main entrance tried to exert some authority and challenged the soldiers of 16 Air Assault.

'Who the fuck are you lot?' asked an inspector.

'Social services,' muttered one soldier.

'Two Para,' said the corporal. 'You need to evacuate the building. Now!'

'No way,' replied the 'mod-plod', 'let's see your ID cards.' As he scrutinised the cards, he continued to interrogate them. 'The blokes on the roof – do they belong to your lot, Corporal?'

'Don't know what you're talking about, mate.'

'Mate? Sir or Inspector will do.'

The corporal was having none of it: 'I don't remember the MoD's Mickey Mouse police force being in my chain of command.'

'Look, only building security and three duty desk officers are here at this time of day. The cleaners arrive in thirty minutes. What's the nature of the threat? We've received no warning.'

The corporal shrugged: 'Why does this come as no surprise to me?'

'Look, if this is an exercise, we are going nowhere,' said the inspector, handing back the ID cards.

'This is no exercise, mate,' came the reply.

Fire alarms wailed the length of Whitehall as the handful of Downing Street workers hurried out of the main door. Last to leave was the police constable. He did a double-take as he walked past the driver of the Land Rover; the soldier was carrying what looked like an M16 rifle instead of the standard-issue SA80. More than that, the man's face seemed vaguely familiar. At the gate he met up with the policemen manning the barrier, paused and looked back again. Soldiers in camouflaged fatigues were climbing from the back of the second Leyland-Daf four-tonne truck; some of them were also carrying M16s, others MP5s – the counter-terrorist weapon of choice. None of them were wearing berets.

'What's up?' asked a colleague, and he gestured to start walking down Whitehall towards the Palace of Westminster and the conference centre.

'I was in the army with the driver of that Land Rover. Fourteen years ago. I'm sure of it.'

'The sappers?'

'No... We were in the Black Watch. After a few years he passed something called selection. He joined the SAS.'

Recruiting to the Cause

As we have pointed out many times, the whole principle of the *coup d'état* is the use of a small number of people applying force to achieve regime change. But it is possible to have too few people to cover all the bases and that will oblige you to recruit to the cause. When engaged in this process, keep in mind the essential tenet that it *only takes one conspirator to betray a conspiracy*.

'Leverage' is important; it is obviously better to sign up a colonel with about a thousand loyal soldiers behind him than a captain and his one hundred followers. Balanced against this, of course, has to be the consideration that the brigadier brings along ten times as many faint-hearts who might give the game away. Also, if you choose the right captain, he is likely to attract much more loyalty from his company than any commander would from a whole battalion. Leverage also applies to any force specialisation; a mortar platoon here, a little armour there.

Cherry-picking these leaders and key individuals is going to be a nail-biting process. There you are, leaning against the bar in the officers' club with Candidate No. 1... Consider how you might put this to him. What are your feelings about the present government? (Oops, no politics in the mess!) Are you up for joining our *coup d'état*, old chap? Or, more obliquely, what are you doing next Thursday? Take a tip from an experienced journalist: never ask a question you don't already know the answer to. Check the background of the person you are going to approach. Has he already hinted at his loyalties to an old friend? Is he related in some way to someone in government? Or to someone in opposition? Or maybe to someone already in the conspiracy? And is that relationship by blood, by marriage or by tribal kinship? What would be the consequences of him turning you down? Would he turn you in? Or, at least, would he just hedge his bets and keep quiet?

Another key factor is deciding who is going to make the approach. Obviously, don't do it mob-handed or you will all end up in a cell arguing about what went wrong. The perfect nominee for making any uncertain approach is (a) the one most likely to win the candidate over (obviously), (b) the most dispensable, in case you have miscalculated, or (c) the one least likely to crack under torture (when he falls into the hands of the president's secret police). More seriously, the bonds between soldiers who have seen combat together are particularly strong; this will reduce the chances of betrayal in the case of a turn-down.

Finally, try to make the approach in innocent surroundings such as sporting or social events. Clandestine meetings at remote seafood restaurants or out-of-the-way bars will take more explaining away than a supposedly chance encounter at the CO's summer barbecue. And don't do it over the telephone or Internet (see Chapter 5).

Training Coup Teams

If you have the resources to train your coup team, train them. And then train them some more. In the build-up to the Uganda coup of 1971 (see Chapter 6), MI6 officer Beverly Barnard had five hundred mercenary soldiers, mostly recruited from southern Sudan, in a training camp in the north of the country. He even used his own single-plane airline, Southern Airmotive, to supply them with food and *matériel*. You might not need that many extras but Barnard was so unimpressed with the Ugandan army, and so uncertain that it would support the putsch, that he decided to hedge his bets with a short battalion of additional troops.

Assuming that the soldiers you are using are beyond the essentials of basic fitness, weapons handling and fire-and-manoeuvre, what are the new skills they should have to make the coup a success? These include urban warfare, patrolling in a peacekeeping role and dealing with civil disorder. Do not assume that any modern, well-equipped army will be able to undertake these tasks – as the US Army and US Marine Corps proved in Iraq. The philosophy of overwhelming force can easily backfire and needs to be replaced by one of *escalating* force. Remember, you want to keep the population on *your* side.

Ken Connor: Reading and Writing

The US Army recently announced that is was encountering a serious problem with new recruits: in the world of high-tech warfare they could not read the manuals that told them which buttons to push.

Illiteracy cannot be tolerated anywhere in the Armed Forces. Civilians hoping to join the British Army, but unable to read and write, are sent to Remedial Education Centres, where they are expected to graduate with a certificate in literacy. I came across such a centre when I was serving in the SAS. We were visiting the depot of another army unit and, because we had driven a long way, decided to go to the club on the base before having an early night. I was taken aback to see a soldier in uniform reading a children's book while having a pint of beer and a cigarette. My mate, much less inhibited than me, went across and chatted to the guy. After finding that he was being taught to read and write, he spent the next few nights reading *The Cat's Adventures* with him while they both enjoyed a pint.

The thing I found most intriguing was that neither of them was embarrassed. The other guy needed help and my mate could help him, so they just got on and did it. Perhaps there's a lesson for the mainstream teachers amongst us who are responsible for more than 10 per cent of school leavers being illiterate.

Philosophical Stuff

In this section we will be discussing the skills and tactics that will be used by your troops when you finally decide to do the dirty deed. The most important resource is troops with the correct skills to achieve the mission you have set them. You do not need enough troops to occupy an entire country or thousands of tanks and tons of military hardware, just a simple plan. And we do mean a simple plan, nothing complicated: *soldiers do not do complicated.* Then you need troops with the correct skills to carry out your plan. Where will the troops get the knowledge they need?

Civilians are not encouraged to look too closely into what goes on inside military training establishments. This has led to an almost childlike belief outside of the armed services that military training can achieve miracles. Most civilians think there is some sort of a black art which the military use to turn male and female teenagers who can't get out of bed before teatime into model citizens who are clean and tidy and get a difficult job done. Also, most civilians do not have any contact with the military. The only time they see them is on the evening television news in Iraq or wherever, trying not to look too scared.

When they are told that their particular army is the best in the world, they accept it at face value. They do not have a yardstick to measure the statement against. But not every army can be the best and several can lay claim to the title depending on what criteria are applied.

How do you judge if your guys have the right skills? Ask the guys in the ranks; anyone who wears his rank on his shoulder will not be able to judge. Try to have a few guys around who have been under fire; they will have an air of competence and confidence about them that other soldiers will react positively to.

Another point to remember is that training establishments in the military are synonymous with discipline. These are the places where, before you can learn to fire an intercontinental ballistic missile, you must learn how to carry out archaic drill movements which were last used in anger in the time of Cromwell. Retired red-faced colonels from the Household Division nod sagely and pronounce on the importance of drill in forming the character of soldiers and regiments. Well, SAS soldiers forget any drill they learned on passing selection and neither they nor the regiment are any the worse for it. With limited time and resources available, having your coup team march up and down all day in the baking sun will do nothing more than destroy its motivation.

The base-line for all training staff in any conventional 'green' army is to assume that the trainees are as thick as the proverbial pig shit. That way, when they are planning to teach anything slightly complicated they will never ask anyone to do anything they are not capable of achieving. The trick here is to break down the activity into as many small moves as possible. After each move the person carrying out that move shouts loudly that he has finished. Then the next man moves, shouts, then the next man moves, and so on until the objective is achieved. At the end every individual feels as if they alone achieved the whole thing, and there is a great feeling of satisfaction all round. This is how units such as the artillery can get semi-educated soldiers to fire intercontinental missiles. It is very wasteful of manpower but manpower is cheap and there is never a bottom line to worry about. It also has the added advantage that the individuals are not thinking too much about the consequences of what they are doing.

In the SAS, however, training was very different. We started by giving the guys the training objective. Then we asked them how this could be achieved. A training plan was then developed jointly. It was not my plan, or theirs, or the Rupert's;[38] it was *our* plan. And because it belonged to all of us, it was in all of our interests to make sure that it worked. Once you start developing the idea, you do not stop until you have a system with which you are all happy and which works! It may take hours or it may take weeks but you keep on practising, ironing out even the tiniest of wrinkles. When it is foolproof, then you put it to bed.

Part of the process is to discuss the impact on others at the sharp end of what you are planning to do. This makes you take into account the most important military lesson of all, 'know your enemy'. When you are forced to consider this, you can then factor in the likely reaction of the enemy and plan your counter-reaction. This was how the regimental motto, 'Who Dares Wins', became a reality.

Ken Connor: Harvey Point

When I went on the SAS entry selection course in 1963, I was an experienced soldier in the Parachute Regiment. I was already a corporal after a couple of years' service, I was used to being in charge of men in tough situations, I knew how to keep my nose clean; but, most importantly, I knew how the army system worked.

When I arrived at the barracks in Herefordshire, close to the Welsh border, where the SAS was based, there was an immediate dislocation of expectations. There were no parades, no roll calls, no long-winded briefings, just the minimum information to allow you to function.

A typical day started at 0400 when the army truck left the barracks and headed west into the Welsh mountains. The only information you were given was the time the truck left and the minimum weight to carry in your pack. If you were not on the truck, you did not want to participate any more so you were returned to your parent unit (RTU'd), or if your pack was not heavy enough, again you were RTU'd. No, you were not given extra brownie points for having a pack which was too heavy, they just thought you were an idiot and RTU'd you anyway.

At some point in the mountains you were dropped off alone and told to make your way to a rendezvous (RV), many miles away over the mountains. You were not asked if you knew where you where, it was your responsibility to know or to find out. This entailed, for me anyway, a climb up to the nearest high point to identify landmarks from which I could calculate my position. Very early on I realised that whenever I climbed to a high point it was always in the opposite direction to the one in which I had to travel to get to the RV. This forced me to attempt to follow the route the truck was travelling after leaving the barracks, a difficult task when we did not have the map coverage for the majority of the journey and compass readings were affected by the metal and electrical machinery of the truck.

The sheer frustration and injustice of the staff not telling me this most crucial piece of information irritated me beyond belief. In the army I had left behind it was compulsory for your immediate superior to keep you informed. It did, however, imprint indelibly on my brain the importance of knowing where I was at any given time.

The reason for this apparent injustice became clear shortly after I joined an SAS Sabre squadron. When an SAS four-man patrol has a brush with the enemy it will always be outnumbered. The guys rely on a complex system of RVs to disengage from the enemy, check for casualties and then get on with the mission. If you do not know your position immediately the contact starts you will be slow hitting the RVs, endangering the rest of the patrol and ultimately, prejudice the success of the operation.

Twenty years after being on the selection course I and a few of my colleagues were invited to visit the United States as guests of the CIA to discuss the merits of our respective explosive techniques. The only information we were given to contact the agency was to fly to Washington DC, go to Dulles airport on a given Monday morning and ask for Maze Airlines. We flew from the UK on a Friday, on the weekly Royal Air Force VC10 shuttle, presumably to save money. After arrival we were put in a nice hotel in Georgetown and left to our own devices. We were young, red-blooded and had a reasonable amount of beer money provided by the regiment. Instinctively, we gravitated to the Fish Market in Old Town Alexandria and pitched camp for the weekend. Over the course of the next couple of days we attempted to drink Washington dry and almost succeeded.

The result was that we arrived at Dulles on the Monday morning slightly the worse for wear. We went into the General Aviation terminal as instructed to find everything shut down. After searching for several minutes the only guy we could find was a janitor who looked as if he had spent the weekend doing much the same as we had. Very tentatively, fully aware of the security implications, I asked if he knew where I could find Maze Airlines. In the loudest voice imaginable he shouted, 'Maze Airlines, that's the CIA outfit. They're outside on the tarmac.'

We slunk outside, my mates glaring daggers at me for this seeming security gaffe, feeling the gaze of a thousand hidden eyes upon us. There in front of us was a small turbo-prop airliner, with the pilots checking their watches. We were given a safety and security brief by the co-pilot before boarding. He stressed that the facility we were being flown to was top secret and it was imperative we did not try to identify its location. The blinds on the aircraft were to remain down and any attempt to open them would result in the aircraft being flown immediately back to Washington and a report made to the appropriate authorities.

After boarding, as I took my seat I glanced forward and noticed that the co-pilot had not fully closed the curtain separating the cockpit from the passenger cabin. During the flight I was able to see the aircraft instruments and could do a dead-reckoning estimate using compass heading, airspeed and the time of flight, so we knew roughly where we were. But in the SAS roughly was never good enough, we had to know exactly.

For the first few days of the symposium I am sure that the CIA operatives were puzzled by the nervousness of their guests. Every spare moment the SAS contingent would disappear to all points of the compass, telling their hosts they were hiking to keep fit. We quickly found we were on the coast, close to a beach. After a while I went strolling in the woods under the same pretext and stumbled upon a number of graves. The inscriptions on the headstones were of members of a family named Harvey who had died in the early 1700s, when the US was still a colony. That was the final piece of the jigsaw. All we needed now was a map and there was one on the wall of the mess hall.

There we were, at Harvey Point, North Carolina, site of the top-secret CIA training facility, where Cuban exiles had trained for the Bay of Pigs fiasco and which other innumerable groups had visited prior to being launched on unsuspecting countries up and down South America and the Caribbean. Presumably, very few of these had deduced where they were because it is not until recently that the name Harvey Point has appeared in the media. We knew it from very early on in our visit.

A small triumph of deduction for the Brits because we have never been told officially where we visited, and it all started in the mountains of Wales with the SAS selection course.

Fighting in Built-up Areas

If your military coup is to be successful you have to start your assault at the primary centres of authority and government control. These power bases are invariably in urban areas; coups are not won in deserts or paddy fields.

If there is any measure of armed resistance to the coup then this will mean having to fight in built-up areas. This is known by British officers as FIBUA (British troops call it FISH – Fighting in Someone's House). If you are forced to do this street-by-street then you may as well pack up your tents and go home, because large numbers of civilians will be killed, many buildings will be destroyed and everyone will blame *you* for it. There is now a verb for this process: to 'Falluja' a place.

The accepted military dogma is that you require numerical

superiority of 10:1 to be successful in assaulting a fixed, defended building. The military method of clearing a room is to throw in a hand grenade and after it explodes you follow it in with lots of automatic fire. If there are six rooms in the house, then you have to do this six times; so, by the time you have cleared the house, you have also demolished it and killed everyone who may be inside. The trouble is, grenades do not differentiate between friendly people and bad guys so you could end up with a lot of citizens hating your guts. A FIBUA team, therefore, does not employ the same tactics as a special forces or police unit rescuing the ambassador from an expensive downtown restaurant. One British training sergeant announces at the beginning of his course, 'There are no good guys in there. A passing friendly tank is an acceptable substitute for what I am about to teach you.'

We can only offer you a couple of crumbs of comfort if you find yourself standing in the street outside the radio station and someone is trying to shoot you from the second-floor windows.

- Get your troops to assault from the top of the building downwards.

- Have them use gas grenades instead of high explosives.

- Do not use stairwells because these are death traps; rappel down to each floor.

It worked at the Iranian embassy siege in London but it still did not stop the building from being totally trashed.

While you are thinking about the problem of getting onto the roof of the location, consider this: do you really need to make an entry with guns blazing? Why not wait? Cut off the electricity, water and telephone lines. Contain the situation; they will probably be as reluctant to come out as you are to go in. Before long, the defenders will become hungry and thirsty and will start to reconsider where their best options lie.

Vehicle Checkpoints

Of all the television news coverage of military coups a good half is of vehicle checkpoints (VCPs). This is not because the cameraman sees

93

'art' or some kind of 'street theatre' in such situations but because when the coup kicks off, sensible folk will hunker down with the wife and kids and watch a movie while they wait for developments.

Film crews, on the other hand, will pile out of the bar at the Intercontinental Hotel, tape 'TV' on the windows of their Toyota Landcruisers and head off in search of the action. If they don't go for the airport road, they will try the government district downtown. Theirs may well be the vehicles you stop first at your roadblock and, when you do, they will start filming and asking questions you are not going to answer. They may prove to be a nuisance, but shooting at them is not a favoured option – especially if one of them gets away with the tapes.

VCPs are an effective way of monitoring and controlling the movement of civilians and military during the immediate post-coup situation. Are soldiers trying to regroup? Are small-arms and ammunition being transported? Are some of the coup targets trying to avoid arrest? They are also a productive way of showing your presence on the streets.

In Iraq in 2003, the Americans found that roadblocks could also be a productive way of spreading your presence all over the streets. When they started setting up VCPs they would block the road with a couple of Humvees and stand around, M16s more or less at the ready, and wait for the first customer. More often than was desirable the customer would be an agricultural IED (Improvised Explosive Device) driven by a guy looking forward to being a martyr in paradise. Bang! And the whole section would be taken out, bodybags and smoking Hummers starring on that night's early-evening news.

Understandably, everyone got really twitchy and any approaching vehicles which didn't seem to be slowing down fast enough were met by a hail of automatic fire. Any temptation to exchange 'high-fives' was stilled when the bullet-riddled corpses of Abdul the shopkeeper, his wife, three children, and their grandmother were found in the vehicle. But no bomb.

What is really disgraceful is that soldiers, any soldiers, should be ordered to undertake such a potentially hazardous job without appropriate training. It does not take a whole section to search a vehicle. The only people standing in the road should be *one* soldier and, if needed, an interpreter. The other members of the section should be positioned well away from the roadblock ready to provide covering fire. To make a chicane, use commandeered civilian vehicles – or anything else that comes to hand – instead of your own jeeps and trucks, which you are going to need later. This approach does not stop suicide bombers, but it is effective in minimising friendly casualties.

Arresting the Bad Guys

A particularly important task is having your good guys arrest the government's bad guys. Take off the top and you are left with a headless dragon. Everyone will be waiting for orders that will never come. To do this requires a number of skills and specially trained personnel, who are not so easily acquired.

First, there are the surveillance teams who will need to shadow the target until he or she is at the perfect time and place for the abduction. Where are government ministers and military commanders going to be on the planned day of the coup? Attending a UN conference in New York? At home in bed? Working late at the office? Working late at their lover's apartment? Once a pattern of activity for each target has been documented, the 'watchers' will brief the hard-arrest teams. These are the guys who will spirit the target away to a place where they can be kept incommunicado until you decide what you are going to do with them. Regular soldiers (short haircuts and blazers) are not always the best for this task, but will supporters from the security services be any better? In Papa Doc's Haiti the Tonton Macoutes (in dark suits and Ray-Bans) were hardly inconspicuous.

If the target has bodyguards (BGs) then it makes the problem harder but not impossible; you just need more resources. The job of the watchers will be to identify the BGs and how they are armed. The hard-arrest teams will then make sure that they have bigger and better weapons than the BGs. If the bodyguards go for their guns during the arrest they can be taken out clinically leaving the target unharmed and unprotected. Armed bodyguards have never prevented a determined assassination attempt on the principals they were guarding, including Presidents John F. Kennedy and Ronald Reagan and Italy's Prime Minister Aldo Moro.

Prime-Time Interrogation

Once you have the deposed leaders under lock and key you can decide in slow time what you will do with them. It will always be prudent to subject them to a little interrogation, if only to get the passwords to their numbered Swiss bank accounts. Always question detainees as soon as possible after you have arrested them, while they are still in shock.

Much nonsense has been written about interrogation. To be successful requires either time and patience or extreme methods. For instance, if it is absolutely vital that someone talks straight away, put two prisoners together and shoot one of them. Then invite the second one to talk – you won't be able to shut him up.

If, however, you are bound by things like the Geneva Convention or you think you may be visited by Amnesty International then you need to be more subtle and patient. The most certain way to get someone to talk is to use drugs because the mind and body just cannot resist them; eventually when you get the dose right, they will work.

Troops with the necessary surveillance, arrest and interrogation skills are rare. We have them in the UK and there are some in the US military inventory, but elsewhere these skills will probably be retained in the counter-intelligence agencies and this could cause you a major problem.

Ken Connor: Torture

If you have to interrogate detainees then take it from me that torturing prisoners is counter-productive. Any pain inflicted will usually make an uncooperative prisoner even more determined to resist. Sleep deprivation and white noise are often useful but they are not quick acting. Threats only work if you carry them out. So be patient and when the prisoners do not have a reason to resist any longer, then they will talk.

Tailoring Your Tactics

When it comes to tactics these have to be based on the skills your troops already have. It will be difficult to suddenly start training troops to carry out tasks which are completely alien to their supposed role.

There is yet another military acronym which sums up everything you need to know about tactics: KISS (keep it simple, stupid). Senior military staff officers often feel they have a date with destiny and write plans with one eye on how they will be viewed by historians. Soldiers are simple people; if they could do something else, would they be in the business of 'kill or be killed'?

As a general strategy you can't go far wrong if you take out the top echelons of the other side and give their lower ranks the opportunity of joining you. Give as many people as possible the option of *not* fighting. Tell them there will be amnesties for everyone except the very senior officers and politicians, but if they continue to resist, then the consequences will be dire.

Never underestimate the difficulties of the task ahead, but if you trust your troops then trust them to get the job done. Tell them what to do and then let them get on and do it; nothing irritates soldiers more than being constantly checked on by the hierarchy. If you are going to interfere, then do the job yourself.

And remember – know your enemy! The biggest miscalculation in recent military history must be US Secretary for Defense Donald Rumsfeld and his 'Shock and Awe' campaign in Iraq. It provided great evening-news viewing for television audiences around the world, and it really did induce feelings of shock and awe in those viewing the footage. But the people it was really supposed to terrify just ran away and hid in the urban areas of Iraq and continued the struggle. The war was won but the peace was lost.

Chapter 5
Keeping Your Coup Covert

The club's main door was both anonymous and unremarkable; he stubbed out the cigarette under his polished shoe, climbed the three steps and pressed the button on the entry-phone, the only external indication of any security.

'Hello?'

The colonel gave his name and the lock buzzed open. Inside, he was met by a white-jacketed steward who braced up, snapping his arms straight to his side in a 'civilian salute'.

'Good evening, Sir. Your party is waiting for you in the library.'

'Thank you,' the colonel said, shrugging off his raincoat. The club's walls were covered with a mixture of framed photographs and paintings, all showing the famous and infamous from the history of unconventional warfare. A new photograph caught his eye; in pride of place next to the notice board, it showed his predecessor as commander of the regiment and evidently marked his election as president of the club. The colonel hadn't voted for him.

Walking to the left of the wide staircase which led up to the bar, he hung his coat on the half-empty row of hooks and went through the door at the end. Down a flight of stairs in what used to be the servants' quarters was the recently opened library. Converted to accommodate a large donation of military books, it was dominated by a conference table. There was one door and no windows. The two men got to their feet as he entered.

'Colonel,' said the taller, older one, 'great to see you. Howya doing?'

He extended his hand: 'I'm fine, Max. How are you?'

'Fine, just fine,' the tall man replied. 'This is Chester. He's our senior analyst at the embassy.'

'Pleased to meet you, Sir' said Chester, offering a firm handshake that belied his weedy, bespectacled appearance. The three sat down and, as the older men exchanged small-talk about families, the young analyst tried to match the man across the table to the biography he had earlier pulled from his files. Expelled from Rugby School for some unrecorded misdemeanour but which was rumoured to have involved a science teacher's wife, he had still sailed through his A-level exams under his own steam. He joined the army as an officer cadet, did well at Sandhurst and joined an English county infantry regiment after being commissioned as a 2nd lieutenant. It seemed as though his career in the established army was preordained. Where his path diverged was when he elected to attend a special forces selection course and surprised everyone – including himself, he later admitted – by passing.

Having finished his time as a troop officer in Britain's renowned 22 Regiment Special Air Service he left and attended Staff College where, by the skin of his teeth, he scraped through and then wangled a job back with the SAS, eventually becoming a squadron commander. Then, rather than going back to what the Brits called 'the green army', he secured a job in the SF Directorate attached to the Ministry of Defence. For the rest of his career he never left the rarefied atmosphere of Special Forces. In Indonesia and Malaysia he had operated in deep jungle. That was followed by several years as a liaison officer attached to Delta Force in Fort Bragg in North Carolina. He also spent time in The Gulf training and working with the newly formed Special Forces regiments of the Emirates and Omani governments. His circle of friends was international and deep. In the world of special operations he was both well known and well respected. He could call in favours from the many people who owed him. In a lecture to the senior command of US Special Forces he had declared: 'When they are in base they should be treated like thoroughbred racehorses, fed the best fodder and oats and cosseted and rubbed down every day. But on operations they can then be thrashed because there is no point in coming second in the race of their lives.' He was, thought Chester, one of those eccentric and charismatic officers that the British Army has always accommodated so well.

The small-talk about sons and daughters dried up and the colonel glanced questioningly around the room.

'We did that earlier,' said Max, leaning to one side to retrieve a portable radio-frequency scanner from his briefcase. Earlier that day, his technical department had programmed it with all the VHF and UHF bands likely to be used by microphone and camera bugs. He placed it on the table between them, set up a stubby antenna, switched it on and pressed the 'Scan' button. If they were being monitored, they would hear the transmission through the speaker. Nice show, thought the colonel, but what about the tape recorder still in the briefcase?

Max tapped the table with his middle finger: 'However this turns out, it will terminate any political options you have in mind.'

The colonel tilted his head to one side: 'Oh, thank you. "He knows nothing and thinks that he knows everything. That points to a political career."'

'George Bernard Shaw,' said Chester, winning an approving smile from the British officer.

'Since you mention it,' said Max, 'can I assume that you have ruled out a political solution to the present situation?'

'Yes.'

'It will be the end of your military career, of course.'

'They just made me up to full colonel – that's a dead-end street, a way of telling me that I'm not going to make brigadier. You can assume that I have worked through all the options.'

Max thought for a moment: 'So what will be the likely outcome of the next Brussels Heads of State conference?'

'Bottom line? The withdrawal from NATO and the closure of all US military bases in the European Union. They'll say it's not anti-American, just pro-EU manufacturing industry. But what they really want is to be able to stop Britain ever again getting involved with the wilder excesses of US foreign policy.' The CIA station chief grunted. 'And I blame you guys, Max.'

'Us? How come?'

'Yes,' said the colonel, smiling again, 'all that crap you fed the White House about weapons of mass destruction.'

'They didn't need our crap, they'd have done it anyway.' The station chief thought for a moment. 'You will obviously be opposed by the political establishment, but what about the average Brit in the Dog & Duck?'

'For many years, the British Army has been ranked in opinion polls as the most popular and respected institution in Britain. You know that.'

'Yes,' said Max, 'but that's when you're racing around someone else's country in a "Pinkie".'

'Recent political polls and election results suggest that the British are happier with "the Special Relationship" – one-sided as it is – than with the idea of being run by a bunch of bureaucrats in Brussels. We might even claim we are defending the Constitution...'

Chester leaped in at that point: 'But you don't have a constitution, not a written one. It's... uncodified.'

'In that case, no one is likely to argue, are they?'

The two Americans looked at the officer and, seeing a twinkle in his eye, realised he was rather enjoying all this.

'Are we talking about treason here?' asked Max.

The colonel nodded: 'Oh, I should think so.'

'And isn't that about the only thing you can still be hanged for here?'

'Yes, but they'll only do that if they want to make matters a lot worse. When they are commissioned, British officers swear an oath of allegiance to the Queen, not to the government. And it is not our intention to overthrow Her Britannic Majesty, bless her. A half-way decent barrister could have a great day in court arguing that one.'

There was a gentle knock at the door and Max opened it. The steward wanted to know if he could get them some drinks. The colonel ordered a large whisky and soda while the CIA men asked for beers. Once the steward had gone, Chester asked how he planned his takeover of Whitehall and Westminster.

'How will it be done? It will be done with a fine blend of audacity and attention to detail, Chester – and maybe with a dash of flair.'

'And which units will be involved?' But this was asked without conviction; the young man knew he was unlikely to progress down this line of enquiry.

'Of course,' volunteered the colonel, with a casual sweep of his hand, 'the SAS had a coup all planned as long ago as the mid-1960s.' He paused for effect. Chester was the first to react.

'No shit? Really?'

Max shook his head: 'Was this connected with the *Spycatcher* thing? Peter Wright? The supposed MI5 plot against the Wilson government?'

'Well,' said the colonel, relishing the moment, 'it was a Brown Study.'

'What's a 'Brown Study', Sir?' asked Chester.

'Every so often, on the rare occasions when we had everyone

back at Stirling Lines, we'd set a planning exercise. See who was coming up with the sharpest ideas.'

'The whole of the SAS?' asked the young analyst.

'Yes. But we only had two squadrons at that time – two hundred badged members. We also planned the robbery of Barclay's Bank. And the kidnapping of the Queen.'

There was a knock at the door again and the steward walked in with a tray of drinks. Max signed the bill; like an officers' mess, no cash changed hands in the club. Chester swigged his beer from the bottle, an affectation that slightly irritated the colonel.

'I got it,' said the analyst. 'The same thing happened in 1992 at the US Army War College. Some guy wrote a paper for the college journal called "The Origins of the American Military Coup of 2012"[39].'

'His name was Lieutenant-Colonel Charles J. Dunlap, Jr,' added his boss.

'Yes, that's him. He said that it was a dramatisation of his concerns about the way the services were becoming increasingly involved in policing and other domestic security matters. This all pre-dates 9/11 and the "War on Terror", of course. He also wrote that it was in no way a prediction.'

'He probably wanted to keep his pension,' observed the colonel.

'But he did predict the Military Tribunals – he called them the "sedition trials",' added Max.

The colonel sipped his whisky and leaned forward.

'So, am I going to get your support?' he finally asked.

'Do you mean is the president of the United States going to appear on the White House lawn and welcome your takeover of the British Government as a blow for liberty and democracy?' said Max. 'No,' he added, answering his own question. 'If you're asking whether we see your action as being in the best interest of the United States, the answer is yes.'

'What does that mean in practical terms, Max?'

'We won't do anything to stop you.'

The colonel leaned back again and took a longer pull at his drink. This was much less than he had been hoping for.

'Has this been discussed in the White House?' he asked.

Max shook his head: 'Not with the president. We met with a couple of trusted National Security Council members and although they are in support, they were unable to guarantee that the president wouldn't squeal on you to the prime minister. So, the Pentagon is with you, of course, so is the NSC, Langley and the rest of the intelligence community. And certain key members of Congress are on-message.'

'That's reassuring, I suppose. But some practical help on the ground might be a damned sight more useful.'

'Sure, but you need to understand that we have to be on the winning side – that's the *realpolitik* of any situation like this. If you are three goals up at half time, then... "Ask, and it shall be given you; seek, and ye shall find; knock, and it shall be opened unto you."'

'Matthew, Chapter 7...' said Chester, hesitating.

'Verse 7. Matthew, Chapter 7, Verse 7,' added the colonel. 'But if you're inclined to get scriptural... "Nought is given beneath the sun; nought is had that is not won." Old Swedish hymn.'

Watching the Watchers: Counter-Surveillance

It will take more than one committed soldier to guarantee a successful military *coup d'état*. However, it will take only one well-placed traitor to ensure that your plans come to nothing and you and the other leaders all end up in some stinking jail instead of the president's lakeside palace. Getting a reliable and trustworthy team together is one of the hardest parts of coup-plotting and we dealt with it at greater length in Chapter 4. But once you have a well-disciplined and well-motivated coup team, you are then faced with the challenge of keeping the conspiracy secret.

If a coup fails, it will probably fail before a single shot has been fired. We estimate that more than 30 per cent of coup-attempts stall because they are betrayed, but another 30 per cent because security is breached. Communications are essential to effective plotting and we deal with that below in sections on telephone and email security. But not everything can be done by passing furtive messages; you also need face-to-face confrontations among the coup leaders in order to brainstorm the right tactics, share information and resolve disputes.

In some societies, *any* meetings outside the official mainstream of events are going to attract suspicion and the unwelcome attention of the government's security service or secret police. So, let us start by considering the opposition. State security services fall into two general categories: (a) those that are well-trained and pretty nigh invisible and

(b) those who *might* be well-trained but who are all too visible. A classic case of the latter is the Tonton Macoutes types in Haiti with their dark trousers, polished shoes, white shirts and fake Ray-Bans. They might just as well be wearing T-shirts with 'spy' written on them in big letters. Such characters certainly carry out a surveillance function but their primary role is one of intimidation. They might look stupid, but they are dangerous and no one is laughing.

We can't tell you what the other guys look like because that is the point – you don't know, and by the time you find out, it is too damn late. They are the clever ones who will have had some decent training overseas by one of the major intelligence agencies. A member of any of these security services would be a perfect member of your conspiracy, but the risks associated with recruiting him, or her, are appalling. It is even worse if *they* make the approach. How will you ever know whether they are an *agent provocateur*?

So there you are, a small group of staff officers, say, who want to overthrow the government and save the constitution etc. You meet individually from time to time on a professional or social basis but the only time a larger group of you meet is when there are outsiders, non-members of the plot present. One of you has to start making decisions about this issue of communications and meetings and how it's all going to be done without giving the game away.

First of all, where are you going to meet? You might have a few ideas here; you need a semi-public place. That rules out bars and restaurants but includes, for example, the golf club, a clay-pigeon-shooting range or an upmarket bordello. Consider these issues.

- Will you all be behaving as you would normally behave?

- How will you deal with non-conspirators asking if they can join your great new club?

- Will this new activity raise suspicions on the part of your partner? Especially regarding the brothel?

- Can most of you get to such events on a regular basis, maybe once a week?

- Is the venue likely to be secure and, if you are not certain, can you get it swept for bugs? Or would that in itself be insecure?

Clearly, a busy whore's bedroom is going to be easy to bug, unlike a sports-fishing boat trolling thirty kilometres (nineteen miles) offshore. The advantage of having 'open' meetings such as this is that the participants don't have the problem of getting to the rendezvous without being followed. Nor do you have the problem of communicating to the group the time and place of that rendezvous – especially if it has to be changed at the last moment. All this kind of fieldcraft demands the use of codewords for all the likely locations; far more complicated than saying, 'See you at the dock at seven.' Also consider this: the very process of trying to 'lose a tail' is insecure in itself. If a surveillance team reports that the four people attending the meeting were all 'aware', the question will be asked, 'Why?' So don't do it unless you really have to.

Occasionally, however, you will still need to have a one-to-one encounter with someone else on the team. If the two of you meet professionally as a matter of routine, then there should not be a problem – so long as you can supply a reason for the meeting if challenged: 'We were choosing the president's birthday present.' If you don't normally meet, then you could opt for a 'chance encounter'. Arrange, perhaps through an intermediary, to be dining in the same restaurant on the same night. Sit where at least one of you can see the door to the toilets and try and ensure it is clear before you head for it. Sometimes this kind of thing is safer done in the car park when leaving, but you need to get your dinner partners to chat about each other's hairdressers while you put the finishing details to the plan for the overthrow of the government. Wherever you meet, say hello to the other party; ignoring someone with whom you should have a passing acquaintance is going to set off alarm bells.

Planning a deniable meeting is the hardest undertaking. You do not want anyone to follow you to the rendezvous and you especially do not want the two of you to be seen together. A good example of this might be a meeting between a senior military officer and someone with a face familiar to the public, an opposition political leader, for instance. Some things will just look odd: why is the commander of the 2nd Armoured Division talking to a trade-union leader? Well, he's merely arranging for a couple of minor street protests to block off parts of the administrative district of the capital on the day of the coup. But they wouldn't want to be in the same photograph on the front page of the government-controlled newspaper, nor indeed be in the same cell.

A head-to-head encounter through the open windows of a couple of cars might work, so long as neither vehicle can be associated with the two players. A rendezvous at the house of a trusted mutual friend is also a favourite, especially if either participant can be concealed in the back of a car which can drive straight into a garage. These and all other rendezvous-points come with the same problem – you have to reach them unseen and unfollowed.

If you are untrained and inexperienced in counter-surveillance techniques you will need the help of someone who knows fieldcraft – and they will probably work for the opposition. Anyone knowledgeable about these matters will tell you that it's impossible to follow someone who doesn't want to be followed. This, however, begs a crucial question; by using techniques of evasion you are telling the watchers that you are up to no good. You only really have one safe way of dealing with this problem. If you have the slightest suspicion that you are being followed, call off the meet and try again another day.

The worst thing that can happen is that the watchers have placed a GPS tracking device on your vehicle and are watching you move from meeting to meeting in the relative comfort of their own office, hot coffee to hand. The best thing that can happen is that you find such a device while carefully checking your car. If you do find a mysterious box clamped to the chassis, leave it where it is! Technology such as this makes watchers lazy and vulnerable to being diverted by someone else driving your car; the highly trained surveillance team could waste a lot of time monitoring your Mercedes heading for a shopping centre while you head in the opposite direction unobserved.

Finally, make sure that you monitor the security discipline of the other team members. They might be trustworthy, but they might also be careless or stupid, or both. Does one of your cohorts see his mistress every Friday night? Who is seeing her on Saturday night?

A Message for Our Listeners: Telephone Security

It will be tempting for the plotters of any coup to make extensive use of cellular telephones; they enable planning and co-ordination to take place away from easily tapped land-line networks used at home and in the garrisons. This is not only a First-World issue. Cellphone networks are now common in developing countries because they are quicker and cheaper to install than traditional telephone systems. One of the first things the British Army does in a war zone is to set up a cellphone network using prefabricated antennas and modular exchanges linked by microwave and satellite dishes. A special reservist team manned by engineers from British Telecom (BT) can set one up over a weekend, it is claimed.

You have probably been told that relatively new cellular telephone systems – known in Europe as the Global System for Mobile Communications (GSM) – are encrypted to a high level. The advantages, therefore, are clear; you can stand in the middle of a field, away from prying ears, and so long as your co-conspirator is doing something similar you can plot away to your heart's content.

So, the days of tabloid newspapers publishing a royal prince's raunchy late-night chats with his mistress are over? Well, not quite. A radio ham might no longer be able to listen to your coup plot, but some intelligence services certainly can. And they can definitely work out which field you are standing in.

As long ago as 1994 someone called Ross Anderson at the University of Leeds in the UK posted a message to a newsgroup on the Web. It started by saying: 'The GSM encryption algorithm, A5, is not much good. Its effective key length is at most five bytes [80 bits]; and anyone with the time and energy to look for faster attacks can find source code for it at the bottom of this post.'[40] Anderson was right in the middle of an interesting Catch-22 dilemma. If the cryptologists insist that a scrambling system is 100 per cent uncrackable, then the manufacturers would not be allowed to sell the phones to, say, Kim Jong-il. On the other hand, if anyone says the code is easy to break, then no one will buy them! The whole topic gets political very quickly and Anderson reported: 'On June 3rd [1994], Dr Simon Shepherd of Bradford University was due to present an attack on A5 to an IEE colloquium in London. However, his talk was spiked at the last minute by GCHQ.'[41]

GCHQ – Government Communication Headquarters – is the British equivalent of America's National Security Agency, both of whom operate worldwide eavesdropping operations against friend and foe alike.

In spite of the determined attentions of the academics it was some nine years later that GSM scrambling was finally and definitively broken. This was achieved by a research team at the Technion-Israel Institute of Technology in Haifa in 2003. Suddenly, according to the prestigious *New Scientist* magazine, 'The encryption system that protects the almost 900 million users of GSM cell phones from instant eavesdropping or fraud is no longer impregnable.'[42] This assumes that it was always 'impregnable'; GCHQ and the NSA can certainly muster more resources than an Israeli college you hadn't heard of until now. Maybe the system was compromised from the start – hence GCHQ's attempt to stop academics investigating it too closely. The bottom line is that it doesn't matter what it says on the sales brochure – your calls are not safe from the very people you don't want to listen to them.

It is possible to buy mobile phones with an increased level of security. The Security Systems A-034 uses an encryption key of 1,024 bits compared with the old GSM standard of 80 bits. That is not 944 bits more secure; in practical terms it is 2^{944} more secure and that is the kind of number used to measure the distance to remote galaxies. Consequently, A-034s cost a galactic three thousand dollars each and you are going to need at least two of them. We are pretty sure your sponsor, the CIA or whoever, will not buy them for you. If they do offer to supply any kind of 'secure' cellphone, do not under any circumstances take up the offer; they will almost certainly have 'gimmicked' the handsets to bypass the encryption. How else will they know what you are getting up to?

Be aware also that there is a serious dislocation between Hollywood fantasy and the reality of all modern telephone systems. Scriptwriters love the tension they can build when the victim's parents take a call from the kidnapper: 'Keep him talking for as long as you can!' implores the FBI agent. Then there are glum faces all around when the guy wearing headphones says: 'He beat the trace.' This is unmitigated rubbish and has been for a long time; but don't let the truth get in the way of a great plot device.

Computer-controlled digital telephone exchanges make it possible to 'trace' a call as it is being switched through the network from caller to receiver. Indeed, this is the basis of a service extended to subscribers; there are many handsets available on the market which will display the number of the caller *before* you even answer the call. If you have the caller's name in your phone it will even display that for you. And don't tell us that a prefix code can suppress that information! It only stops the called subscriber from seeing it, and the telecom company can easily override it from a computer keyboard. We have seen this in operation at a monitoring centre which deals with 'nuisance calls'. The telephone number of the subscriber making the complaint is entered into the system. Each time that number is dialled by anyone, anywhere in the country, the caller's number *and name and address* are displayed on the screen after the first couple of rings. That includes the address of pay phones. Locating mobile phones takes a little longer, maybe a few minutes, but co-ordinates can be displayed based on the cells (antenna zones) with which the phone is registered – or was previously registered if the call was made from a moving car or train.

In some parts of the world, hand-held satellite phones are almost becoming commonplace. We recently saw a man in a remote Afghan village chatting away on one. Was he an al-Qaeda operative? No, he was a shopkeeper ordering fresh produce from his supplier in Kabul; the region was too mountainous for effective cellphone coverage. If he had been a targeted al-Qaeda operative, his days could be numbered; the Americans have triangulated the position of satellite phones accurately enough to kill the user with a missile strike. That's another way of dealing with nuisance callers.

What is the message in all this? There are no secure communications by any kind of telephone. The only safe assumption you should make is that your calls *will* be monitored and traced.

Gentlemen Don't Read Each Other's Email

Even the poorest developing country will have some form of Internet service, if only in the capital and major cities. Using the Internet as a means of communication between coup plotters at home and abroad has many distinct advantages:

- It can be accessed from anywhere that has a computer, a telephone line and, of course, a reasonably reliable supply of electricity.

- It is fast to the point of being instantaneous, even with international connections.

- If something needs to be in writing, it can be printed off – but note our warnings about the risks of doing this.

- It can be much less hazardous than having the coup plotters meet every Thursday night in the back room of the Café Grande.

But there is a downside: the Internet is not wonderfully secure and the format in which information such as emails is transferred on telecommunication links makes it easy for well-resourced agencies to harvest large tranches of message traffic. The biggest of these is the US National Security Agency (not to be confused with the National Security Council or NASA) and Britain's Government Communications Headquarters

(GCHQ). The two bodies work closely together under the terms of the top-secret 1947 UKUSA Pact and share what might be the world's biggest 'listening station' at Menwith Hill in North Yorkshire, England. However, the monitoring of Internet traffic can also take place at a local level. So, if you are going to use email to plan your plot, you must take precautions.

You need to make use of encryption, a technique for 'scrambling' information (computer files as well as emails) in such a way that they can only be read by the intended recipient. This book is not the right place to explore encryption in any detail, but if you are interested we recommend Simon Singh's *The Code Book*.[43] Fortunately, you do not need to be able to build a television to be able to watch a soap opera and you can use quite advanced coding techniques that would make it difficult, if not impossible, for the opposition to read your private mail. We would only ever entrust our messages to a system called PGP – 'Pretty Good Privacy'. It is actually *very* good privacy and the OpenPGP encryption standard is recommended by GCHQ for use by Secret Intelligence Service (MI6) field agents when filing reports via the Internet (no more sitting in dark attics in Riga tapping out Morse code).

This is the simplest way to send a secure email. From a web browser go to www.hushmail.com. HushMail provides a secure email facility and the basic service is free.

- First click on 'open new account' and type in a name. Not your own, of course, not the dog's and certainly not 'coup leader'… use something obscure. Your new HushMail address will look something like this: 'delta100@hushmail.com'.

- You will then be prompted to provide a 'pass-phrase'. This needs to be as long as you can manage to remember without having to write it down. It is recommended that you include random shift changes, numbers and odd bits of punctuation but the next time you enter this, it will have to be 100 per cent correct. How about a line from a song?

- You then need to generate some random data by moving the mouse cursor over a panel on the screen. This is used to produce the 2,048-bit keys that are needed to protect your messages.

The whole process takes about ten minutes. Any attachments you send (including orbats and surveillance photographs) will also be encrypted. To send and collect mail you will need to visit the HushMail web-site and log in using the name and pass-phrase you provided. You can, however, have HushMail send you a regular email to tell you that you have secure mail to pick up.

The HushMail service does not hold any of your messages in clear text, but your own computer will, of course. This means that you are at risk from a dawn raid and all those neatly filed emails describing your plot will next appear at your treason trial. So here are some precautions you should take.

Do not use your office computer. *Even if you are sending an encrypted message, do not use your office computer.* Under the Regulation of Investigatory Powers Act in the UK and the Patriot Act in the United States, the authorities – your employers or superior officers – can legally monitor and read your telephone calls and email. Most countries with laws now have laws like this in order to defend liberty and freedom... The Management might not be able to read your encrypted messages but the very fact that the emails are encrypted is going to raise their suspicions. This might be a problem if the documents you want to copy are in your office computer (e.g. the army Order of Battle and current deployments). Copying them onto a removable diskette would be one solution, but many office PCs are no longer fitted with diskette drives as standard. Take a closer look at your desktop machine and see if it is fitted with a USB port. If so, you have the option of buying or borrowing a portable Zip drive, a CD-burner with a USB interface, or even one of those nifty little memory-sticks (easy to conceal, especially the type that look like a pen) for as long as it takes you to copy the material. Remember to uninstall the driver software once you have finished.

Do not use your home computer unless you invoke a few security measures first. Implement any password procedures available to restrict access to the PC. Any forensic IT consultant worth his or her salt will have little trouble getting past this, but it will keep any casual sleuths out. *Don't keep any sensitive materials on your PC in clear-text (readable) form: encrypt it or delete it.* A handy program for this purpose is KPKFile, available from www.geocities.com/john52612000. This easy-to-use program provides three functions: file encryption and decryption (using, I think, the Blowfish cipher with a 400+ bit key); file erasure (using up to nine passes to destroy latent magnetic images of files); and a 'Private Folder' mechanism providing password protection for access to file folders. Not only will KPKFile encrypt your files, it will also hide them for you inside other files; very clever. If you are going to keep sensitive documents on your PC, then you should encrypt them. If they are not needed any more, *erase* them using software like this – simply clicking on 'delete' is not secure!

An alternative to using the office or home computer is to get in the car and find a cybercafé. Keep in mind that it is possible to trace email messages back to a specific location – so don't keep returning to the same place, no matter how good the Colombian stuff is. A quick glance around will also enable you to spot the security cameras. So, change cybercafés, change hats and keep changing your HushMail account.

Chapter 6
A Word from Our Sponsor

The man stood in the door of the Hercules being buffeted by the slipstream as the plane flew very low, jinking left and right, stressing the man's knees until they ached. Even with the baffle in front of the door extended, the slipstream of the aircraft as it flew at over two hundred knots was blowing the cheeks of his face, making them flap. The dark-green and brown camouflage cream had broken up the planes of his face. The parachute harness was digging into his shoulders, so he rested the pack he was carrying on the lower D-rings to the floor.

On the higher D-rings of the pack was his reserve parachute. Fat lot of good that's going to be, he thought. From the height we are jumping, combat height five hundred feet, if my main chute doesn't open I'm certainly not going have to time to deploy any reserve. He was dealing with the stress of what was about to happen in the time-honoured way that soldiers have always dealt with extreme stress; he was putting himself into a semi-hypnotic state, thinking of anything but what was lying ahead.

His mind slipped back to Iraq. He had been in Iraq with the regular SAS, thinking that as a Territorial Army part-timer he would learn a lot. In fact, on his two tours of duty with UK Special Forces, he came out of the theatre of operations very disappointed. He found that the attitude within the regular units was cynical. The young guys were coming in, working hard and getting out. The career soldiers were getting so far up their superiors' arses that the joke in the unit was that they needed to have their initials painted on the soles of their boots so that people would know where to find them. Sad, really, as he had looked forward all his life to being a regular.

After going to university and graduating as a solicitor, he set up a practice in Harrogate not far from his home in the market town of Pateley Bridge in the Yorkshire Dales. It was a bizarre coincidence that, on his daily commute to work, he always drove past what was now going to be their target, the US National Security Agency's listening post at Menwith Hill. He had often seen the many 'golf balls', satellite dishes and antenna farms which landmarked the top of the hill. He had seen at a distance the very high security fences topped with razor wire and the armed MoD Police who patrolled the area in their distinctive Ministry of Defence vehicles. This did not faze him. He knew from local gossip that the standard of security around the place was minimal. Even sixty-year-old peace-protesters routinely broke into the site. A television presenter had even flown over the location in a hot-air balloon. It was all show and no bite.

They were going to do a combat-height drop five hundred feet into a reservoir on the Yorkshire moors, and make their way across country to the Menwith Hill Station. In their packs they had the latest microwave explosive-initiation devices. These worked on line of sight. You could set up as many of these rebroadcasting units as you could carry. Once the rebroadcast unit had received, downloaded, boosted and retransmitted the signal on to the next unit, in theory this could go on *ad infinitum* so long as you did not break the line of sight.

They had been told to take on targets of opportunity *en route*. From the maps and their own local knowledge they had identified two chains of electricity pylons. He knew that the secret of bringing down the high-voltage overhead wires was to attack two legs of a pylon which was on a bend. If you tried to take out one in a straight line it would just hang on the wires. If you attacked the corner one it would drop and would take many weeks to repair. Obviously, the station would have stand-by generators, but it was unlikely that they would have enough spare capacity to power the electrified security fence.

But the real target was the fibre optic cable that fed the station with targeted UK telephone traffic. This ran underground from the Hunterstones microwave relay station north along the B654. All they had to do was lift a couple of the manhole covers and drop in timed charges to sever the link for the foreseeable future.

The buzzword from the briefing that stuck in his mind was CHAOS – they had to cause chaos. Well, they would cause chaos – let them try watching fucking *Emmerdale* without power, he smiled grimly to himself. He could feel his patrol commander pushing in his back. Everyone was keen to get going. When Lockheed designed the C-130 they solved the noise problem by putting it all inside. Everyone was keen to get out of this smelly contraption. Again, they were doing something they had never done before. They were going to jump without lights. The aircrew were all wearing passive night goggles which gathered ambient so that they could see through the moonless night sky. Any outside bright light would interfere with their working, so there were no lights on the plane.

He could see and almost touch the trees; he could see the individual branches and leaves that they were flying over, the aircraft was so low. His patrol commander was a roofer from Hartlepool. He should feel at home here, he thought. He goes up higher than this aircraft is, on a ladder every day, to mend tiles. Then, suddenly, water. Swinsty Reservoir, he thought, nearly there. There was change in the aircraft noise. The airbrakes slowed the plane down dramatically. He could then see out of the right-hand corner of his eye the flaps being extended. The crew tensed – they were as nervous as the guys who were going to jump. They were going to have to get the aircraft to stalling speed, or just above stalling speed to make this drop as safe as possible.

The Hercules jinked left. He glanced forward and, beyond the dam, could make out the dark outline of Fewston Reservoir, the next in the chain. Oh shit, he thought. He could see the thin white mist rising from the surface in the cool of the summer night. This was going to make it even worse – he wasn't going to be able to see the surface of the lake and brace himself for his entry. What they had to do in the space of a very few short seconds after the parachute deployed was to lower their equipment and to brace themselves for the entry into the water. Then get rid of the chute, swim ashore, stash the kit and make their way to the first target. He knew from his training that the only thing he could do to brace himself was to roll himself into a ball, shit the rest as long as he got into the water safely.

Suddenly he heard the klaxon. He didn't have time to react; the rest of the patrol literally pushed him out of the door. He could feel on his back the ties braking systematically as the parachute deployed at a rate it was not designed to do. Suddenly he swung like a pendulum below the deployed canopy. Never mind stabilising, he dropped his kit. As the kit descended on the end of its nylon rope it straightened him with a jerk. He rolled himself into a foetal ball and bombed into the freezing-cold water.

Invasion or Intervention?

In terms of regime change there is a fine but distinct line between direct military intervention (as was the case of Iraq in 2003) and the external sponsorship of a military *coup d'état*.

Military intervention is a polite way of saying that the military forces of one country have invaded another sovereign state, guns blazing. This is done in the full glare of publicity; warnings in presidential speeches, intelligence assessments made public, UN Security Council resolutions forced through, deadlines set and CNN tipped off about the landing-beach. On the other hand, the sponsored coup is a covert operation using internal armed forces. Any external support will be mercenaries or troops from a neighbouring state also a client of the sponsoring country. The sponsorship will usually come in the form of arms, intelligence, training and cash.

In this chapter we set out two examples from the early 1970s; the CIA-sponsored coup in Chile and the MI6-sponsored coup in Uganda.

'Made to Scream': Chile 1973

Probably the most infamous *coup d'état* of modern times was the one which resulted in the overthrow of elected President Salvador Allende of Chile and his replacement by General Augusto Pinochet. Although Pinochet himself was forced out of office in 1990, his 16 October 1998 arrest in London on a warrant issued by a Madrid judge (citing crimes against Spanish nationals) made the affair headline news once more. In the summer of 2004 a Chilean court ruled that the 89-year-old was fit enough to stand trial in his homeland.

Chile is a long ribbon of a country, starting at its border with Peru in the north and ending 4,300 kilometres (2,672 miles) to the south; it leans back against the Andes, its toes in the Pacific Ocean. Rich in mineral resources – nitrate, copper and iron – if it has oil, the black gold has not yet been discovered. The population is mostly mestizo, of mixed Spanish and Indian blood and a small (not very Indian) oligarchy used to dominate the economic and political scenes. In the 1960s socialist and social democratic parties combined forces in a new political alliance called the *Unidad Popular* (Popular Unity) and backed the Marxist Salvador Allende Gossens for election as president. The Allende platform was fairly predictable; agrarian reform, the state ownership of all mining and banking and the redistribution of wealth would lead to something called 'socialism'.

The Americans were not at all happy with this situation. The Cold War was still at its height and Allende was seen as the gate-keeper for Soviet influence in South America. At a more practical level, the copper mines were owned by US interests and copper was needed to make wires for the burgeoning telecommunications industry. Centre-right Christian Democrat President Eduardo Frei had already acquired 51 per cent control of the American copper-mine companies; wisely, he called this 'Chileanisation', rather than 'socialism'. But enough was enough and, accordingly, the White House approved a dirty-tricks campaign by the CIA station in Santiago. Much of this bordered on the ridiculous – rumours were spread among the peasants that, under an Allende government, all children would be required to have the hammer-and-sickle tattooed on their foreheads. Religion would be banned, even the animistic faiths of the native peoples.

In the 1970 presidential elections, the voters responded to this scary stuff by electing Allende by a majority that George W. Bush would have died for. The incumbent, President Frei, called on the colourful US Ambassador Edward Korry for help in blocking Allende's ratification by the Chilean Congress. At the instigation of Nixon's National Security Council, the CIA stepped up a gear and formulated a twin-track solution to the problem. Project *Fubelt* comprised Track I, the blocking of the inauguration, and Track II, an outright military *coup d'état*. For a long time, Washington tried to deny direct involvement in any coup, but the lying stopped once the document shown in Figure 3 was declassified.[44]

The secret cable was written by CIA Deputy Director of Plans Thomas Karamessines and sets out operational orders for Henry Hecksher, the Agency's station chief in Santiago. The orders are effectively from Henry Kissinger, President Nixon's National Security Adviser, and are determinedly unambiguous: 'It is firm and continuing policy that Allende be overthrown by a coup.'

'We are to continue to generate maximum pressure toward this end utilizing every appropriate resource,' the cable continues. 'It is imperative that these actions be implemented clandestinely and securely so that the [United States Government] and American hand be well hidden.'

Some practical matters were put in hand with expediency: 'By a special (and unique) arrangement requested by CIA, the US Army Attaché in Santiago was placed under operational direction of the CIA station chief there. His assistance and Chilean military contacts were invaluable in this program.'[45] The Army Attaché would have invested many

RESTRICTED HANDLING

CLASSIFIED MESSAGE

SECRET

ORIG:
UNIT:
EXT::
DATE: 16 October 1970

DECLASSIFIED - E.O. 12356, Sec. 3.4
With PORTIONS EXEMPTED
E.O. 12356, Sec 1.3 (a) (1)

LESNA

(CLASSIFICATION)   (DATE AND TIME FILED)

SECRET   422   CITE HEADQUARTERS 802

IMMEDIATE SANTIAGO (EYES ONLY)

16 14 08z Oct 70

1. POLICY, OBJECTIVES, AND ACTIONS WERE
REVIEWED AT HIGH USG LEVEL AFTERNOON 15 OCTOBER. CON-.
CLUSIONS, WHICH ARE TO BE YOUR OPERATIONAL GUIDE, FOLLOW:

2. IT IS FIRM AND CONTINUING POLICY THAT ALLENDE
BE OVERTHROWN BY A COUP. IT WOULD BE MUCH PREFERABLE
TO HAVE THIS TRANSPIRE PRIOR TO 24 OCTOBER BUT EFFORTS IN
THIS REGARD WILL CONTINUE VIGOROUSLY BEYOND THIS DATE.
WE ARE TO CONTINUE TO GENERATE MAXIMUM PRESSURE TOWARD
THIS END UTILIZING EVERY APPROPRIATE RESOURCE. IT IS
IMPERATIVE THAT THESE ACTIONS BE IMPLEMENTED CLANDESTINELY
AND SECURELY SO THAT THE USG AND AMERICAN HAND BE WELL
HIDDEN. WHILE THIS IMPOSES UPON US A HIGH DEGREE OF
SELECTIVITY IN MAKING MILITARY CONTACTS AND DICTATES

COORDINATING OFFICERS   ....CONTINUED....

RELEASING OFFICER   **SECRET**   AUTHENTICATING OFFICER

THIS FORM FOR USE BY AUTHORIZED RESTRICTED HANDLING MESSAGE USERS ONLY!

3205

Figure 3: CIA Operating Guidance Cable

rounds of golf and much small-talk at cocktail parties to develop his contacts with Santiago's high command; he was the obvious short-cut to identifying the officers likely to support the coup. One of these was a Chilean admiral who is referred to in the declassified documents as the 'Cooptee'.

No provision is made in Thomas Karamessines' Operating Guidance cable for a bloodless coup. Nor was that an option being considered in theatre. General René Schneider was a senior officer who had made no secret of his opposition to the military jumping into the snake-pit of Chilean politics. The plotters could not take the risk of him splitting the army. A group of soldiers commanded by General Camilo Valenzuela told the CIA that they would deal with Schneider; they would 'neutralise' him with 'sterile' weapons and blame the murder on Allende supporters, thus provoking a military takeover. This sounded good to the Santiago Station and on 18 October a special request was cabled to CIA headquarters at Langley.

[STATION COOPTEE] MET CLANDESTINELY 17 OCT WITH [TWO CHILEAN ARMED FORCES OFFICERS] WHO TOLD HIM THEIR PLANS WERE MOVING ALONG BETTER THAN HAD THOUGHT POSSIBLE. THEY ASKED THAT BY EVENING 18 OCT [COOPTEE] ARRANGE FURNISH THEM WITH EIGHT TO TEN TEAR GAS GRENADES. WITHIN 48 HOURS THEY NEED THREE 45 CALIBER MACHINE GUNS ('GREASE GUNS') WITH 500 ROUNDS AMMO EACH. [ONE OFFICER] COMMENTED HAS THREE MACHINE GUNS HIMSELF BUT CAN BE IDENTIFIED BY SERIAL NUMBERS AS HAVING BEEN ISSUED TO HIM THEREFORE UNABLE TO USE THEM.[46] (Redactions by CIA declassification personnel.)

Langley agreed to dispatch the 'grease guns' by courier but was confused about why they were needed:

IF [COOPTEE] PLANS LEAD COUP, OR BE ACTIVELY AND PUBLICLY INVOLVED, WE PUZZLED WHY IT SHOULD BOTHER HIM IF MACHINES GUNS CAN BE TRACED TO HIM. CAN WE DEVELOP RATIONALE ON WHY GUNS MUST BE STERILE? WILL CONTINUE TO

MAKE EFFORT PROVIDE THEM BUT FIND OUR CREDI-
BILITY STRETCHED BY NAVY [OFFICER] LEADING HIS
TROOPS WITH STERILE GUNS. WHAT IS SPECIAL PUR-
POSE FOR THESE GUNS?[47]

It seems that the guys running the CIA's Latin America desk didn't get out much. We don't have Santiago's answer to the last question but it might have pointed out that the guns were going to be used to commit a capital crime.

Through the efforts of the National Security Archive[48] under the Freedom of Information Act, the minutiae of the Agency's planning are now available. For example, the author of an 18 November 1970 internal progress report on Project *Fubelt* clearly never dreamed that he would ever reach an audience of millions. (See Figure 4.)

But even within the scope of secure communications between Langley headquarters and the CIA's Santiago Station, some things were clearly better left unsaid. No mention is made of the Agency's involvement in the 22 October murder of General René Schneider, who was shot, not by Valenzuela's team with their sanitised grease guns but by another group of CIA-sponsored plotters commanded by retired General Roberto Viaux. It probably did not make any difference to René Schneider, who died needlessly. Indeed, the stunt may have even backfired; the military didn't rise up and the country rallied to support the president-elect. On 24 October 1970, two days after Schneider's death, the Congress of Chile ratified Salvador Allende's elevation to the presidency.

While the Christian Democrats allied themselves with the right-wing Nationalist Party and started to cultivate the army, Popular Unity got on with cultivating the land under the agrarian-reform programme. The changes yielded good results for the left alliance in the 1971 municipal elections and the 1973 Congressional elections. But this manifestation of democracy counted for nothing with Chile's élite and its American allies; Allende was a dead man walking.

Richard Nixon had ordered that the Chilean economy should be 'made to scream'. This was primarily achieved through a boycott by American capital. Copper revenues suffered, manufacturing output declined and middle-class support deserted the government. The inevitable coup struck on 11 September 1973 and Allende was killed during an attack on the presidential palace by air force strike jets. One

18 November 1970

SUBJECT: Report on CIA Chilean Task Force Activities,
          15 September to 3 November 1970

1. General

    . On 15 September 1970, CIA was directed to try to prevent
Marxist Salvador Allende's ascent to the Chilean presidency on
3 November. This effort was to be independent of concurrent endeavors
being undertaken through, or with the knowledge of, the 40 Committee,
Department of State, and Ambassador Korry.

    b. Briefly, the situation at that time was the following:

    -- Allende had attained a plurality of only some 40,000
        in the Chilean popular vote for president. Jorge
        Alessandri, a conservative and the runner-up, would
        face Allende in a Congressional run-off on 24 October.
        The run-off winner would be invested as president on
        3 November.

Figure 4: CIA Report on Project *Fubelt*

account was given in a report sent to the Pentagon by US Naval Attaché
Patrick Ryan:

> Allende was found alone and dead in his office off the inner
> courtyard. He had killed himself by placing a sub-machine
> gun under his chin and pulling the trigger, messy but efficient.

The gun was lying near his body. A gold metal plate imbedded in the stock was inscribed 'To my good friend Salvador Allende from Fidel Castro'. Obviously Communist Cuba had sent one too many guns to Chile for their own good.[49]

This has always seemed too good to be true for supporters of Allende. Exactly how Allende died remains uncertain, but from the following transcript of a radio conversation between General Augusto Pinochet and Vice-Admiral Patricio Carvajal, it is clear that Pinochet did not care one way or the other.

PINOCHET: 'Unconditional surrender! No negotiation! Unconditional surrender!'

CARVAJAL: 'Good. Understood. Unconditional surrender and he's taken prisoner. The offer is nothing more than to respect his life, shall we say?'

PINOCHET: 'His life and... his physical integrity, and he'll be immediately dispatched to another place.'

CARVAJAL: 'Understood. Now... in other words, the offer to take him out of the country is still maintained?'

PINOCHET: 'The offer to take him out of the country is still maintained. If the plane falls, old boy, when it's in flight...'

CARVAJAL: (Laughter.)[50]

Allende was replaced by a junta composed of army commander-in-chief General Augusto Pinochet Ugarte, General Gustavo Leigh of the air force, General Cesar Mendoza of the *Carabineros* and Admiral José Toribio Merino of the navy, the CIA's 'cooptee'. Pinochet was nominated as president of the junta and the National Congress was dissolved. The old constitution was torn up and the new one written by the navy auditor-general stated that the purpose of the junta was to 'restore the ruptured Chilean identity, justice and institutional framework'; it was a sufficiently vague remit to suit all purposes.

In quick succession, the right-wing parties pledged support, the US formally recognised the new regime and the killing started. The ploy to justify the repression showed a rare deftness; on 17 September, the junta announced the discovery of 'Plan Z', a supposed plot by the deposed

Popular Unity government for a counter-coup. Allegedly, the secret documents were found in offices of the Interior Ministry. These made provision for the acquisition of guns and explosives and listed leading political figures for assassination. Published in a *Libro Blanco* (White Book), the documents were used by the junta to justify its wholesale persecution of left-wing activists.

A folk singer is found dead, his body showing signs of torture. Thirteen people are gunned down on a bridge in the town of Orsono by a civilian death squad after being 'released' by the *Carabineros*. A catholic priest involved in the workers' movement is found dead on a river bank, ten bullets in his back. Nineteen employees of a pulp and paper mill near the towns of San Rosendo and Laja are loaded into a company truck and driven away by soldiers; they are never seen again. All this happened on the same day – 18 September 1973.

Political opponents were rounded up and herded into Santiago's National Stadium. According to the Red Cross some seven thousand people were imprisoned there by 22 September. A similar pattern of detentions using sports grounds and military barracks was followed throughout the country. When they started to overflow, concentration camps were set up away from the cities in remote places such as Pisagua, Chacabuco and Dawson Island.

One junta death squad specialised in making housecalls; this was the notorious 'Caravan of Death'. Led by General Sergio Arellano Stark, the team would carry out summary arrests, trials and executions of opponents. During the first week of October 1973 it flew by helicopter to five cities in the north of Chile and shot seventy-two political prisoners without any form of legal trial. Naval Attaché Patrick Ryan described this process as 'Armed Forces pursuing known terrorist groups'.[51]

The junta proved remorseless in hunting down its enemies, real or perceived and wherever they might be. General Carlos Prats Gonzalez had been Pinochet's predecessor as Commander-in-Chief of the Army and was a supporter of the Allende government. Immediately after the coup he and his wife decided that discretion was the better part of valour and decamped to Buenos Aires. In the small hours of 30 September 1974, as they were arriving home from an evening with friends, their car exploded: 'The scorched remains of the car and the victims' bodies were scattered over a radius of 50 metres... Autopsy reports indicate that General Prats died from trauma, multiple visceral-vascular injuries, and internal and external haemorrhaging. His wife Sofia Cuthbert died as the consequence of the multiple bone-organ-vascular destruction [and] internal haemorrhaging.'[52] As Patrick Ryan might have put it, it was 'messy but efficient'.[53]

According to subsequent investigations the crime was committed by agents of Pinochet's newly formed, US-trained *Dirección de Inteligencia Nacional* (DINA, National Intelligence Directorate) with support from an Argentinian ultra-right terror group called 'Milicia'.

On 13 October 1973, the junta banned all political parties and sequestered their assets; so much for the introduction of freedom and democracy. In the aftermath of Project *Fubelt*, the Pinochet regime murdered some 3,197 people according to a report commissioned by the new civilian government in 1990; a further thousand 'disappeared'. In November 2004, The National Commission on Political Prisoners and Torture presented its report on a further study to President Ricardo Lagos. It had not been published at the time of writing, but it estimates that 35,000 people were abused in some way during military rule and includes hundreds of new accounts of torture methods employed including 'sexual abuse using dogs' and 'forcing suspects to watch as family members were sodomised or slowly electrocuted'.[54]

Richard Nixon's National Security Adviser, Henry Kissinger, was later awarded the Nobel Peace Prize.

'Caravan of Death' 2: Operation *Condor*

By 1976 right-wing regimes throughout South America had agreed to extend Pinochet's 'Caravan of Death' concept to a global scale. The intelligence agencies of Chile, Brazil, Argentina, Uruguay and Paraguay decided to share resources on left-wing opponents. Nothing too controversial about that, but they also decided that they would hunt them down, anywhere in the world, and assassinate them. With the Americans on their side they had decided they could get away with anything.

'Legal Attachés' in US embassies are FBI agents. Robert Scherrer, the Legal Attaché in Buenos Aires, had obtained information about Operation *Condor* from a confidential source and his report about what he had learned was couched in somewhat concerned tones; there is no love lost between the FBI and the CIA. Sent to the Director of the FBI on 28 September 1976, the report read in part as follows:

A third and most secret phase of 'Operation Condor' involves the formation of special teams from member countries [Chile, Argentina, etc.] who are to travel anywhere in the world to non-member countries to carry out sanctions up to assassination against terrorists or supporters of terrorist organizations from 'Operation Condor' countries. For example, should a terrorist... be located in a European country, a special team from 'Operation Condor' would be dispatched to locate and surveil the target... A second team would be dispatched to carry out the actual sanction against the target.'[55]

Apart from the minor technicality of the lack of due legal process in this activity, there are many people who would be unconcerned if the targets were dyed-in-the-wool terrorists of the type who would murder more than three thousand people in an office complex in New York or more than three hundred children and adults in a school in southern Russia.

Scherrer, however, goes on to reveal his suspicions that the murder in Washington DC of former Chilean Ambassador Orlando Letelier might have been an Operation *Condor* sanction. Whatever Letelier had done to upset the Pinochet junta, he was not a terrorist; nor was his American assistant, Ronni Moffit, killed by the same car bomb.

The Kampala Strangler: Uganda 1971

The story of Uganda in the 1970s is the story of Idi Amin, or 'President for Life Field-Marshal al-Hadj Doctor Idi Amin Dada, VC, DSO, MC, Lord of All the Beasts of the Earth and Fishes of the Sea, Last King of Scotland, Conqueror of the British Empire in Africa in General and Uganda in Particular', as his wives called him in more intimate moments.

Amin gained power in 1971 by overthrowing Milton Obote in a British-backed military coup; his reign of terror lasted until Tanzanian troops and refugee Ugandans finally ejected him from the capital, Kampala, in 1979. It is estimated that at least 300,000, possibly 500,000 of his people were butchered in the intervening eight years. Amin became a guest of Colonel Qaddafi, then Saddam Hussein before settling in Saudi Arabia, where he died in 2003 aged between seventy-eight and eighty. Few grieved his passing.

But it is the circumstances of his rise to power and the involvement of Britain's Secret Intelligence Service (MI6) in sponsoring the coup that is of interest here. Uganda is a land-locked state in East Africa, its capital, Kampala, on the northern shore of Lake Victoria. Until it gained independence in 1961, Uganda was a British colony. It was a country with potential; a sound agricultural economy was boosted by copper, a nice foreign-currency earner. The political structure was fairly typical; a multi-party parliamentary system in the European pattern overlaid a more traditional tribal structure. In the 1960s, Milton Obote's nationalist Uganda People's Congress (UPC) held sway over the country and Obote held sway over the UPC. He clearly thought that one party was enough to hold sway over at any one time, and put the rest out of business and introduced a one-party state. He ousted President Sir Edward 'King Freddie' Mutesa four years later and rewrote the constitution so he could take the job for himself.

The British shrugged; such was the way of things in the new post-colonial Africa. Then Obote decided to nationalise business and industry, starting with about eighty UK-owned companies. The British stopped shrugging and decided that this Obote chap had gone too far – it was time for a *coup d'état*.

The man for the job was MI6 officer Beverly Gayer Barnard. He had prior experience (see Chapter 3, Iran 1953), was already operating in nearby Sudan and ran a useful one-plane cargo airline. By all accounts – and we concede there are not many of them – Barnard was an interesting character. In 1938, at the age of twenty-two, he was working for the British Broadcasting Corporation as what has been described as a 'researcher'. It is hard to believe that this means 'researcher' in the sense we understand it today, especially as he was working in the infant field of television. When the war with Germany broke out, he moved to Bristol, where he worked for Westland Aircraft, now a helicopter manufacturer. The fact that he was not conscripted into the army or air force suggests that he was in a 'reserved occupation'; in other words he was a scientist or technologist whose skills would be invaluable to the war effort. This is confirmed by his later move to the Royal Aircraft Establishment, Farnborough, which was, and still is, Britain's premier centre of aeronautical research.

It is not known when Beverly Barnard became an intelligence officer, but towards the end of 1944 he was selected as member of the Control Commission. This had the task of governing the British sector of post-surrender Germany and, given that it oversaw the process of 'de-Nazification', was considered to be a somewhat spooky operation. During his three years in this job, Barnard must have joined the Secret

Intelligence Service and in 1947 was sent to Tehran, where he was given the quasi-diplomatic cover post of 'Civil Air Attaché'. As his brief covered Iraq and the Gulf States as well as Iran, MI6 gave him a small aircraft, which suggests he had learned to fly before leaving RAE Farnborough.[56] It is not clear how Barnard kept himself busy in the following years but we could speculate that, in addition to Iran 1953, he took a professional interest in other Middle East coups: Yemen 1955, Iraq 1958, 1959 and 1963, Syria 1963, Sudan 1964, Abu Dhabi 1966, Yemen 1967, Iraq 1968 and especially Sudan 1968. Certainly, in 1959 he had 'Middle East Consultant' on his business card.

Small, intelligent and bespectacled, Barnard had the job of cultivating a man who was almost entirely his opposite. Idi Amin Dada was a giant of a man in everything but intellect. His behaviour the first time the British put him in a position of authority should have been a warning sign. Amin was a sergeant in the King's Africa Rifles during the 1950s and served in Kenya during the colonial power's bloody conflict with the Land Freedom Army, the 'Mau Mau'. While working as a guard at an internment camp, his favourite party trick was to grab a prisoner by the throat and lift him bodily from the ground, earning himself the nickname, 'The Strangler'. For seven years he was heavyweight boxing champion of Uganda.

When Obote came to power, Amin was rapidly promoted through the ranks to general and made commander-in-chief of the armed forces. His power base in the army was a large group of Sudanese mercenaries who had been recruited by the British. These soldiers were exclusively from the Christian and animist area of southern Sudan and were battle-hardened from the long and bloody war with the Muslim-led north of the country. Also owing allegiance were the Anya-Nya guerrillas, the military wing of the Nile Liberation Front from the Ugandan–Sudanese border region, home base to Amin's tribe, the Kakwa. This alliance was useful to MI6; the Sudanese fighters were loyal to Amin, not particularly to the state of Uganda, and certainly not to Milton Obote.

Idi Amin was Beverly Barnard's first choice for coup leader. He had Obote's trust and a considerable power-base. And, as military commander-in-chief, he had only one place to go – head of state. As the MI6 man reported to London, Amin was 'intensely loyal to Britain' although 'a little short on the grey matter'.

By the end of the 1960s, Barnard had set up a training camp over the Sudan border and his airline was delivering *matériel* to the five hundred irregulars being put through their paces there. The weapons and ammunition were being supplied by Anthony Divall, a British arms dealer and contract MI6 agent based in Hamburg. The UK spooks had also managed to solicit the support of Mossad, the Israeli intelligence service. Its interest was not in the overthrow of the Obote government but in undermining the Islamic regime in Khartoum, which they considered a threat in the wake of the 1967 Arab–Israeli War. (Until 1969, the British had a military training team in the north supporting the Sudanese army. This arrangement ended with that year's coup and the Brits were replaced by Egyptian and Soviet teams. Nonetheless, it may have been, for a short time at least, that the UK was backing both sides in the civil war.)

On 11 January 1971 President Obote was out of the country, having decided to attend the Commonwealth Heads of State conference in Singapore. This was a particularly unwise decision on his part; trouble had been brewing for some time and, only eighteen months earlier, he had survived an assassination attempt. At the conference, Obote made an impassioned speech condemning Britain's decision to renew arms sales to the apartheid regime in South Africa. In response, Prime Minister Edward Heath prodded his finger at Obote and said, 'I wonder how many of you will be allowed to return to your own countries from this conference.'[57] It is hard to believe that Heath was unaware of the coup being orchestrated by his intelligence service in Uganda as he spoke.

Indeed, Beverly Barnard's plan went smoothly. Amin's troops sealed off Kampala's airport at Entebbe and tanks and infantry took to the streets of the capital. The presidential palace was seized and vehicle checkpoints set up on all major routes. And the plotters didn't forget to take over the radio station! A national broadcast announcing Idi Amin's self-elevation to head of state also accused government ministers and senior civil servants of widespread corruption; the army had acted in the belief that bloodshed would result from the president's policy of giving preference to his own tribal region.

Alarmed at hearing all this, British High Commissioner Richard Slater rushed around to Amin's office. There, with his feet metaphorically on the general's desk, was the Israeli Defence Attaché Colonel Bar-Lev. (The two were old chums, Amin having facilitated the shipment of Israeli arms to the rebels in southern Sudan in return, no doubt, for a considerable commission.) In a recently declassified cable to London, Slater stated: 'In the course of last night General Amin caused to be arrested all officers in the armed forces sympathetic to Obote...

Amin is now firmly in control of all elements of [the] army which controls vital points in Uganda... the Israeli defence attaché discounts any possibility of moves against Amin.'[58] The reason why it wasn't Beverly Barnard's polished shoes on Amin's furniture was obvious: at that time MI6 didn't officially exist; nor therefore did its officer Barnard. What is clear from the incident is that the High Commissioner had been kept in the dark, a common practice among British and American coup plotters. Amin showed his appreciation by making his first official overseas visit to Israel, where he alarmed Prime Minister Golda Meir by demanding enough munitions to keep her country's arms industry busy for a decade. Within months 'The Strangler' was having lunch with the Queen at Buckingham Palace. God only knows what they chatted about.

Not in the dark about developments in Uganda was a colourful Kenyan businessman–politician and World War II fighter pilot called Bruce McKenzie. McKenzie had astutely backed jailed opposition leader Jomo Kenyatta during the build-up to independence and was later rewarded with the influential post of minister for agriculture. He was the ultimate wheeler-dealer, his interests extending to the ownership of Cooper Motors, which held the Kenyan and Ugandan distributorships for Volkswagen Beetles and British Leyland trucks, including the ubiquitous Land Rover. His sales team could also rustle up a squadron of armoured cars, should you have the need and the cash.

These business activities were helped by a wealth of political contacts. He was a close friend of Colonel David Stirling, the founder of the British Special Air Service, then active in African politics. (At the time, in the late-1960s, 22 SAS was training Kenyan special forces in return for the provision of a bush camp near Nyeri, sixty miles north of the capital, Nairobi.) When in the UK, McKenzie was a regular house-guest of Maurice Oldfield, Barnard's ultimate boss as 'M', the director-general of MI6.[59] Indeed he had also been McKenzie's 'boss' since 1963 when the businessman had signed up as an agent of the Secret Intelligence Service.

Alarmed by the threat of Obote's policy of nationalising foreign businesses, Bruce McKenzie was a keen supporter of 'Amin for president' and those views were undoubtedly impressed on Oldfield and Prime Minister Harold Wilson. When he lost his job as agriculture minister in 1970, he remained the most influential white man in East Africa, taking the opportunity to expand his business interests by becoming chairman of Kenya Airways.

An excellent coup... shame about the consequences. Less than two years later Amin had 'ethnically cleansed' Uganda's Asian population and wrecked the economy. With the benefit of hindsight the country's middle-managers, professionals and traders were better off out of Africa; the 'President for Life' started slaughtering his own people on the slightest whim and at a rate that was once estimated to be seven thousand per week.[60]

On Sunday, 27 June 1976, Air France flight number AF 139 was hijacked by four terrorists affiliated with the Popular Front for the Liberation of Palestine (PFLP), two of them actually members of the German Baader-Meinhof Gang. After a short stop in Benghazi, the plane took off again and headed for Entebbe Airport, where the group was joined by three others already in-country. The hijackers announced they would start killing the Israeli and Jewish passengers if fifty-three terrorist prisoners in five countries were not released. It was clear from his behaviour that Amin was supporting the PFLP and so the Israelis activated their Sayeret Matkal special-operations unit. What happened next made Amin look an even bigger buffoon, should such a thing be possible. The Israelis managed to land three C-130 transport planes unchallenged and unopposed. With the help of a limousine and an Amin look-alike, they stormed the terminal building and freed the hostages with minimal loss of life – except among the terrorists and Ugandan soldiers.

The Israeli team with its liberated and relieved hostages exfiltrated to Nairobi Airport in Kenya, where refuelling facilities, food and medical assistance for the wounded were on stand-by; all courtesy of Bruce McKenzie. Whether McKenzie was motivated by remorse at the havoc he'd helped unleash in Uganda is less important than the fact that he'd supported the Israeli operation with the full backing of MI6 and the British Government. A grateful Israeli government showered him with honours. But it was a decision that was to cost him his life.

By May of 1978 the lure of the big government contract – or pressure for intelligence from MI6 – had got the better of Bruce McKenzie's judgement. That month he flew with two business associates in his own light aircraft to Uganda for a meeting with Amin at Entebbe airport. By all accounts, the get-together in the VIP lounge was congenial enough. As the visitors were about to leave, Amin asked McKenzie to deliver a gift of an antelope skin to an address in Nairobi. The MI6 agent tucked the parcel under his arm and shook the president's big hand. Amin stood on the apron and waved his visitors off as the plane taxied to the end of the runway. There was, no doubt, a huge grin on his face. As the small plane reached five thousand feet it exploded, killing Bruce McKenzie and his two passengers.

An article in the London *Sunday Times* of 11 December 1980 revealed that Amin had brought in some help to achieve this brutal revenge murder. Also in the airport at the time of McKenzie's visit were two renegade CIA operators, Frank Terpil and Edwin Wilson; both were more than capable of making an improvised bomb that would trigger at a predetermined altitude. Terpil was later indicted by a New York Grand Jury on charges of illegally supplying arms to Uganda but he skipped bail and disappeared. Supposedly, he died in the Lebanon, hopefully not before his time.

By 1979 the British had had enough of the thug it had sponsored as the saviour of Uganda, and the Labour Foreign Secretary Dr David Owen (now Lord Owen) proposed that MI6 be ordered to assassinate Idi Amin. Speaking on BBC radio shortly after the tyrant's death in 2003 he admitted that his proposal was seen as an outrageous suggestion, but: 'I'm not ashamed of considering it, because his regime goes down in the scale of Pol Pot as one of the worst of all African regimes.'[61]

Perhaps David Owen was influenced by the fact that, ten years earlier, MI6 had actively planned for the assassination of President Milton Obote as an alternative to the coup plot. In addition to Barnard's camp in the north of the country, there was another one in which Ugandan security personnel were being trained in the fine art of assassination by use of Improvised Explosive Devices (IEDs) – home-made bombs.

The tuition must have been excellent; the team doing the job was from MI6's own training facility at Fort Monkton near Gosport in Hampshire. 'The Fort' was one of a string of four coastal defences built by Henry VIII in 1545 to protect the strategic city of Portsmouth from foreign invaders. Its fascinating history has reflected the needs of the day; by 1944 it had become the communication centre for the invasion of occupied Europe. The Royal Engineers took it over and, when they moved out in 1954, the SIS moved in (conveniently forgetting to tell the Ministry of Defence, who continued to pay the bills for thirty years).

All MI6 recruits, some from the military, some from university, would have to pass IONEC, the Intelligence Officer's New Entry Course at Fort Monkton. It was here that they would learn their 'tradecraft', the lore of dead and live letter boxes, bump contacts, agent handling, surveillance and counter-surveillance.[62] Special Air Service Regiment instructors took on the job of teaching the trainees weapons and explosives handling. So it was a team from Fort Monkton who found themselves in the East African bush teaching the practical differences between the 'culvert bomb' and the 'car bomb'. As it turned out, the training was not needed because Beverly Barnard's coup worked just fine.

Nor was Lord Owen's proposed assassination of Amin needed. Milton Obote returned to power that same year (1979) when Tanzania lost patience with Amin's repeated armed assaults across their border and invaded the country with the support of Ugandan exiles. To show willing, the British paid the Tanzanian Government for the cost of the operation; hence paying to restore the man they had previously paid to dislodge. In the aftermath severed heads and a huge library of pornography were discovered in 'Big Daddy's' house. When accused of cannibalism he responded by saying, 'I ate them before they ate me'. He also said, 'Sometimes people mistake the way I talk for what I am thinking.' Most politicians are faced with that problem, of course, but in this case few people had any doubt that he meant exactly what he said.

Short of cannibalism, Obote was almost as much a tyrant as Amin and he didn't last, being overthrown in yet another military coup a few years later. Beverly Barnard died in 1973, aged fifty-seven.

The coups of Uganda 1971 and Chile 1973 had one important thing in common: a bloody aftermath for the ordinary people of those countries and one which later proved embarrassing to their foreign sponsors. Certainly in the case of Chile, resentment towards the United States by many ordinary people throughout South America remains irreparable.

Chapter 7
Strategically Situated Exotic Islands

The man dressed in civilian clothes walking round the large windowless room was, in fact, an army major. He ran a critical eye over his centre of operations. The room looked like a large business call-centre with banks of display screens showing real-time images from various points around London and the Home Counties. In front of each bank of screens, desk officers sat with earphones on their heads monitoring messages that were coming in from a variety of sources checking the CCTV pictures and occasionally barking out instructions across the ether.

The building had started life as a storage bunker for high explosives being manufactured at the Royal Ordnance Factory in Rotherwas, Hereford. When the factory closed in the 1950s the storage areas, deep in the Herefordshire countryside, had been taken over and converted to other uses by the Ministry of Defence. To the uninitiated, the SAS camp in Credenhill in Herefordshire is the nerve centre of the regiment's worldwide operations. To those in the know, however, these old ammunition-storage bunkers were where it all happened. The width of the walls and the strength of the ceilings meant that no sound went either in or out. The only exits were small doors set in each end of the building. It was ideal for the covert operations that dominated the lives of Special Forces.

Each of the banks of screens and consoles was providing information on a person under surveillance. The desk officer could call up real-time video and audio signals. The electronic teams from 14 Intelligence Company had placed listening microphones and minute cameras in the homes and workplaces of the 'x-rays' – the jargon within the company to cover the real identity of the targets under watch. Other cameras and devices were watching from overlooking flats and houses, from inside vans with blanked-out windows, from parked cars with cameras set in the headlights and taillights. They had even placed cameras in litterbins.

The airborne early-warning Nimrods were intercepting and passing all telephone calls from the x-rays direct to the bunker.

The radio transmissions of the surveillance teams were also coming into the earphones of the desk officers. The constant talk on the air when a foot- or mobile-team using cars, motorbikes, taxis – whatever was suitable for the area – were moving, the transmissions on the radio net were continuous, providing a non-stop commentary on the location of the x-ray, what he was doing, and trying to anticipate where he might be going. This would enable them to bring together the rest of the team and to hound the x-ray wherever he may be travelling to.

The desk officer had at his fingertips up-to-the-second intelligence on what the target was doing and where he was going. When the orders came to detain the target, snatch squads would go into action, arresting the so-called pillars of society. They would then be transported to another bunker similar to the control room and adjacent to it, but one with a more sinister use. This was the SAS holding and interrogation centre, used by the regiment to test and train its own people in the most recent developments in this strange trade. The guards and equipment were in place. The guards were the inscrutable Gurkhas, who have a very close affinity with the SAS, having worked around the world in different operations in support of the unit. As far as the soldiers of the Gurkha Rifles were concerned, this was just another exercise, *Pilgrim's Progress*, one of many that they had participated in during the year. It was not for them to know what the real reason for the exercise was.

Temperature Rising

For reasons to do with the geography of empire-building, many coups take place in tropical climes. And a fair proportion of those take place on exotic archipelagos. The popular ideal of the paradise island is far remote from the political reality of being in a strategic location. In this chapter we cite the cases of the Comoros, Fiji and the Seychelles. Exotic coups attract exotic characters and here we introduce 'The Frightful One', 'Mad Mike' Hoare and a man called 'Horse'.

The Teenage Coup: Comoros 1978

Broadcasters recently aired yet another variation on the 'reality television' theme. They would rig a large, well-furnished house with hidden cameras and then fill it with a bunch of teenagers who would be left to their own devices for a week or so. Viewing, we heard, was not for the faint-hearted. Now imagine the same teenagers, armed with AK-47s, taking over a whole country... It was only the Comoros, but it is a country of sorts. What you are about to read will make you appreciate the lump under the duvet upstairs.

There are four small islands in the Indian Ocean between the northern tip of Madagascar and the mainland border of Mozambique and Tanzania. Three of the islands, Grande Comore, Mohéli and Anjouan, are volcanic in all senses of the word. The fourth, Mayotte, is French but the other three islands think it should be part of their Union des Comores. In common with most of the East African coast, the economy has been traditionally dominated by Arab slave-traders and spice-dealers from the north, and French-colonial farmers took over in the mid-nineteenth century. The 500,000 mostly Muslim population was governed from Madagascar.

In 1973 France agreed to a five-year plan for all four islands to be given independence but the locals could not wait and, in 1974, voted for immediate self-rule. All except the people of Mayotte, that is. They decided to stay under French control and the Union des Comores started as it continued, with disunion and discord. President Ahmed Abdallah declared the whole archipelago independent on 6 July 1975; he was deposed later that year for his troubles.

In 1976 power was seized a young tearaway called Ali Saleh (sometimes spelt 'Soilih'). Terror may be defined as a drunken teenager with an AK-47 and an attitude. Whole gangs of them raped and looted their way across the islands with impunity; and impunity came in the shape of the fifteen-year old whom Saleh had just appointed chief of police. Insanely, he had put his teenage buddies in charge of whole government departments.

The madness continued for two years. One day in May 1978, Saleh was chilling out in the presidential bedroom with three naked schoolgirls. They were smoking ganja and watching a flickering 8-mm porn film projected on a wall when the door burst open. Standing in the doorway was Bob Denard. Now if you are the nasty self-imposed leader of a nasty self-imposed African government and, sooner or later, are going to be shot, there is no one more suitable for the job than Bob Denard. Denard pulled the trigger of his machine pistol and Saleh's reign ended in a pool of his own blood.

The story of the Comoros is the story of this renowned French mercenary, the self-styled 'Colonel' Bob Denard. Born in Bordeaux in 1929, his real name is Gilbert Bourgeaud. He claims he joined the French army after World War II and served in Indo-China and North Africa before becoming a mercenary after the Revolutionary War in Algeria. Denard was very much an Africa hand who played a part in conflicts in Angola, Benin, Gabon, Zimbabwe, the Congo and Nigeria. It is unclear on which side he fought in the Nigerian Civil War, but Frederick Forsyth denies meeting him there. In spite of this busy and well-travelled life, Denard found time to father eight children with seven wives, some of whom he forgot to divorce before marrying the next one. This may be how he picked up his nickname, 'The Frightful One'.

It was no disadvantage to Denard that he had the quiet support of the French home security agency, the DST, and the foreign intelligence service, the SDECE, for as long as France wanted to maintain influence over its former colonies. When a group of Comoran businessmen went looking for someone to serve an Anti-Social Behaviour Order on Ali Saleh and his underage government, they chose Bob Denard and offered him a substantial six million dollars to make it happen. The DST watched as he recruited old comrades from old wars and the SDECE tracked his ancient arms-laden freighter as it headed towards the Cape of Good Hope through the South Atlantic. The journey around Africa can't have been comfortable for them but, being French, at least the food must have been good. SDECE watched Denard and his team, but it did nothing to block the venture.

On a moonlit night in 1978, the mercenaries went ashore near the capital, Moroni, on inflatables and met up with local troops. According to one account, the city was secure enough by daybreak for 'Colonel Bob' to drape Saleh's corpse across the front of a jeep and drive around the capital showing the remains of the tyrant off to the delighted Comorans. For planning and execution, the Comoros *coup d'état* of 1978 scores a good seven out of ten.

In the aftermath Ahmed Abdallah – usurped three years earlier – was re-elected president. He survived three coup attempts by his own military and was elected yet again in 1984. But in November 1989 he was assassinated, allegedly by the recently sacked army chief. Ah, you say, Colonel Bob is back! No, he never left; the original 1978 coup team was renamed the Presidential Guard and Bob invested the surplus from the project fund in a range of business enterprises. He didn't need to pay wages because the apartheid government of South Africa had seen

136

the Frenchman as a some kind of stabilising influence – that must have been a first – and sponsored him and his Dogs of War for a decade. According to some sources, Denard was *de facto* leader of the country, the real power behind the throne.[63]

The army commander vehemently denied having anything to do with killing the president and attention focussed on Denard and another senior officer of the Guard. They had been seen walking with Abdallah in the garden of his official residence only hours before the assassination and Colonel Bob later admitted that he had been in the president's office when he was killed. Mere coincidence, perhaps? No, said Denard, it was 'an accident due to the general state of confusion...'

On 29 November Denard added to the confusion even further by launching a coup against provisional President Haribon Chebani, who, as head of the Supreme Court, had automatically succeeded Abdallah. In his place, Denard gave the job to Said Mohammed Djohar, who was now the Comoros's third president in five days. Along the way, the mercenary 'Presidential Guard' had shot and killed twenty-seven policemen, arrested hundreds of protesters and forced all foreign correspondents to stay in the bars of their hotels. It must have been hell for them.

There was outrage throughout Africa at the murder of Abdallah and pressure was put on France to do something about the bizarre and unpleasant situation. Paris was fearful of losing a considerable volume of arms sales on the continent and sent in troops via the still-friendly island of Mayotte. Denard was arrested and flown to South Africa, where he was held under house arrest while the French investigated his involvement in the assassination of President Abdallah. He was flown to France in February 1993, arrested, charged with the murder and found not guilty. Colonel Bob said it was all history and that he'd retired to a quiet life.

Two years later, in September 1995, thirty-three mercenaries stormed up the beach near Moroni after disembarking from an old freighter called the *Vulcain*. At their head was Colonel Bob Denard, obviously bored with early retirement. It was Groundhog Day in the Comoros. The invaders were mostly former members of the Presidential Guard and the locals, especially the women, greeted them warmly. They knew their way to the presidential palace and the Kandani garrison blindfolded. President Said Mohammed Djohar was killed during the putsch – Denard's third dead head of state on the island and one he had himself had put into power in 1989. African states protested once more but didn't seem able to put a counter-coup operation together. Again they threatened the French with a suspension of arms deals and the French rolled over.

Operation *Azalée* swung into action. Troops and equipment of *Commandment des Operations Speciales* (COS) were airlifted to Mayotte on 1 October. On the planes were soldiers of 1st RPIMa special-forces regiment, a *Commando Jaubert* navy assault team, gendarme special units and, for good measure, *Hubert* combat swimmers. A flight of Puma special-forces helicopters was also put in place. Two navy vessels were used to move the main assault force to offshore Grand Comore. On the evening of 3 October, *Commando Jaubert* used the beach adjacent to Hahaya Airport to insert a reconnaisance team. At 0200 on the 4th three Pumas flying directly from Mayotte delivered units of 1st RPIMa to capture the airport. Two other Pumas flying off one of the support ships landed at an airstrip called Iconi with the objective of securing the French embassy. Simultaneously a battalion-strength assault took place using Zodiac inflatables. The soldiers deployed according to plan and set up vehicle checkpoints. No one shot at them, so they held their fire too.[64]

Bob Denard had thirty-three mercenaries and four hundred Comoran troops but, at the age of sixty-six, had little heart for an all-out battle with his fellow-countrymen. Faced with the well-equipped COS, it was a battle he was bound to lose; this wouldn't be the same as his famous rout of the Congolese army in the 1960s. He surrendered.

On 21 March 2000, the wire services reported that small-arms fire had been heard in the north of the capital and that the telephone system was briefly disconnected. Shortly after, a spokesman announced that the army had prevented the nineteenth coup attempt since independence and there were no casualties. He went on to say that the alleged coup leaders were the two sons of former president Ahmed Abdallah, whose assassination in the 1989 coup was witnessed by Bob Denard. The target of the putsch was President Colonel Azali Assoumani, who himself had taken power by means of a *coup d'état* in April 1999; he was busy breaking the rule about not leaving the country while under threat by being in Saudi Arabia for the Hajj. We hope you have been paying attention.

Fiji 1987: Take 1 and Take 2

Much as the Fijians would like to tell you they were created by the gods on this beautiful archipelago of three hundred islands, the truth makes a much better legend. The people of Fiji are of South-East Asian origin, members of a race of seafarers who, sailing over a period of three or four millennia, progressively inhabited Micronesia, Melanesia and Polynesia. Stretching to Easter Island in the east, Hawaii in the north and New Zealand in the south, it is an area greater than the land mass of North America. It was a remarkable feat of navigation, unrivalled anywhere, even by the Vikings. The driving force behind these serial migrants was one of survival; they would settle each new island and, for a time, enjoy its natural resources. But, over maybe ten generations, the population would grow and those natural resources shrink until it was time for the pathfinders in their fast sailing canoes to search out new lands. And so it continued. There is no consensus regarding the date when the would-be Fijians discovered Fiji; some time between 1800 BC and AD 1 – choose a date. The population settled for a while, before there was an even bigger wave of migration from Melanesia between AD 1000 and 1800.

From a European perspective, Fiji was 'discovered' by Dutch explorer Abel Janszoon Tasman in the seventeenth century. He also discovered Tasmania. But he only sailed past Fiji and didn't bother with a stop-over. (Forget about cartoon desert islands consisting of a hump of sand, a solitary palm tree and a sad-looking castaway; Viti Levu, the biggest island, is 150 kilometres – 93 miles – across.) In the eighteenth century the redoubtable Captain James Cook passed by *en route* to discovering there was an even bigger island north of Tasmania. Strangely, none of the usual suspects, Britain, France or Spain, bothered to colonise Fiji but by the 1860s it had plenty of European carpetbaggers arriving on its beaches to set up plantations; cotton was a big thing, the market being stirred by a shortage resulting from the American Civil War. These rival groups of expatriates would often fight among themselves.

And so would the Fijians. The indigenous society was hierarchical; chiefs headed tribes and each tribe was divided into clans called *mataqali* with even more sub-clans below that. Inter-tribal and inter-clan rivalry would cause alliances to be forged and broken on a regular basis. Internecine warfare was endemic. From that point of view, nothing much has changed, it seems.

By 1874, the Fijians decided that even they had had enough of constant bickering over land and politics and, on 10 October, signed a deal with the Brits and became a Crown Colony with Sir Arthur Gordon as governor. Gordon set to in his new job, grittily determined to make a bad situation worse. Believing he was acting in the interests of the

Fijians, he barred them from all business and commercial activity and effectively kept them out of politics by requiring them to have their interests represented by the chiefs through the tribal system. The scheme was based on 83 per cent of all land being registered as *mataqali* property in perpetuity. This was then available for lease; the Fijians didn't even have to collect the rent, a government agency did that, deducting an administrative charge and handing the balance over to the clans for the benefit of the community.[65]

Clearly, such a feudal system was going to take the economy of the islands nowhere. Gordon determined that there was a market for sugar and got a company called the Colonial Sugar Refining Company to put up the capital. Considering cane-cutting to be beneath the Fijians (and the Fijians agreeing), the Brits imported indentured labour from another colony – India. The critical date was 14 May 1879 when the SS *Leonidas* arrived off Suva carrying 463 immigrants. Between then and 1916, sixty thousand people came to work as 'coolies'.[66] According to Fijian academic and Indian community leader Dr Ahmed Ali, 'privacy was nonexistent, marriages fragile, morality a luxury, over-tasking widespread, violence, including murder and suicide, not infrequent'.[67] But, on the up-side, it was better than India.

The Indian workers were encouraged to stay after the completion of their contracts, but they had limited political rights and no rights at all to buy land on which they could set up their own farms. Even today, when they have a slight majority of the population, they own only 1.7 per cent of the land. This has been a bone of contention since 1920 but not with the Fijians; the Indian population targeted its ire at the small European community which owned key parts of Fiji's economy and dominated its politics. Although colonial rule by the British was considered to be benevolent, industrial unrest grew after World War II and the trade unions became stronger. A general strike at the end of 1959 resulted in rioting by both Fijian and Indian workers against European property and employers. Another strike the following year climaxed in a march on Suva by thousands of sugar workers. They were stopped on the outskirts of the capital by the Fijian army backed up by soldiers from New Zealand.

The British decided it was time to withdraw from the colony and started the build-up to independence by scheduling the first popular elections for 1963. Members of the legislative council had previously been appointed by either tribal chiefs or influential businessmen. Now, everyone would get to vote, including the women. A Council of

Ministers was formed and they set to trying to thrash out a constitution for the newly autonomous Fiji. The main bone of contention tended to be whether the country should stay loyal to the British Commonwealth and the Queen or become a republic. A large part of the Indian community – but by no means all of them – supported the latter option. These and other constitutional matters were resolved in time to meet a deadline and, on 10 October 1970, the outcome of the negotiations became evident when Prince Charles represented the Queen at the handing-over ceremonies.

Fiji had a strong leader in Ratu Mara, whose Alliance Party won a fourteen-seat majority in the 1972 elections. Paramount chief Ratu Sir George Cakobau became the country's first post-colonial governor general. Fiji settled down for a while and, by South Pacific standards, even prospered somewhat. In 1978, as if to make a mark with the international community, Fiji sent a battalion of soldiers to Lebanon as part of the United Nations Interim Force in Lebanon (UNIFIL). As usual, they served with distinction, some of them losing their lives.

It was on his return from duties as commander of the Fijian force in 1987 that Lieutenant-Colonel Sitiveni Rabuka decided to get into politics. The Methodist lay preacher became Staff Officer in charge of Operations and Training. He ranked third in the hierarchy of the Royal Fijian Military Force (RFMF).

Parliamentary elections had been scheduled for 11 April that year and it looked as though the ruling Alliance Party was going to lose. The Alliance was a conservative group supported by the traditional Fijian tribal chiefs and it had been in power since independence in 1970. Rabuka and his supporters claimed that the traditional system had the support of 98 per cent of indigenous Fijians. But some caution is needed here; this figure derives from the views of the chiefs multiplied by the number of people in their tribes. Given that the chiefs were certainly in favour of keeping their inherited powers and that there was no overt dissent within the tribes, 98 per cent seems fairly predictable and fairly meaningless.

The opposition National Federation Party had teamed up with the Labour Party to form a coalition. Sure enough, the Labour–NFP Coalition won by twenty-eight seats to twenty-four, a majority that cannot be explained by the slightly superior number of Indians in the population. But Rabuka was having none of it. He talked of Fiji being in the hands of the 'immigrant race' (the Indian one, that is) and declared, 'The only option now is the military option. I must act.'[68]

141

On 14 May, 38-year-old Lieutenant-Colonel Rabuka did indeed act. The opening gambit was the seizure of the parliament building in the capital of Suva and the arrest of leading members of the new government. Operations Order 1/87 (obviously not a busy year for the RFMF) is reproduced at the end of Eddie Dean's book. It is headed 'The Neutralisation of the Coalition Government of Fiji' and shows (in Rabuka's handwriting) lists of primary objectives that include: Government House, FM 96 (yes, the radio station), the *Fiji Times*, various sugar mills and government buildings.[69]

The coup plan was put seamlessly into effect and not much more than dignity was damaged in the process. The entire cabinet of the new government was arrested and taken into custody. The following morning, Ratu Mara himself declared he would join Rabuka's junta, an act which many Fijians considered a betrayal of his democratic values.

Much of the credit for the smoothness of the putsch needs to go a very interesting RFMF officer who had served most of his career with the British Army; we will call him 'Horse'. There was an important difference between Rabuka and Horse when it comes to respect. Horse had seen action with the British SAS over many years (see The Incredible Horse, page 147). Rabuka, on the other hand, had seen action with, er… UNIFIL. In that posting, the main threat against him came from a fellow blue-bereted Norwegian officer in the Lebanon: 'He cocked his gun. He saw my UN badge, but he wouldn't believe I was a UN soldier. He kept his gun pointed at me. I advanced across the fully lit helicopter pad towards him.'[70]

We will spare you the rest, but be assured that no one got hurt in that particular incident. In Eddie Dean's uncritical biography of Rabuka, Horse is called 'Captain X', which makes him sound like a comic-strip super-hero, tights and all. In reality, he was probably the most well-trained and operationally experienced soldier in the South Pacific. He is depicted as doing the hard graft, training and more training; checking the radios and then checking them again to ensure they worked in the area around Government House. He was exercising a level of attention to detail that had 'SAS' written all over it. 'I asked him to choose sixty top men,' wrote Rabuka, 'to undergo intensive training in the use of arms and in close-quarter battle. This is the use of weapons inside buildings, in confined areas, or in urban streets and lanes. No questions were to be asked.'[71]

Horse, though, stayed well in the background while Rabuka did the press conferences and speeches. 'The Fijian's power-base is his land or 'vanua', which he guards jealously,' he told the foreign media, and explained, 'Any threat to his land rights is defended vigorously because it is the only material thing that he owns.' Just to be sure, Rabuka also played the God card:

> The main driving force is my belief in God, and that made me brave enough to see what I saw, made me brave enough to do what I did... I am not a good Christian, in that I am like most people, I pray a lot, and perhaps I can say that I also sin a lot. I do not despair when I do something wrong, because I know that the love of God overcomes everything. I come back to Him, and confess. He is there! He says: 'Get up and go again.'[72]

So Rabuka believes that God made him do it. But there are a lot of Fijians who believe the Americans made him do it.

A long-term resident of Fiji told us that the 'ethnic thing' was something that took considerable effort to stir up. 'Whenever there [was] a dispute between the Fijians and the Indians, they would get together for grog. The matter would get resolved during the process of getting very drunk. Then they would all stagger off into the night, the best of friends. I never saw it done any other way.' Rabuka's categorisation of 'left-wing parties Indian, right-wing parties Fijian' also looks like wishful thinking. Except perhaps for the nationalist Taukei Movement, both sides of the political spectrum seemed to draw support from all parts of the ethnic mix. Dr Timoci Bavadra, the new prime minister, was elected on a platform which promised the creation of an Institute for Fijian Language and Culture and greater access for indigenous Fijians to Fiji Development Bank loans that had previously been earmarked for foreign-owned businesses. He was also committed to an expanded programme of free medical care, and undertook to protect timber resources. Non-Indian Fijians were appointed to a majority of cabinet posts (and it may have passed Rabuka's notice that the new prime minister was an ethnic Fijian).

'We have done in four weeks for poor people,' said Bavadra, 'what [the] Alliance Party could not do in 17 years.' So, if we are going to discount Divine Intervention to block an invasion by Colonel Qaddafi – and we think we are – what were the real motives behind the Fijian coups of 1987? Enter stage right former Deputy Director of the CIA General Vernon Walters.

Rabuka was certainly making all the right noises to keep the United States happy. This was still the height of the Cold War and Fiji's new leader was saying that, because half the population was Indian and because India was a neutral country with good relations with the Soviet Union, then the Labour–NFP coalition would introduce communism. This he coloured up a bit by encouraging the rumour that Libya was plotting to invade Fiji – though no details were provided about how Qaddafi and his team of shapely female bodyguards would actually carry this out.

On a more serious level, the Reagan administration was growing concerned about the increasing opposition throughout the Pacific to allowing US nuclear ships – and ships carring nuclear weapons – berthing and bunkering facilities. The tiny island republic of Belau had recently voted to confirm its unprecedented anti-nuclear constitution. Even New Zealand was in favour of a non-nuclear Pacific. Just to make matters worse, the Republic of Vanuatu (formerly New Hebrides), had signed a fishing treaty with the USSR.

Fiji's defeated pro-West prime minister, Ratu Sir Kamisese Mara, had previously reversed a no-nukes policy, but his incoming replacement, Dr Timoci Bavadra, was planning to fall in line with the growing mood in the rest of the Pacific. Most island communities consider their land to be sacred and would prefer not to see it glow in the dark. American intentions in this regard are not a by-product of the usual anti-US hysteria; former Ambassador to Fiji, William Bodde, Jr, removed all doubt on this when he said 'a nuclear free zone would be unacceptable to the US, given our strategic needs,' adding, 'the U.S. must do everything possible to counter this movement.'

'Doing everything possible' covered a lot of bases. Washington started by jacking up aid for Fiji through projects such as the International Military Education and Training Program, Pacific Armies Management Seminars and the Weapons Standardization Program; not much there to cover land reform and improved health care.

More aid came in the shape of Lieutenant-General Vernon Walters, who arrived in Suva on 30 April 1987 – two weeks after the election and two weeks before the coup. Walters had a very public career as US Ambassador to the UN and former Deputy Director of the CIA. He also had a somewhat less well-known career as a coup plotter, starting with Iran 1953 (Chapter 3) and progressing through Brazil 1964 to Chile 1973 (Chapter 6). The writing was on the wall of the arrivals hall at Nadi International Airport.

After a short, uncomfortable meeting with the new prime minister, General Walters moved on to hector Foreign Minister Krishna Datt about the no-nuclear-ship policy. No doubt the envoy lectured him about the American policy of 'strategic denial' under which Washington was determined to prevent, by whatever means necessary, South Pacific island states from entering into any foreign relationship of which the US did not approve.[73] Next on the schedule was a protocol-busting meeting with Lieutenant-Colonel Sitiveni Rabuka; the minutes of that encounter have never been published.

As early as 1953, in Iran, Walters would have learned that money is a great way to lubricate the wheels of a *coup d'état*. In the case of Fiji it seems that 200,000 dollars of oil was needed. The pipeline was the South Pacific regional office of the US Agency for International Development (USAID) in Suva. This was not the first time USAID has been accused of providing a cover for less reputable activities and its regional director, William Paupe, won't be the first to be accused of actually working for the 'Agency for Central Intelligence'. An adviser to Dr Bavadra called him 'a barefoot Ollie North running around the US embassy in Fiji'.[74]

During the planning of the coup Rabuka had an unusual 'accidental' encounter with the ultra-nationalist Taukei Movement (which was tied in with the Alliance Party). On the spur of the moment, as it were, he dropped by for a 'grog' at the Suva house of the party's leader, the Reverend Raikivi, and was astonished to find the place full of people.[75] Rabuka recognised most of those present as well-connected political leaders from the indigenous community, 'but I could not see everyone clearly because it was fairly dark in the lounge room. Nobody asked me to leave.' He might not have been able to see all the party-goers, but he could certainly hear them planning street violence against the Indians and the government. Rabuka warned them not to attempt it because they'd be up against the army.

The Taukei Movement took Rabuka's advice, for the time being at least. But on the day of the coup, 14 May, they saw their opportunity and launched a vicious campaign of intimidation, riots, fire-bombing and eventually murder – all targeted against the Indian population. Amnesty International reported that, for the first time in Fijian history, it had identified cases of illegal detention and torture. Worldwide condemnation put tremendous pressure on Fiji and Rabuka soon handed power over to the governor-general.

However, it wasn't all bad news and there was a very positive response to the overthrow of a democratically elected government from at least one quarter: 'We're kinda delighted,' said a Pentagon spokesman. 'All of a sudden our ships couldn't go to Fiji, and now all of a sudden they can.'

But the cork was out of the bottle and the race riots continued. If Rabuka was opposed to this activity, and with both the army and the police under his command, why didn't he put a stop to the Taukei Movement's campaign of terror? It did eventually end when, on 25 September, Rabuka led another *coup d'état*. This time he declared Fiji a republic – originally an 'Indo-Fijian' policy – and demanded a new constitution which guaranteed untrammelled ethnic Fijian control of any government. At the end of 1987 Rabuka appointed Ratu Mara prime minister of an interim government and gave himself the job of minister for home affairs in charge of the military and the police.

For most of the 1990s, Fiji developed into a pariah state with an economy that was going into reverse. In 1997, ten years after the original coup, Rabuka signed an agreement with the leader of the Indian community for the introduction of a new electoral system. When this was first tested two years later, Rabuka's party was defeated by a landslide; even the ethnic Fijians had had enough of the soldier-preacher. A new government was formed by the Labour Party, led by Mahendra Chaudhry, the country's first Indian prime minister.

Three Coups and You Are Out: Fiji 2000

George Speight was a bankrupt businessman who thought he'd have better luck running a country. On 19 May 2000 a group of armed supporters stormed the parliament building and took Mahendra Chaudhry and other representatives hostage. During a long stand-off that made the evening news on television stations around the world Speight recited the Rabuka creed about immigrant takeovers, thus proving he was also bankrupt of ideas. It looked as though international approbation and sanctions would become the order of the day again.

There was trouble on the streets once more and parliament had to be suspended; the Great Council of Chiefs appointed Laisenia Qarase as the head of a provisional government. Eventually the coup petered out and Speight was arrested. Once law and order was restored, sanctions were lifted and life in Fiji returned to what passes as normal again. But the damage had been done; inward investment had collapsed, the sugar industry was in decline and skilled and professional Fijians left in despair, in droves. The health service now has to encourage immigration by foreign doctors and nurses.

Fiji is further proof that veto coups, even ones that start off 'blood-less', invariably cause an inordinate amount of grief. The events of 1987 and 2000 were not just a couple of traditional inter-tribal skirmishes; unless, that is, you count the whole of the Indo-Fijian community as a tribe and Lieutenant-General Vernon Walters as some kind of honorary visiting chieftain. Playing global politics with a super-power is a bit like sleeping with a gorilla; potentially exciting, inevitably dangerous.

In a move that suggested all Fijians wanted to see an end to *coups d'état* as part of their political lives, George Speight was tried and convicted of treason. He is now serving a life sentence on a small island not far offshore from Suva, maybe one with a single palm tree and a shark circling it.

Ken Connor: The Incredible Horse

At the beginning of the 1960s the British Army changed from being a conscript to a fully Regular Army. It quickly became apparent that it would not be possible to recruit the number of soldiers to keep the army up to strength if those soldiers were recruited solely from the British Isles. The recruiting sergeants cast their nets ever wider until, eventually, someone had the very bright idea of recruiting from the former colony of Fiji.

The two main criteria for the new recruits were that they must be physically fit and be able to speak and write English. This narrowed the recruiting base down to young men who had just left school or college. Eventually two hundred successful candidates arrived in the UK, where they were sent to various military training depots. They very quickly developed a reputation for bravery, excellence at rugby and having a good time. Eventually from this group, twelve went on to join the Special Air Service. Over the next couple of decades, the SAS Fijians served the Crown with distinction. They were always where the action was thickest and the danger greatest. Many were decorated and an even greater number were killed or wounded in action. They have left an indelible impression on the people they served with and on the people of Herefordshire, where the SAS is based. Now, in the new century another generation of Fijians is serving with similar distinction with the unit. Not a bad record for individuals who are technically mercenaries.

'Horse' was the first of the original twelve to join the SAS. This is an attempt to show how his time in the regiment shaped his development from a schoolboy in the South Pacific to the organiser of military coups *par excellence*.

In 1964 the regiment was heavily engaged in two theatres of war, fighting insurgents in Borneo and rebellious tribesmen in South Arabia. The skills needed to excel and survive in these operations were diverse and challenging. The operations covered a range from deep-penetration patrols into Indonesia to fight regular troops of the Indonesian army to sneaky patrols, disguised as local Arabs, in the back streets of the Crater quarter of Aden. Although the casualties we suffered were relatively small, the impact they had on a regiment of less than fifty fighting troops was immense. We were all very, very close in temperament and when we lost a comrade the shock waves reverberated around the other patrols.

Into this anarchic, insane and dangerous environment came the legend that was soon to be called Horse.

I walked into 17 Troop 'basha' early one morning after a night on the tiles, to be confronted by a dark-skinned, heavily built guy lying on one of the beds. I immediately turned tail and went to find Bill, our troop sergeant. He explained that the guy has just successfully completed the selection course and was posted to the troop on probation. At that time even applicants who had got through the very demanding entrance test were only admitted to the squadron on probation. They had to cut it with the rest of the blokes on operations before they were considered part of the regiment. This was a severe test of everyone's ability because most of the troops were less than ten strong and the close interaction between personalities made any defects difficult to hide.

Later that day we travelled down to Falmouth to do boat training. To the trogs' minds this was a euphemism for winding down before the next deployment to Borneo. Unfortunately, along with Horse, we had also acquired a new troop officer. Some officers are fine and fit into the system because they are sensible enough to see their place in it. Others are a constant source of annoyance because they know they have been specially selected as leaders and that they have a sense of infallibility which is only shared by the Pope. They know with certainty that they are always right, and that a senior NCO with twenty years' experience will always be hanging on the officer's word to learn how to carry out the trade...

When we arrived in Falmouth we met up with a converted trawler which was to be our safety boat. The ship had a crew of three and was captained by Skipper 'Fearless' Brown. Old Fearless had served in the navy throughout World War II; he was approaching retirement and all he wanted was a quiet life.

Also, the crew were paid the same if they were in port or at sea. The SAS hierarchy was very safety-conscious about training in open water, having recently had two guys die of exposure in the Irish Sea because a safety officer made a bad decision.

The time in Falmouth became a constant game of the new Rupert being very gung-ho and wanting to be at sea at every opportunity and the trogs wanting to be in the pubs. The trogs won because Fearless has a taste for navy rum and the troop had rum in plenty. We were issued the grog for cold, wet-weather training and it was a challenge for us to get it out of the army accounting system even if we were training in a heat wave. Every morning we would set sail with the officer at the bow of the trawler surveying the waves, day-dreaming of deeds of daring-do, and Fearless in the wheelhouse steering the boat.

Once we hit the open sea one of the trogs would enter the wheelhouse with a full mug of rum and let the fumes waft under the nose of the intrepid Fearless. The trog would say how much better it would be if we could make our way back to the quay because the weather might turn nasty and most of the trogs were suffering from hangovers, letting Fearless have the occasional sip of the brew. We never got very far before the trawler would start to pitch and roll alarmingly and Fearless would explain to the Rupert that he would have to return to port because the sea was turning rough and conditions were dangerous. There were some terrific arguments between the two but Fearless had the power of veto over anything he considered a danger to the ship. On returning to Falmouth, Fearless got his rum ration and we got our time in the pubs.

It was on this trip that Horse acquired the nickname which was to stay with him the rest of his life. For the training we had inflatable boats which were powered by forty-horsepower outboard motors. These engines were a two-man lift on land but when we were attempting to manhandle them on a heaving deck at sea they often required three or four pairs of hands. Horse would politely move everybody aside and carry an engine on his own. His strength was phenomenal. At the time there was a popular TV programme called *Bonanza* which featured a character who was immensely strong and gentle; he was called Horse. It was inevitable that we would nickname our Fijian friend after him.

One of the squadron's trips to Borneo coincided with the Commonwealth Military Far East Rugby Sevens. There were competitors from all over the region including a team of New

Zealanders who were the reigning champions. Over a few beers we decided to enter a team even though we did not have seven guys who had played rugby. We sent a team of six and Horse, and to everybody's surprise and the Kiwis' chagrin, we won the trophy. To be more accurate, Horse won the trophy almost single-handed. It transpired that he was a player of such skill that he had been offered a very substantial sum to join Rochdale Hornets Rugby League team before he had transferred to the SAS.

Another illustration of the madcap world of the SAS occurred in Aden. Again we had a new officer and this particular guy had a hang-up about camouflage. We did not subscribe to the military doctrine of wearing camouflage cream, preferring the more natural way of not washing or shaving. At every opportunity the officer tried to make this an issue and would seek allies to support his position. He particularly liked Horse because he was invariably polite and listened to the Rupert's arguments and would agree with his points of view on the subject. What he did not appreciate was that Horse was invariably polite to everybody, including his worst enemies. Eventually, the Rupert insisted that we all put on the cam cream, citing Horse as being in agreement with his position. The first one to wear it was Horse even though his skin was as brown as a coconut. He felt that he had got us into it and only by showing the Rupert how ridiculous the whole thing was, could he get us out of it.

Horse spent several dangerous months walking the back streets of Aden along with the other Fijian troopers disguised as Arabs. They were there to entice the terrorist gangs to attack other SAS patrols and then intervened and took out the bad guys. As a tactic it had limited success and the mental strain on the guys was enormous, but they did it uncomplainingly and cheerfully. The only redeeming feature from the Fijians' point of view was that because the Fijians were too big and bulky the white guys had to dress as women. Loud and often were the laughs when tough unshaven Geordies and Jocks put on figure-hugging dresses and high heels.

In Northern Ireland, Horse found himself in the ignominious position of being arrested for illegally crossing the border into the Republic of Ireland. He was on patrol with other soldiers in South Armagh when, after they were picked up, the guy driving the lead car took a wrong turn and drove into southern Ireland. They were quickly arrested by the Gardai and taken to Dublin. There has always been a suspicion in my mind as to whether there was collusion between the Gardai and the IRA on this occasion, because they were never as alert as this at other times.

Horse, in his position as the first of the Fijians, was uniquely placed to be influenced by the happenings around him. When he joined the SAS he was little more than a schoolboy, used to formality, structure and deference to authority. In the SAS he found himself in situations where, if the wrong decision was made, people were going to get hurt. The trogs for the most part were quite happy to forego a career for the privilege of serving in the regiment, but one or two of the officers used the SAS to promote and forge their way onwards and upwards in the military. It was one of these Ruperts who caused the downfall of Horse.

A Parachute Regiment officer serving with the SAS had the bright idea of sending all SAS corporals to be trained by the Paras before they could become sergeants. The idea was ludicrous. Most of the SAS corporals had several years of combat experience while the Para instructors had only seen active service in Northern Ireland if at all. To send your best guys to be trained in large-scale airborne-unit tactics when the role of the SAS was small reconnaissance patrols was another, even greater, reason for not going ahead with it. The only good that would come out of it, as far as most of us could see, was that it would further the career of the Para Regiment officer who first came up with the proposal. When Horse was made to attend the course the inevitable happened; he rebelled, and refused to finish the training. The Paras very reluctantly gave him a 'failed' grading. After all, he did know more than the instructors who were supposed to be teaching him. The result was that he was told that he would not be considered for further promotion within the regiment. Horse finished his time in the British Army and returned to Fiji, with this disgraceful episode fresh in his mind, to start a new career, where he put his military expertise and experience to other uses.

Finis Coronat Opus: The Seychelles 1977–1987

In the Seychelles there is no dispute over who is and who is not an incomer. From the pirates who arrived in the early 1700s to the mercenary coup-makers of the late-twentieth century, they are all immigrants.

With seven full coups or coup-bids since independence in 1976, we could have put the Republic of Seychelles into the 'Serial Offenders' chapter. However, unlike Nigeria, it has become a popular package-holiday destination and so we have placed it in the 'Exotic' category. This widespread group of 115 islands north-east of Madagascar in the Indian Ocean has a flashy Latin motto: *Finis Coronat Opus*. This translates literally as 'the end crowns the work' or 'the end justifies the means', which is the motto of coup plotters throughout the world and a good alternative to Colonel Rabuka's 'there is no other way'. (See Fiji 1987, this chapter.)

The country was ruled from Paris until 1814 and French is still one of the official languages. Britain took over while France was licking its wounds in the aftermath of the Napoleonic Wars. For a long time, the Seychelles were a dependency of Mauritius but in 1903 the islands became a Crown Colony. The population is mainly of African and European origin and mostly live on the main island of Mahé. Work in the cinnamon and copra plantations was the main source of income before 1971, when an upgraded airport led to a surge in commercial air traffic and a burgeoning tourist industry. This new source of foreign earnings supplemented revenues from the sale of licences to fish the one million square kilometres (386,000 square miles) of ocean it controls; the domestic fleet harvests the tuna crop for export through a cannery co-owned with a French company. The consequences of this are that the eighty thousand population does quite well by the standards of most developing countries. Citizens benefit also from such social welfare as free healthcare and education. And travel agents describe the islands as one of the most beautiful places on earth.

So, what was the problem? Well, it seems that the United States determined that the Seychelles lay in an area of strategic interest. Hold on, you say, wasn't that the Pacific? Actually, it was anywhere America wanted it to be. But let's start at the beginning, in the late seventies with the declaration of independence. James Richard Marie Mancham became the founding president of the republic and soon developed a reputation for the jet-setting high-life. As ever, it was not a particularly smart idea to spend too much time abroad when you have an enemy within. During the 1960s and in concert with the British, Mancham had been instrumental is allowing the US to construct what purported to be a satellite tracking station on top of a big hill at *La Misére* on Mahé. His political opponents were opposed to alliances with any of the super-powers (or so they said) and certainly didn't like the idea of the Americans having as much as a burger joint on the islands. South Africa's apartheid regime also had an interest in the archipelago;

Pretoria considered the Seychelles to be a potential cut-out for sanctions-busting oil shipments from the Middle East. It would also provide a useful strategic base from which to destabilise Marxist Tanzania.

At the beginning of June 1977 sixty Seychellois supporters of the opposition Seychelles People's Unity Party returned from protracted military training in Tanzania, thus confirming the worst fears of South Africa and the other players. The team was to play a key role in the 4-June coup which overthrew Mancham and put leftist politician France Albert René into power as *de facto* head of state. René claimed he had no knowledge of the plot and two years later was elected president with a convincing 98 per cent majority. The other two per cent must have voted for their favourite goats, because René was the only candidate. As head of the only permitted legal party, the Seychelles People's Progressive Front ('the Front'), he was to hang onto unilateral power by his fingernails for fourteen years.

This doesn't mean to say that René was able to rule without opposition, but that opposition came in the form of a succession of unsuccessful *coups d'état* backed by the deposed James Mancham in London, the CIA in Virginia and a mercenary called 'Mad Mike' Hoare in South Africa. The first coup took place in 1978, the year after René's takeover. If Mancham's supporters had been trained by France, Britain or America, they might have been better off going to Tanzania; the whole thing was a flop, despite René being on a state visit to China and North Korea. Clearly, he had also failed to learn a fundamental lesson from many previous coups.

It was decided to bring in the professionals and this is when 'Mad Mike' appeared on the scene. Ireland-born Colonel Michael Hoare had lived in South Africa since 1946 and that country provided a base for his many escapades throughout the 'Dark Continent'. He first came to international prominence, along with Bob Denard (see Comoros 1978, Chapter 7), during the bloody chaos that was 1960s Belgian Congo.

Hoare's first try, in November 1979, was stymied by someone in the Seychelles blowing the whistle and causing the arrest of eighty supporters in Mahé. It was a strange business; the eighty detainees were later released without charge and rumours spread that the French were behind the plot. No one, however, could explain why. An attempt to reverse the British takeover of 1814 seems improbable.

But the island state didn't stay quiet for long. On 25 November 1981 a South African rugby club called 'The Ancient Order of Frothblowers' arrived on a Royal Swazi flight at Mahé International. The forty-five hard-drinking heavies had already consumed all the alcohol on the plane and seemed in a good mood as they passed an oval ball to and fro in the baggage-claim area. Most were already through customs unchallenged when one of the sportsmen was stopped for a routine check of his hold-all. The mood changed suddenly when, from under the jerseys, boots and jock-straps, the customs officer pulled out a folding-stock assault rifle. Realising the game was up, the rest of the team of South African special forces reservists, former Rhodesian soldiers and various ex-Congo veterans produced their own weapons and seized the terminal building.

Seychellois police and army units responded and opened fire. There were remarkably few casualties; 2nd Lieutenant David Antat and a police sergeant were shot and killed by the coup team, which lost only one man. Some airport staff were taken hostage, but the South Africans realised that Operation *Anvil* was another non-event and decided to get out of the country the only way they could – by hijacking a plane. On the apron and fuelled up was Air India Flight 224. With a little encouragement the pilots were persuaded to make an unscheduled departure towards the south-west with forty-four freeloading passengers on board. Back in the capital of Victoria, the Seychelles Government arrested six men and a woman who had formed part of Mike Hoare's advance party and who had missed the unscheduled flight home. In Durban, South Africa, a few hours later, the South African police met the Air India jet and arrested all the mercenaries including their leader.

When the group was eventually brought to trial, the defence was predictable: 'We were all working for the South African government.' Two of the defendants had thrown their lot in with the prosecution and swore that no one had told them about working for the government. This was backed up by an opposition group called the *Mouvement pour la Résistance* (the Movement for Resistance), which announced that one hundred of its wealthier émigré members had funded the coup. At first it seemed that the Pretoria government would let them all free as a way of avoiding any embarrassing disclosures in court but there was international outrage at the idea that the mercenaries could get away with the hijacking.

Several of the mercenaries, including Colonel Hoare, served time in jail for their involvement in Operation *Anvil*. But Justice Neville James told the court that there was no evidence to support Hoare's claims that the South African Government was involved in the coup. Strangely, though, all charges against Hoare and the others were dropped except for the relatively minor one of endangering the plane and its passengers. All were found guilty. 'Mad Mike' Hoare was, the judge observed, an unscrupulous man with a highly cavalier attitude to the truth'. He went to jail but, on 7 May 1985, he was released as part of a presidential amnesty.

For a time, it looked as though the coup team left behind in the Seychelles would be considerably less fortunate. Although the woman was released, one of the men was jailed in June 1982 for ten years and another for twenty; the remaining four were sentenced to death. However, the South African Government secretly negotiated their release and, after paying a considerable amount in 'compensation' and agreeing not to support any future military actions against the island nation, they were all released a year later. It later transpired that President France Albert René had forgotten to mention to his cabinet that he'd been paid three million dollars.

Tanzania had had a military presence in the country since shortly after René's own post-independence coup. In 1981 there were two companies of the Tanzanian People's Defence Force (TPDF) on the islands. Reinforced by a further two hundred troops, these soldiers had proved useful in taking control of Mahé International Airport on the day after Mike Hoare's failed coup attempt. They also proved useful in August 1982 when René asked them to suppress a mutiny by his own Seychelles People's Defence Force (SPDF), thus blocking a rare internal bid to overthrow him.

It was four more years before the next coup. The United States, France and the UK were named as the backers of a 1986 plot known as Operation *Distant Lash*. This involved thirty mercenaries and a considerable 350 insurgents in the Seychelles itself. The leader this time was a local politician, Defence Minister Ogilvy Berlouis, who, backed by a group of army officers, was promoting himself as having policies favourable to the Western powers. Government security forces rumbled the coup before it was really off the drawing board and Berlouis was busted. Ironically, the army officers had been trained by the Tanzanians. This time, René was attending a Commonwealth Heads of State conference in Zimbabwe and still wilfully ignoring all the lessons.

In July 1987, London's Metropolitan Police Special Branch was tipped off about a plot being hatched in Britain by four former members of the Special Air Service Regiment. It's possible to understand why the police were so twitchy; two years earlier, Seychelles opposition leader Gerard Hoarau had been murdered outside his London home. In the

1987 case it was alleged that, before setting off to overthrow the René regime, the plotters intended to kidnap leaders of the South African opposition movement, the African National Congress (ANC), who were also based in London. This could have been a cunning plan to win over the sympathies of the apartheid government. However, as they were only dreaming of spending the summer sunning themselves on the beaches of the Seychelles, the four mercenaries were charged with no more than conspiring to abduct the ANC members. But it all came to nought and even those indictments were dropped in the face of a paucity of evidence. We suspect that the leader of this group might have been the infamous 'Mercenary Fink'. (See page 188.)

By this time, France Albert René seemed to get bored with foreign coups disrupting his well-ordered rule on these paradise islands and things began to settle down. The North Korean 'advisers' who had trained his personal guard left in 1988; they weren't much fun anyway. At the start of the next decade the Soviet Union withdrew its support, citing a need to deal with a coup of its own. In 1992 James Mancham returned from exile for the first time, but with a team of ex-SAS bodyguards in tow. His incentive was the forthcoming Commonwealth-supervised multi-party elections and a chance to throw René out legitimately. He failed by small margin and grumpily claimed the ballot had been rigged.

Probably unconnected with the election, Pretoria then paid the Seychelles a large amount of money in settlement of previous disputes and the two countries kissed and made up; on 8 November 1993, diplomatic relations were established. Malaysian businesses have made a big investment in the tourist industry and the islands have been turned into an offshore tax haven. France Albert René won another vote in 2001 but retired in 2004 when his loyal supporter James Michel became president.

Even the Americans are now friendly. The Pentagon provides military assistance (such as biodiversity, air-sea rescue and dog training) in return for facilities of a strategic nature (such as the tracking station at *La Misère*).

Chapter 8
The Coup That Never Was

The two Nimrod electronic warfare aircraft were cruising at eleven thousand feet over the Oxfordshire countryside, endlessly repeating a lazy oval pattern. They were running on two engines after making the dash from their base at Kinloss in Scotland to arrive on station above southern England.

The pilots were careful to avoid sharp turns, making sure the crew in the back were not thrown about as they carried out their delicate task of operating the complex electronic equipment packed into the back of the plane. The Nimrod had first been designed to protect the UK during the Cold War. It then went through various changes until the last time it was used in anger, during the Iraq war, when it was used to identify targets for the UK Special Forces operating deep beyond enemy lines.

Now, in the rear of the aircraft, the fingers of the air electronics officers were whizzing across computer keyboards. On the screens in front of the operators were visual displays of electronic transmissions and call signs. On the port side of the aircraft were all the civilian and emergency-services transmissions. On the starboard side were similar displays showing all the military call signs. The highly skilled operators, probably the finest in the world, allowed the signals and transmissions to start before interrupting or blocking a signal altogether. They showed great skill in imitating an intermittent electrical equipment fault rather than deliberate interference.

As the various agencies on the ground whisked around the electronic spectrum in search of a clear channel, the airborne team above them deftly blocked any full signal from going between one call sign and another. With the use of in-flight refuelling and on-board sleeping and feeding facilities the Nimrods could, in theory, stay on station indefinitely. They could also, in theory, interfere with all the radio communications on the UK mainland indefinitely.

The Middle East before it Became a Way of Not Saying 'Palestine'

The Arabian Gulf forty years ago was a different world from the present high-rise coastal-strip development populated by newly oil-rich locals and expatriates. At that time there were very few permanent settlements. There was the famous Gold Souk in Dubai, a very small permanent settlement in Abu Dhabi, and the same in Qatar. The place that was most developed was the island of Bahrain, which had an airport, docks and a small refinery that was producing petroleum products for the southern Gulf.

In the whole of the region there were no more than five miles of hard-top roads and very few vehicles. Those that were there travelled along tracks which followed the ancient caravan routes from oasis to oasis. The indigenous population were bedouin, who lived a subsistence life searching the arid desert for a little grazing for the few animals they kept. The bedouin diet consisted of rice and bread which was traded with the merchants who ventured into the desert to visit the oases. They bartered their animals for flour and rice which they ate for almost every meal during the lonely treks looking for water and shrub.

There was very little modern industry on the mainland. The only commercial activity exploited by the locals was some pearl-diving off the coast of Abu Dhabi. The small oil refinery on Bahrain was run by British and Indian expatriate labour while the larger one on the coast of Saudi Arabia at Dhahran was administered and operated by the Americans.

The southern Gulf was administered through a series of ancient treaties by the British. The centre of power was in Manama on Bahrain, where there was a sizeable political residency. There was also a British Royal Navy Base and a Royal Air Force airfield on which was stationed a squadron of Hunter jet fighters with a half squadron of Beverley transport aircraft. Also on the island was a battalion group of British paratroopers and support units. The military forces were the legacy of an Iraqi threat to invade Kuwait in 1958 (yes, 1958). In response to this threat, the British Government had sent a brigade of paratroopers supported by a squadron of tanks to Kuwait where they dug in on the Iraqi border for several months until the threat had receded. Not convinced that the threat had gone away entirely, the British had moved the troops to Bahrain, where they were held in readiness to respond if the Iraqis tried it on again.

Throughout the rest of The Gulf the British military presence was maintained by locally raised militia. These units, British-officered and administered on British Army lines, were housed in Beau-Geste-like forts. The forts were painted white to reflect the sun but also to stand out as an unsubtle threat to the local population in a region where violence was never far away. As late as 1959 there had been a pitched gun battle between the tribes of Abu Dhabi and Dubai which had to be suppressed by using a local military force called the Trucial Oman Scouts. All of the non-commissioned ranks of the Scouts were local Arabs. They did not make the best soldiers on the drill square but they knew the desert and they knew the people.

The centre of the British political web was Manama on Bahrain Island. Outside of that, in areas where there was any population at all, there was a sprinkling of British political residents. These were either newly recruited university graduates or seasoned ex-soldiers. Their brief was simple – get out into the hinterland, get to know the tribes and get to know who was 'in bed' with whom. A common denominator of these political residents was that they all spoke excellent local Arabic.

The other influence at that time came from the international oil companies, particularly the Americans. They sent survey teams in Dodge Power trucks to the remotest parts of the desert. These unannounced excursions threatened relations with the local tribes because, without the tribes' agreement, the prospectors could not gain legitimate access. The oil people generally operated out of Saudi Arabia and were intent on getting the tribes to sign agreements for the extraction of oil and minerals. This activity was countered by the British diplomats working hard to protect UK interests along the coastal area. However, the West-influenced division of areas did not prevent several attempts by the Saudis to subvert the ruler in Oman – a series of events which led to the Jebel Akhdar rebellion of 1958. This was suppressed by the SAS in a feat of arms for which the word 'epic' might have been invented.[76]

Ken Connor: Self-Sufficiency and the Art of Dental Hygiene

For the first three years of their time in Bahrain the Paras lived in tents on the edge of the RAF airfield while the RAF guys lived in air-conditioned brick accommodation with a cocktail bar and, we suspected, a manicurist. On an island where the temperature often hits forty-five degrees Celsius and the humidity is always 100 per cent, even the top brass realised that this situation was not sustainable.

They brought in a British contractor to design and build a camp at Hamala on the far side of the island, as far away from the other residents of the island as it is possible to go. The plans included the unheard-of luxury of communal showers. The intrepid contractor then recruited local labour to build the camp. Progress was painfully slow. The Arabs would only work when the weather was cool, and the weather was never cool! Eventually, the commanding officer of the Para battalion decided to lend a hand. He instituted the 24-hour working system, using each of his rifle companies to work an eight-hour shift, and the camp was completed in a record three weeks. But, as is often the case, there was a down-side.

The Para engineers drilled a borehole to supply the communal showers and, above the showers, they built a large water tank. The Paras regularly stood in the showers for hours on end to escape the blazing heat and, in the usual way, while they were showering they brushed their teeth. Unfortunately, no one had checked the quality of the water coming out of the ground as it was only to be used for washing and not drinking. There was a parasite in the water which attacked the gums, and as a result 25 per cent of the battalion lost their teeth. Yes, I still see people I know from my time in the Paras who have been wearing false teeth for years and, yes, the camp at Hamala is still standing and is used by the Bahraini defence forces for their troops and, no, they don't use the same water tank to service their showers!

Rotting Rupees: Abu Dhabi 1966

The events which led to Sheikh Zayed bin Sultan becoming the ruler of Abu Dhabi have been described as a 'palace revolution', but that doesn't mean the British weren't in the palace at the time.

Look at the south-east corner of the Arabian Gulf on any map and you will see a place called the United Arab Emirates. (You may also be able to smell the oil.) Ninety per cent of this real estate is Abu Dhabi; the six other members of the alliance are tiny statelets dotted around the Musandam peninsula to the north. The city of Abu Dhabi, essentially a small island connected to the mainland by a bridge, is the capital of the UAE. How all this came about does not appear in the official history books; it is a remarkable story of money-eating rats.

There were three different currencies in use in The Gulf in those not-so-far-off times. The currency of choice was the ubiquitous gold sovereign. Any trade using the sovereign was backed by the gold content of the coin. The second preference was the Maria-Theresa dollar, known throughout the region as the MTD. This coin was first minted during the Austro-Hungarian Empire and the attractiveness to the tribal people was its high silver content. The coins were often melted down and used to make the beautiful hair ornaments worn by the female members of the tribe. Both the sovereign and the MTD can still be bought in the souks of the modern Gulf and are remembered nostalgically by older people.

The third currency in circulation was the Indian rupee. The Arabs looked on it with distain and were very reluctant to use it. The problem they had was that the rupee was a cheap option for the British administration and they used it to settle their treaty obligations to the local rulers. This policy directly resulted in the Abu Dhabi coup of 1966.

Sheikh Shakhbout al-Nahayan, who had ruled since 1928, was an unsophisticated man of the desert. Banks and fiscal management were not part of his world and, when the British handed over sackloads of Indian rupees in small-denomination notes, he would, literally, stuff them under his bed. And there they stayed; he was so tight-fisted that he seldom felt a need to give them out to anybody else. After a while, because of the high humidity, the notes started to rot; this attracted rats which came to feed on the mouldering notes. The subsequent indignant protests about the region's shrinking reserves got to the ears of the British political residents, who decided that something had to be done. A *coup d'état* was engineered using the British-officered Trucial Oman Scouts, and Sheikh Shakhbout was deposed to be supplanted by his younger brother, Sheikh Zayed al-Nayahan.

Both authors have met Sheikh Zayed at different times and in different places. We can only agree with Wilfred Thesiger, who, on meeting him in 1948, described him thus: He was a powerfully built man of about 30 with a brown beard. He had a strong intelligent face, with steady observant eyes, and his manner was quiet and masterful.'[77]

After taking power, Zayed ruled the country in an enlightened and benign manner. When the British left the region in 1968 he promoted the replacement of the loose Trucial States alliance with the United Arab Emirates and became its founding president in 1972. Of all the rich Gulf states, Abu Dhabi soon became the richest.

The Sheikh's only failing (he died in November 2004) was to have a much more liberal attitude to banks than his brother, far too liberal, in fact. In the early 1970s he was approached by a smooth-talking Pakistani called Agha Hasan Abedi with a proposal to set up a major new international bank which would be based in Abu Dhabi. Sheikh Zayed gave him his backing. The resulting Bank of Credit and Commerce International (BCCI) was crooked to the core. Only after it had crashed owing billions of dollars to creditors across four continents was it revealed that it had been heavily involved in laundering money for drug traffickers and providing a banking service to various terrorist groups. The affair was embarrassing for Abu Dhabi, but it is not clear whether the Sheik resorted to keeping any of his twenty-billion-dollar fortune under his bed.

Ken Connor: Making House Calls

I remember once, as a young soldier with the Paras in Bahrain, I went to the oasis at Buraimi on a patrol. We were there to show the flag. As part of the patrol we called in at the political residence in Dubai where the two diplomats were sharing a tiny bungalow with the help of an Indian cook and a cleaner. There were thirty of us on the patrol and we were invited to have a bath, an unheard-of luxury in those times. When we had finished the tide-mark around the bath probably had to be blasted away with a flame-thrower, but to spend a couple of hours in the company of people who were so on top of their job was a considerable privilege.

Enough Sa'id: Oman 1970

To the east of the United Arab Emirates, on the Indian Ocean, is Oman. The British Army fought a fierce war here for over seven years with hardly a word about it being printed in the London press. In the south, Oman has a province called Dhofar, which has a border with what was then North Yemen. It was in that south-eastern toe of the Arabian peninsula that the Marxist philosophy had gained a foothold.

That might not have mattered too much if, in the early 1960s, the mountain *jebali* tribesmen of Dhofar hadn't risen against the Sultan of Oman's rule. It was expedient for the Yemenis to help the *jebali* and equally expedient for the *jebali* to accept that help if their campaign was to become more than guerrilla skirmishing. For a while, it looked as though the Marxist philosophy was going to creep around into The Gulf, taking Dhofar as it went. That couldn't be allowed to happen and the British Government, already friendly with Oman, made a commitment to provide military support to Sultan Sa'id.

The uprising was in the hands of an outfit called the Marxist Popular Front for the Liberation of the Occupied Arab Gulf. Later, once it realised that it was losing, it helpfully changed its name to the less ambitious Popular Front for the Liberation of Oman. But after a failed attempt in 1966 to assassinate the sultan, the group started getting the support of the USSR, China, the People's Democratic Republic of Yemen and, yes, Iraq. (Yemen, the former colony of Aden, had only been granted independence by the UK as recently as 1967. So there was no sign of gratitude there.) By the end of the 1960s, the MPFLOAG – or whatever they were calling themselves – controlled 90 per cent of the territory.

Lined up against the insurgent forces was the Sultan's Armed Forces (SAF) and the Trucial Oman Scouts. Well, most of them were lined up against the insurgents. In need of good training, some of the Dhofari rebels would join the Scouts in order to benefit from British Army training in the Northern provinces. During their annual summer leave they would head south for a few weeks' fighting against the sultan's forces. When Operation *Storm* started in 1970, the SAS Regiment was deployed to Dhofar. The approach it adopted was classical and effective. Needing a 'force multiplier' it won the hearts and minds of the locals by doing something the Sultan never did; the soldiers provided much-needed medical and veterinary help to the tribesmen and their families. Then they recruited and trained them to fight the *jebali*.[78]

But, for the British, there was a serious problem from the start; the rebels had a point about the corrupt and anarchic rule of Sultan Sa'id bin Taimur. His isolationist policy needed to be replaced by one that improved the country's infrastructure, developed natural resources and extended basic healthcare and education to his people. The only way that could be achieved was through regime change; a *coup d'état* was called for.

One of the advantages of usurping a despotic head of state is that the plotters' limited resources can be concentrated on taking that ruler out of play. On the other hand it is crucial that an acceptable replacement be ready to move in immediately. You can't remove the old guard and substitute vague promises about elections. Overseeing the conspiracy were the British Consul-General David Crawford, the British political resident Geoffrey Arthur and the Defence Secretary of Oman, Colonel Hugh Oldham. Local support came in the form of Sheikh Braik bin Hamud, the son of the Wali (Governor) of Dhofar. They agreed that Sa'id's son Qabus bin Sa'id was perfect for the soon-to-be-vacant job and they had little doubt he would be acceptable to the tribal elders and the people. But there was a problem. Qabus was a graduate of the Royal Military Academy at Sandhurst and since his return his father had ordered him to stay in his room. Effectively he was under house arrest and all visitors were being scrutinised.

Timothy Landon, the resourceful chief intelligence officer of the SAF first arrived in Oman in 1965 as a 'contract officer' on loan from the British Army. After serving with the SAF in Dhofar he returned to Britain to undertake a two-year intelligence course before rejoining the SAF in a more senior post. Knowing that they needed someone close to Qabus to make the coup happen, Tim Landon did some homework. He checked the files at Sandhurst and came up with the name of the officer cadet who had shared a room with Qabus while they were on the commissioning course. Landon then tracked the room-mate down and discovered he had recently joined 22 SAS as a lowly troop officer. How did you get on with Qabus? Landon asked him. Just fine, was the reply. Landon had found his way through to the young sheikh. The proposition was put to him: Would he take over as head of state if the British removed his father? The answer was 'yes'. All that remained was for the operation itself to be planned and executed.[79]

The date was set for 23 July 1970. The coup team was a mixture of experienced hands from the Trucial Oman Scouts, the Sultan's Armed Forces, the British Army training section and the SAS. For security reasons the group had been kept small – far too small to carry out an assault on the sultan's palace *and* provide perimeter protection while they did it. An exercise was called for the SAF; it was to deploy in a defensive formation around the Salalah compound. Then, bold as brass, Sheikh Braik and six soldiers, led by Tim Landon, strode past the security cordon, walked up to the main gate and demanded to be let in. The guard had already been bribed and he had sent his colleagues off for a break while he looked after things. As the coup team made its way through the complex they noticed considerable stashes of new small arms, machine guns and a couple of Russian BRDM-1 armoured reconnaissance vehicles. The sultan was waiting for them.

The instant the group entered the courtyard, Sa'id and his personal guard opened fire. The gate sentry fell dead and Sheikh Braik was wounded. It has been reported that the team called for air cover and tear gas was dropped into the palace compound, but that never happened.

It all came to an undignified end when the sultan managed to shoot himself in the leg.

Sa'id was flown out of the country in a noisy old Beverley military transport and taken to England for medical treatment. Just to show there were no hard feelings, the British Government put him up in the Dorchester and he stayed there until his death two years later. Immediately after the coup Sheikh Braik took over from his father and became the Wali of Dhofar. The young SAS officer, under the watchful eye of an experienced warrant officer, became commander of the new sultan's personal bodyguard.

Qabus set to modernising the government and the economy. But there was still the matter of the Dhofar rebellion to clear up. The SAS strategy of turning the local tribesmen worked and, with support from Jordanian and Iranian troops and financial backing from Saudi Arabia and the UAE, the tide was turned against the enemy. By the beginning of 1975, the *jebali* were pinned down in an area of ten square kilometres (3.86 square miles). By the end of the year it was all over.

Here is a footnote to the story. At the point at which the borders of Saudi Arabia, Abu Dhabi and Oman meet there is an oasis called Buraimi. In desert regions water is a strategic asset and, in the 1960s, the Saudis occupied the area, claiming it as their own. They withdrew after a few days when the British flexed some muscle and threatened them with air-strikes from the jet fighters based in Bahrain. This part of The Gulf was a sensitive area then and it is still a sensitive area. In 2004 there were largely unreported clashes between Omani and Saudi forces on the edges of the Empty Quarter and there have been military stand-offs between several countries within the United Arab Emirates. These incidents have been driven by the dwindling deposits of oil under the desert.

The CIA Train: Iraq 1958, 1959, 1963 and 1968

At the time of writing, the United States was systematically trashing large swathes of central Iraq. This was a process that had started more than forty years earlier.

The Middle East was awash with politicking and intrigue. In the aftermath of the 1952 coup that deposed King Farouk (see Chapter 1) Egypt made a play for the hand of Syria in some kind of union. This and the supposed attentions of the USSR caused alarm in Washington DC, resulting in plots being hatched for the assassination of President

Nasser. Early in 1957 Director of Central Intelligence Allan Dulles flew to New York, where a General Assembly of the UN was taking place. With him was senior CIA officer Kermit Roosevelt. If Roosevelt wasn't the architect of the Iran coup of 1953 (see Chapter 3), he was certainly the main contractor. The two were in town to make a joint approach to King Saud of Saudi Arabia and Crown Prince Abdul Illah of Iraq. If the CIA were to fund the venture, would the two of them please arrange for the early retirement of Nasser? The Crown Prince would only do it if the British were involved, but King Saud wasn't talking to the British at the time; so that plan came to nothing. As it happened, the Secret Intelligence Service (MI6) had already deployed teams to assassinate the Egyptian leader.[80]

So concerned were the Americans about the growing influence of Nasser in the region that they tried to orchestrate the activities of a ragbag of intelligence services to get rid of him. The stage for these shenanigans was the Lebanon where, a few months after the fruitless encounter at the UN, Kermit Roosevelt was staying at the home of Ghosn Zogby, the CIA Beirut station chief. Intelligence operatives from Britain, Jordan, Iraq, Israel, Turkey and the Lebanon itself traipsed to and fro as schemes were hatched and rehatched. Egypt and Syria went ahead anyway and formed the short-lived United Arab Republic. But the real problem came from an unexpected quarter.

In July 1958 23-year-old King Faisal II of Iraq and his uncle Crown Prince Abdul Illah were assassinated in a particularly bloody *coup d'état*. The body of the Crown Prince was strung up outside the defence ministry. The British embassy was ransacked and burned as people celebrated in the streets of Baghdad. Only six years after the similar overthrow of King Farouk in Egypt, this was seen as an alarming boost for Arab nationalism and fears grew that further unrest could spread throughout the region, threatening the West's strategic oil reserves.

Taking over as Iraq's new prime minister, defence minister and military chief of staff was Major-General Abdul Karim el Qasim. By all accounts Qasim was a nasty piece of work, but no one suspected that it was anything other than business-as-usual. All that changed in 1959 when he pulled out of a Cold-War-style anti-Soviet alliance called 'the Baghdad Pact' and threw his lot in with the Russians. Arms deals were struck and local communists put in government posts. Qasim threatened to invade Kuwait and nationalised the production side of the Iraq Petroleum Company. DCI Allan Dulles declared that Iraq was 'the most dangerous spot in the world'. Just hold that thought for a while...

Egypt had gone, Syria had gone but the Americans decided that Iraq couldn't be allowed to go the same way. The CIA decided that a short-form coup was needed – murder Qasim. In a remarkable volte face, the Agency had not only shifted its attentions away from Nasser but had managed to solicit the support of the Egyptian intelligence service, probably because it needed human assets who could operate under cover in Iraq.

A six-man assassination squad was quickly assembled, trained and briefed. The team was drawn from members of the anti-Soviet (and, therefore, anti-Qasim) Ba'ath Party and set up in an apartment in Baghdad. The rent for the apartment was paid directly from the personal account of Captain Abdul Maquid Farid, assistant military attaché at the Egyptian embassy. Looking out of the window across busy al-Rashid Street the would-be assassins could watch Qasim's movements in and out of the defence ministry building, where he had an office.[81]

The plan was to ambush Qasim as he got into his car and the date was set for 7 October 1959. Accounts of what happened are inconsistent but all agree that the operation was under-rehearsed and badly executed. The team got into position but the target was into his car too quickly. Instead of getting in close, the CIA-backed team opened fire from a distance, killing the driver and drawing the attention of the ministry building guards in the process. In the ensuing firefight Qasim, now huddling on the floor of the vehicle, was wounded. One of the assassins was killed and a 22-year old attacker was shot in the leg, probably by one of the assault team. In the ensuing mayhem they made their escape but Qasim was still alive.

The 22-year-old Ba'ath Party member was Saddam Hussein.

With help from the Egyptian agents, Saddam headed north to familiar ground, his home town of Tikrit. After getting his wounded calf patched up he headed across the border into Syria and from there to Beirut. Now he was in the hands of the CIA again.[82] After being put through a short training course (presumably Assassination 101) he was relocated to Egypt.

In spite of being described by a State Department official as 'a thug, a cutthroat', the tyrant-in-waiting was installed in a flash apartment in the Cairo suburb of Dukki. Still in his early twenties, it is hard to believe that he carried much influence in the Ba'ath Party. But there was clearly something about Saddam that appealed to the Americans; it seemed as though he was being groomed. According to a United Press International report he was taken to the US embassy, where he had regular meetings with CIA station chief Jim Eichelberger and was later interviewed by busy Cold-War warrior Miles Copeland.[83]

Abdul Karim el Qasim was eventually shot and killed during a Ba'ath Party *coup d'état* in February 1963. This successful operation did not involve Saddam Hussein and, remarkably, did not involve the CIA, according to the CIA. The Ba'athists, it seems, were now motoring under their own steam. This does not mean to say the agency was unhappy, far from it. According to author Adel Darwish the newly formed Republican Guard swarmed across the country detaining known and suspected communists, whom they would systematically beat, torture and summarily execute. Presiding over this bloodbath was Saddam Hussein, working from a list of suspected Iraqi communists supplied by the CIA.[84] US intelligence sources have revealed that the killings happened at Qasr al-Nehayat, the Castle of the End. No one kept records, but the body-count may have been as many as five thousand. Saddam, now aged twenty-six, was rewarded for this by being appointed director of the clandestine intelligence organisation of the Ba'ath Party Saddam, the feared *Al-Jihaz a-Khas*.

Do we believe the CIA when it insists it had no involvement in the 1963 coup? Former Ba'ath Party secretary-general Ali Saleh Sa'adi recently said: 'We came to power on a CIA train,' which is pretty unambiguous. He also said that the coup was co-ordinated directly from the CIA station in the US embassy in Baghdad.

Whatever the truth of the matter, the takeover didn't stick and, soon, prison doors were slamming behind prominent Ba'athists throughout Iraq. Saddam went on the run but was eventually arrested and jailed as a political prisoner. He escaped in 1966 and returned to plotting a further power-bid by the Ba'athists. That happened in 1968.

By that time Saddam had risen to become deputy leader of the party under his uncle, Ahmed Hassan Bakr. On taking power, Bakr became president and Saddam vice-president. The CIA was still involved in promoting the rise of Saddam Hussein; Deputy Chief of Army Intelligence Colonel Abdel Razaq al-Nayyef later said, 'For the 1968 coup you must look to Washington.' King Hussein of Jordan also attributed the success of the Ba'ath Party in 1968 entirely to the substantial backing it got from the CIA. With that support, Saddam became president of Iraq in 1979 and there he stayed for twenty-three years.

In the 1980s America's bogeyman in the Middle East switched from the Soviet Union (which in reality had done little to destabilise the region) to the Iran of Ayatollah Khomeini. When war broke out between Iran and Iraq, US support for Saddam actually intensified. Both the CIA and the Defense Intelligence Agency (DIA) put in place mechanisms for supplying Iraq with satellite and AWACS (airborne warning and control system) battlefield intelligence. The support even reached a practical level. In February 1988 the US obligingly blinded Iranian radar during a three-day assault on the al-Faw peninsula in the south.

The cosy relationship between America and Iraq ended in August 1990 when Saddam ordered something Qasim never had time to action – the invasion of Kuwait. Within a matter of months, Iraq had become a card-carrying member of the 'Axis of Evil'.

The Coup That Never Was: Iraq 2003

As we write this in February 2005, nearly 1,500 American and British troops as well as soldiers from other 'coalition' countries have been killed in Iraq since the invasion started in 2003. Estimates of the number of civilian deaths vary between 15,000 and 100,000. The original justification for this toll was that Saddam Hussein presented a serious and immediate threat to the region and to the West from his arsenal of 'Weapons of Mass Destruction'. Both George Bush and Tony Blair have now admitted that the intelligence leading to that assessment was mostly faulty. Where it wasn't faulty it was contrived; but we'll come back to that.

Two substitute justifications have been brought off the bench. The first says that Saddam was hand-in-glove with Osama bin Laden and the al-Qaeda franchise. No more convincing evidence for this has been produced than was shown for WMDs. Iraq has always been a secular state and the Ba'athists considered Muslim extremists of all flavours to be a threat to their power-base. Bin Laden probably hated Saddam Hussein as much as he hated George Bush; more, because Saddam purported to be a Muslim when it suited him.

That brings us to the third argument: Saddam was a really bad guy and we needed to get rid of him. In other words it was all about regime change. What has gone largely unremarked is the fact that the bad guy is still alive – incarcerated, but alive nonetheless – and more than fifteen thousand of the people we were supposed to be rescuing are dead.

But if the objective really was regime change, why was all-out war the only means of putting it into effect? The problem with using the guns-blazing approach is that it has a tendency to Falluja the very country you are trying to save for what George Bush calls 'liberty and democracy'. Was there really no other option? What was wrong with the idea of sponsoring a good, old-fashioned *coup d'état*?

The invasion of 2003 (and the death of thousands of Shiite Iraqis) would have been avoided if George Bush Senior had not stopped the 1991 invasion force long before it had reached the Sunni Triangle. The first to appreciate the enormity of this error was Saudi Arabia. By 1994 King Fahd was trying to get President Bill Clinton to agree to a joint covert operation to rid Iraq of Saddam Hussein once and for all. He failed. But the Saudi royal family and the Bushes were close and the fact that Osama bin Laden and all but three of the 11 September terrorists were Saudi nationals was a source of mutual embarrassment. So, in April 2002, when Crown Prince Abdullah put his money where his mouth was and promised participation in a one-billion-dollar joint action with the CIA, he must have been surprised when Bush turned him down flat.[85] It may well have been that 2002 was too late for a Baghdad coup. At that time it was pretty obvious that all-out invasion was the only option being considered in Washington – regardless of what the UN decided in New York. But the coup idea didn't stop there.

Throughout the 1990s there was clearly dissent within Iraq's ruling circles, with senior Ba'ath Party members, military officers and even Hussein family members more than willing to head for Jordan or Syria should the opportunity arise. On the negative side, Saddam was a veteran of the CIA-sponsored coups of 1959, 1963 and 1968; and you don't survive for twenty-three years as a brutal despot without developing a finely tuned sense of paranoia. The quality of the intelligence coming out of Baghdad was questionable and that was part of the problem with the false WMD claims. Expatriate dissident groups may have their hearts in the right place, and their arguments may be valid, but they have a dire tendency to exaggerate and even lie to get their case across. There may also be a direct relationship between the stories they tell and the scale of the funding they receive from sympathetic governments.

The members of a junta left holding the reins after a veto coup may not have been the sort of people you'd invite home to dinner. But that consideration never stopped the Americans or the British in the past; reference Chile's Pinochet and Uganda's Amin. Would it have been worth a try in the case of Iraq? Well, not only the Saudis thought so. During 2002 a large coup team was in training in a country towards the eastern end of The Gulf. Plans had been drawn up for their insertion, the assassination of Saddam Hussein and the taking of Baghdad. Clearly, if there was to be no involvement by Western forces then the plot was based on the premise that the army in particular and the Shiite majority would rise in support.

It might have been worth a try, but it all came to nothing. Someone was working to a timetable for all-out invasion. Opponents of the war will continue to insist that it was all about oil but any attempts to get the oil industry into safe Texan hands may have been stymied by the Baghdad interim government's adamant refusal to privatise its oil assets. Another little-reported development kept off the news programmes by the continuing daily death toll is the fact that the US – with help of Halliburton and the other PMCs (private military companies) – is building fourteen huge *permanent* military bases across Iraq. The clear purpose of these is to give America a long-term presence in the Middle East, in locations strategically suited to operations against Iran and Syria. Some US troops will come home but it looks as though another generation of young men and women for whom military service is the only way to a university education will pay with their lives to fulfil the neo-conservative dream of domination in the region.

Chapter 9
Outsourcing Your Coup

The Augusta 109 helicopters approached the western edge of the Royal Air Force aerodrome at Northolt, flying at zero feet. At this point the pilots should have done two things: first, contact the London Area Traffic Control and climb to a height where they could be picked up by the ATC Radar; second, turn on their transponders which would transmit a coded signal to the radar screens so that they could be identified in the busiest airspace in the world. The pilots did neither.

Instead, they pressed down tighter on the collective. The two aircraft were flying so close together they could almost touch. In the back of each aircraft there were six men wearing the now-familiar classic uniform of a counter-terrorist team, Starship Troopers in black.

The doors of the Augustas were open. The men in the back stared intently at the ground. They were used to working behind enemy lines and it was important that they knew, at all times, where they were, in case they were shot down and had to continue on foot to the target. The Augustas had originally been designed to move business executives around safely. They had been adopted by the SAS for a new, more specialised role after being captured in the Falklands during the campaign to liberate the islands from the Argentinians.

The two 109s pressed on at rooftop height, flying just south of west, outside the air-traffic control zones. Their noisy passage was setting off a cacophony of house- and car-alarms and barking dogs. Approaching Admiralty Arch the two aircraft separated by a couple of hundred feet. The first flared his rotor above the citadel at the west end of the old Admiralty building. The blockhouse, which had been built at the beginning of World War II, was now covered in ivy. The first aircraft almost touched down, balancing one wheel on the roof of the citadel to give it some stability. Before the pilot could even give the order, the six guys had jumped out onto the roof. It then climbed away allowing the second Augusta to approach. Before the second aircraft had disgorged its cargo the first group had entered through a door on the roof and they were closely followed by the second group.

The team moved silently down a steep stairwell passing three storeys of the old Admiralty building until they were in a labyrinth of corridors and small rooms. It was from here that the Lords of the Admiralty had controlled the major sea battles of World War II. The decline of British sea power had made the size and complexity of the building redundant.

The troopers wore black Nomex overalls, their equipment held by leather straps, because nylon burns. Each had a Heckler & Koch MP-5K strapped across his chest with a Glock pistol on his hip and flexi-cuffs threaded through his waistband. They ran silently on their rubber-soled combat boots. They automatically moved on the balls of their feet to minimise the sounds. As they passed the part of the underground complex which was open to the public, the back four of the group peeled away and headed towards the Thames. They were going to open the emergency exits, which were there to enable their political masters to escape in the event of a terrorist attack on Whitehall.

The other eight headed silently towards Downing Street and the Cabinet Office – the epicentre of British political power. They ran with their passive night goggles down so they could see in the dimly lit corridors. They had practised this operation in the SAS training area in Pontrilas in Herefordshire for weeks on end, by day and night, in sunshine and rain until they could literally do it blindfolded. They had also visited the area before as part of the ongoing SAS responsibility to assist Her Majesty's Government in the security and defence plans for Downing Street and Whitehall. Now they were there as part of a plot to bring about the downfall of the very system they had sworn to defend.

As the team reached the door beneath 10 Downing Street it slowed down. The soldier leaning against the wall stepped on his half-smoked cigarette but didn't raise his M-16 assault rifle.

'Where have you lot been? The party's nearly fucking over.'

Guinea Foul

Equatorial Guinea is a small country on the west coast of Africa. It should not be confused with Ecuador, Guinea, Guinea-Bissau, Guyana or Papua New Guinea.

Three-quarters of Equatorial Guinea's population of 500,000 suffers from malnutrition; the other 25 per cent mostly consists of the extended family and clan of the country's president and they eat very well indeed. Since gaining independence from Spain in 1968 Equatorial Guinea has experienced eight attempted *coups d'état*; the first, in 1972, was instigated by a thriller-writer researching a new book,[86] the second, in 1979, succeeded, and the seventh in March 2004 failed to get over the start line – with disastrous consequences for its British and South African leaders. The first coup failed because the ammunition failed to turn up, the seventh because the mercenaries failed to turn up. The coups in between were probably faked by Equatorial Guinea's president as an excuse to execute or expel political opponents. Then there was the drugs trafficking. And the money-laundering. You could not make this up.

It may come as no surprise that this otherwise-inconsequential country has oil and almost inevitably an unstable political situation. (See also Chapter 2, Venezuela 2002.) It has had only two presidents but between them they have managed to wreak untold misery on a poverty-stricken people. Neither gained power through legitimate elections and both of them were quite mad. The latter condition might be genetic because they are uncle and nephew... But never mind, Equatorial Guinea has *oil and gas*!

When Spain gave up its colony, it didn't know about the crude. The man it put in power was Francisco Macías Nguema, who was born Mez-m Ngueme, but Francisco – or Mez-m – didn't like any of those names and changed them all to Masie Nguema Biyogo Ñegue Ndong because that was more African. Fair enough, you might think, it is a free country, but he ordered the rest of the population to do the same, thus proving that it wasn't a free country after all. No one was going to argue. On becoming president, Masie detained former prime minister Bonifacio Ondó Edu and tried to starve him to death. Edu was not very co-operative and Masie got bored, so he had him shot instead. Malabo prison conditions must have been pretty dreadful because most of Edu's colleagues 'committed suicide' in their cells. By now the international media was describing Equatorial Guinea as 'Auschwitz Africa' and over a third of its people headed for the borders; Cameroon and Gabon were preferable to living under this monster. Even Masie's wife objected to sharing a bed with someone who called himself 'The Unique Miracle' and claimed magical powers; but his magic wasn't powerful enough to stop her leaving too. No one on the international scene took any notice.

While a substantial proportion of the population was departing for a quiet life, a group of mercenaries was trying quite hard to get *into* the country. The attempted coup of 1972 was an odd affair. Equatorial Guinea comprises a mainland province (called Rio Muni) with a few offshore islands plus a much bigger island, Isla de Bioko, some two hundred kilometres (124 miles) north in the Bight of Biafra. The country's capital, Malabo, is on the northern tip of Bioko. The island used to be called Fernando Po and it played a key part in the Biafran Civil War. So did Frederick Forsyth, a British Royal Air Force officer-turned-journalist. After reporting on weddings and funerals for the *Eastern Daily Press*, Forsyth became a Europe correspondent for Reuters and then joined the BBC. In 1967, after only a couple of years with the Corporation, he found himself in Nigeria reporting the nasty that had resulted from the Eastern Region's declaration of independence. With less partiality than the BBC would have preferred, Forsyth threw his lot in with the Biafrans and their leader, Lieutenant-Colonel (later General) Odumegwu Ojukwu. By 1968 he was filing reports criticising the British Government for supporting the Nigerian regime and his employers 'reassigned' him. He quit and wrote a book about the affair.[87] Forsyth then switched to writing well-researched thrillers, the first being about an OAS assassination attempt on France's president Charles de Gaulle;[88] he claimed the book was based on a story he had heard, perhaps from one of the ex-Foreign Legion, ex-OAS mercenaries then working for Ojukwu. (See Chapter 3, Algeria 1961.)

The island of São Tomé was used as a staging post for arms shipments going into Biafra during the civil war; non-lethal aid was routed through Bioko Island. At some point while on Bioko, Forsyth seems to have decided that Masie's government in newly independent Equatorial Guinea was crying out for a *coup d'état*. Forsyth was about to become RAF officer-turned-journalist-turned-coup sponsor. He raised $200,000 of funding and recruited various mercenaries he had met in Biafra as well as Anthony Divall, an interesting Hamburg-based British arms dealer and former Secret Intelligence Service (MI6) officer.[89] The assault team had already boarded an old fishing boat for the trip from Spain down to São Tomé when, realising that a local dealer was not going to deliver the required ammunition, they wisely called the whole thing off. The resulting book[90] and film were called *The Dogs of War*.

President Masie oversaw a murderous regime which was strictly a family affair; his relatives occupied all the key positions of power in the administration, the military and key businesses. Anyone who even hinted that they might be unhappy with that situation was butchered.

Masie's own downfall came in 1979 when he declared himself 'President for Life', the certain Kiss of Death for any ruler (see Idi Amin, Chapter 6, Uganda 1971). On 3 August Masie was usurped by his nephew, Teodoro Obiang Nguema Mbasogo. As if to prove that blood is not thicker than water, Mbasogo had his uncle executed. This in itself turned out to be something of a challenge because Masie had done a great job convincing folk that he really did have magical powers and no one was prepared to pull the trigger. (Why didn't they ask his wife?) In the event, Mbasogo persuaded some Moroccan soldiers in his body-guard detail to do the job. Now boasting the nickname *el Jefe*, 'the Chief', Equatorial Guinea's new president continued political business-as-usual, a fine blend of nepotism, corruption and brutality. According to the US Department of State, he: 'names and dismisses cabinet members and judges, ratifies treaties, leads the armed forces, and… appoints the [provincial] governors.'[91]

Apart from Britain being the first to formally recognise the new government, no one on the international scene took any notice.

Then in 1996 Mobil discovered massive new offshore oil reserves and suddenly the country became very interesting indeed. Crude mineral oil was definitely more exciting than the country's previous crop of palm oil. Production increased twenty-fold in eight years; and so, it seems, did the frequency of coups.

The first one came a year later when leader of the *Partido del Progreso*, Severo Moto Nsa, was caught by the Angolan security services with his hand in the coup till. When he failed to explain his connection to a Russian trawler loaded to its gunnels with arms and ammunition, Moto and his twelve cohorts were expelled to Europe, no doubt relieved that they hadn't been sent back up the coast to Equatorial Guinea. *El Jefe's* corrupt judicial system put them on trial *in absentia* and gave Moto a US-style jail sentence of 101 years for high treason and plotting to assassinate the president. The opposition leader had been through a similar trial – physically in the dock – a year earlier. He was expelled when Spain's King Juan Carlos and Pope John Paul appealed for clemency on his behalf. Today, *el Jefe* probably wishes he'd had Moto 'uncled' after all. In the meantime the Chief celebrated the country's newly found oil wealth by keeping for himself 96 million dollars of the 130-million-dollar revenues from 1998.

Although the president assumed the pretence of introducing multi-party democracy, it was all pretty much a sham. Parties had to be registered but, even if they were, *el Jefe* had become adept at putting them out of business. In March 2002 he had leaders of the *Unión Popular* (registered) and the *Fuerza Democrática Republicana* (Democratic Republican Force – unregistered) arrested in Malabo on their return from a trip to the mainland region of Mongomo. After a doubtless uncomfortable two weeks in Black Beach prison confessions were extracted and a further wave of arrests followed. Of the 150 rounded up, most were relatives of the accused plotters but also included were a handful of retired army officers, some pregnant women and even a few children. Assassination hit-lists were found during house searches. When sixty-eight of the hapless group appeared in court in June that year they showed signs of serious maltreatment: 'the men clearly appeared to have been tortured: they were bruised, some had broken arms or wrists, and several walked with difficulty'.[92] This was a consequence of them having their wrists and ankles shackled and being hung from poles. 'Torture in *incommunicado* detention is a routine practice in Equatorial Guinea,' reported Amnesty International.[93] They were jailed for between twenty and thirty years. The prosecution called for the execution of eighteen of the defendants. Yet, apart from confessions of dubious value, there was no credible evidence that the affair was anything other than a concocted device for getting rid of an opposition group; it was a classic *faux* coup and a particularly dirty one at that.

If the object of this exercise was to send a message to the opposition, it worked; no one stood against *el Jefe* in the December 2002 presidential election and, unsurprisingly, supporters claimed he had won 97.1 per cent of the vote. The US State Department said the election was 'marred by extensive fraud and intimidation,'[94] so the result would probably have been the same regardless of what the opposition had done. It had always been that way; Joaquín Alogo, the president's son-in-law, made the following note about the 1993 legislative elections.

> Santos Pascual Bikomo wins over Obiang with 57.60 per cent of the valid votes given. The President calls on me and threatens to kill me. Thus, I give up my logistic assistance to Mr Bikomo's political party. President Obiang gives orders to all the Election Committees in the big towns to falsify the polls, with a death penalty for non-compliance.[95]

Alogo later died in Colombia in what are called 'mysterious circumstances'. His wife, the president's daughter, published his diaries.

But even more trouble was brewing. November 3 in 2003 was a bad day for Rodrigo Angue Nguema, the Malabo stringer for Agence France Presse. He was arrested after the agency ran a report claiming there had been yet another coup attempt a week earlier. Government officials shrugged it all off saying that there had been a training exercise at various strategic sites in the capital, including the airport and, yes, the radio station. Further rumours of plotting swept through the capital during December; was a coup for Christmas on the cards? But family festivities were cancelled when General Agustin Ndong Ona, the president's half-brother, was arrested along with a group of senior officers and politicians previously thought to have been loyal to the president. Ndong Ona was a fellow Esangui clan-member, a senior army commander and a former defence and security adviser. As such, he should have had enough special knowledge of el Jefe's security arrangements to make the coup-attempt stick; could this have been another *faux* coup?

From Mutiny to Scrutiny

You could understand why the Chief and his family would not want to live in this shit-hole, even if it was of their own making. So, as soon as the oil revenues flowed into the government's coffers, he transferred them out again, mostly to privately held accounts at Riggs Bank in Washington DC. This financial institution is headed by Joe Allbritton, a long-time family friend of the Bushes. It also employs President George W. Bush's uncle Jonathan as a senior executive. Riggs likes to think of itself as 'venerable' and uses the slogan 'the most important bank in the most important city in the world'. A group of researchers from the US Senate Sub-committee on Investigations came to a less flattering conclusion.

> Riggs Bank managed more than 60 accounts and certificates of deposit for Equatorial Guinea, its officials, and their family members, with little or no attention to the bank's anti-money laundering obligations, turned a blind eye to evidence suggesting the bank was handling the proceeds of foreign corruption, and allowed numerous suspicious transactions to take place without notifying law enforcement.[96]

Riggs Bank had helped *el Jefe* to set up the facilities he needed to loot his country's oil revenues. The private accounts were mostly in the names of his sons, his brother, his wife, his wife's brother and various government ministers. All oil companies doing business in Equatorial Guinea made substantial payments into accounts used to pay for the university education in the United States of the children of the president, his relatives and government officials – some 160 of them.

Riggs Bank also loaned *el Jefe* 2.6 million dollars to buy a house in Potomac, Maryland and 1.15 million dollars to his wife, Constancia Nsue, so she could also buy a house in Potomac. Teodoro Nguema Obiang is the president's eldest son; he goes by the nickname *el Patrón*, 'the Boss'. As Equatorial Guinea's Minister for Forestry and sole owner of Grupo Sofana, a company with monopoly rights to timber exploitation, you would think he would spend his time in West Africa overseeing the country's second-biggest export earner (after oil); but no, he wanted a penthouse apartment in Los Angeles and Riggs Bank loaned him 7.5 million dollars to buy it.[97] In California the Boss was able to keep his hand on the tiller of his music company, TNO Entertainment, where, it is said, his employees wished he did spend more time in West Africa.

But there seemed to be other sources of revenue apart from the oil companies and contractors. In 1999 Riggs Bank helped President Obiang to establish an offshore company called Otong SA in the Bahamas. Although the president used his mother's maiden name, he gave the account-holder's address as: 'The Presidential Palace, Malabo, Equatorial Guinea,' which was a bit of a give-away. Then the Riggs opened a 'money-market account' for Otong SA at the bank. A few months later, serious cash deposits began. These were the deposits made over a period of just two years:

20 April 2000	$1.0 million cash
8 March 2001	$1.0 million cash
20 March 2001	$1.5 million cash
5 September 2001	$2.0 million cash
17 September 2001	$3.0 million cash
12 April 2002	$3.0 million cash
Total	$11.5 million

By December 2002 there were two Otong SA accounts, one containing 11.7 million dollars and other 4.4 million dollars. Millions in non-US currency were also paid into accounts in the name of *el Jefe's* wife, Constancia Nsue, or held jointly by her and her brother, the ambassador. Riggs Bank officials did not even raise an eyebrow, never mind the paperwork required by US banking regulations.

An even more serious allegation against President Obiang, if there could be one, is that he is heavily involved in international drug trafficking. It is claimed that the heroin is bought in bulk from Nigeria and Pakistan and then distributed in diplomatic baggage. Senior diplomats have been detained with large quantities of narcotics in their possession in Spain (three times), Brazil, Thailand and France; once expelled they usually end up with ministerial jobs back in Malabo.[98] Accepting that legitimate money from the oil companies was paid into the oil account at Riggs Bank by wire transfer, the drugs business might explain those large payments in cash that attracted the attention of the Senate investigators. They talked to a bank employee who told them:

> on at least two occasions in which he [the employee] was present, the cash was brought into the bank in suitcases transported by Mr Kareri [the Riggs account manager] who said he had obtained the cash from senior [Equatorial Guinea] (EG) officials such as the EG President or Ambassador. The employee indicated that most of the cash was in unopened, plastic-wrapped bundles which did not have to be counted, while the remaining bills were counted using high-speed machines. Since $1 million in hundred dollar bills weighs nearly 20 pounds, the currency brought into the bank would likely have weighed at least that much on each occasion. On the last two occasions involving $3 million, the bank would've had to accept nearly 60 pounds in currency. The bank employee indicated that the large cash deposits he witnessed were not treated as unusual or requiring additional scrutiny.[99]

Malabo's senior press officer, Alfonso Nsue Mokuy, responded on state television, saying, 'The investigation that led the American Senate to Riggs Bank has nothing to do with our government, nor with our dignitaries...' Viewers may have been confused about what dignity had to do with any of this. 'Consequently,' Mokuy continued, 'there is no problem between the State of Equatorial Guinea, the Senate and the Congress of the United States of America.' That's all right then, no mention of narco-trafficking and the people being robbed blind.

Whatever was said publicly, Obiang may have wondered what possessed him to conduct his corrupt financial affairs in a country with such strict banking controls and an inquisitive administration. Was it stupidity, arrogance or a combination of the two? Switzerland is not what it used to be, but the intimate details of suspect cash transactions would not have ended up on the Internet. The best way to choose a country that will not ask too many questions of you and your bankers is to visit the web-site of the Organisation for Economic Cooperation and Development's Financial Action Task Force on Money Laundering.[100] Then look for the list of 'Non-Cooperative Countries and Territories'. In 2000 the list included: the Bahamas, Cayman Islands, Cook Islands, Dominica, Israel, Lebanon, Liechtenstein, Marshall Islands, Nauru, Niue, Panama, Philippines, Russia, St Kitts and Nevis, and St Vincent and the Grenadines. As a result, no doubt, of the 'War on Terror', the July 2004 list was down to: the Cook Islands, Indonesia, Myanmar, Nauru, Nigeria and the Philippines. In other words, your options for laundering your dirty money are becoming very limited. A final cautionary note; do not put all your eggs in one basket.

Hiatus in Harare

One of the consequences of the incumbent regime being in the hands of a single close family, extended family or tribe is that it is very difficult to dislodge by a straightforward *coup d'état*. A veto coup with foreign sponsorship and foreign troops or mercenaries is probably the only way to go.

That is what appeared to be happening on Sunday, 7 March 2004 when Captain Neil Steyl pulled back the throttles of a private Boeing 727 and touched down at Harare International Airport in Zimbabwe. According to the flight plan the ageing aircraft, N4610, was *en route* to the Democratic Republic of Congo. The ground movement controller ordered Steyl to proceed to the restricted military side of the airfield. The South African was unconcerned as he eased the throttles open again and followed the taxiway. The seventy mercenaries in the passenger cabin realised that something was seriously wrong when they saw military trucks pull up and Zimbabwean soldiers jump out to surround the aircraft. Their rifles were pointing in, not pointing out. Everyone was arrested and bundled off the plane. On board, the authorities found a variety on non-lethal military equipment and two bundles of cash; 30,000 dollars and 100,000 dollars. Three other people were arrested at the airport, two South Africans and a former British soldier called Simon Mann; they had arrived in-country on a commercial flight twenty-four hours earlier.

The following day, Monday, 8 March, a group of fifteen foreigners was arrested in Malabo, in Equatorial Guinea. It was a cosmopolitan bunch of men from South African, Angola, Armenia and Germany. Their leader was a South African called Nick du Toit. Mann and 48-year-old du Toit have lengthy rap sheets when it comes to the mercenary business.

To his credit it has to be said that Simon Mann could have had an easy, risk-free life; but that might be the last thing we say to his credit. As a member of the Watney-Mann brewing dynasty it was perhaps inevitable that he would be sent to Eton, the boarding school of choice for Britain's richest families. Mann then attended Sandhurst before being commissioned as an officer in the Brigade of Guards. Bored with overseeing the changing of the guard at Buckingham Palace, he applied to join the élite 22 Special Air Service Regiment. Mann failed to make much of an impression at Stirling Lines in Herefordshire, except with an NCO who summarily 'decked' him. The officer complained to the CO, who determined, after due consideration, that the appropriate action was no action. Mann got the message and retreated to the family home at the New Forest estate of Inchmerry (which, during the latter years of World War II, had been the Special Operations Executive's base for the insertion of Polish agents into Nazi-occupied Europe).

Mann went on to form Executive Outcomes, a South Africa-based company which was very involved in the s of Angola and, in the 1990s, Sierra Leone. It was during that time that he met Nick du Toit, a former commander of South Africa's 32 Buffalo Battalion, a tough mixed-nationality counter-insurgency force which operated illegally in Namibia and Angola in the 1970s and 1980s. It was later alleged that most, if not all, of the mercenaries on board N4610 were veterans of 32 Battalion.

While Simon Mann was trying to convince the Zimbabwe authorities that he and his team were heading to the Democratic Republic of Congo to provide security for a diamond mine, Nick du Toit was singing from a different song-sheet at a televised press conference in Malabo. 'It wasn't a question of taking the life of the head of state,' he declared, 'but of spiriting him away, taking him to Spain and forcing him into exile and then of immediately installing the government in exile of Severo Moto Nsa.' That, of course, is the same Severo Moto Nsa whom Angola had expelled after the 1997 coup plot. The Information Ministry added that the real sponsors of Moto's coup were the CIA, MI6, 'Spain's intelligence service' (obviously forgetting that it is called 'el Centro Nacional de Inteligencia') and multinational companies and that du Toit had been paid ten million dollars. Once the mercenary had established that no harm was intended, he added a little detail about the planning: 'The group was supposed to start by identifying strategic targets such as the presidency, the military barracks, police posts and the residences of government members. Then it was supposed to have vehicles at Malabo airport to transport other mercenaries who were due to arrive from South Africa.' So far, so good. 'But at the last minute, I got a call to say that the other group of mercenaries had been arrested in South Africa as they were preparing to leave the country.' Du Toit's informant was not quite right in the geography, but the consequences were the same; the coup had stalled as the lights turned to green.

So far, the story seems to have been one of unbridled incompetence but later revelations proved that there was intrigue a-plenty. During his August 2004 trial, Simon Mann admitted that he'd considered the arms purchase to be 'safe'. The week before the aborted flight, he had visited Harare and negotiated a deal with Colonel Tshinga Dube, the director of Zimbabwe Defence Industries. He had handed over 180,000 dollars for a consignment of Kalashnikov AK-47 assault rifles, mortars and thirty thousand rounds of 7.62-mm ammunition. The plotters would have had trouble acquiring the *matériel* in South Africa, where mercenary activities had been illegal since 1999.

Zimbabwe Defence Industries (ZDI) is one of the busiest no-questions-asked arms suppliers on the continent of Africa. It is a state-owned and -operated business with a top management staffed entirely by military officers. The marketing manager is Group Captain G. H. Mutize and its directors include General Vitalis Zvinavashe (former Chief of Staff), Air Marshal Perence Shiri and Lieutenant-General C. G. Chiwenga, the present Chief of Staff. ZDI rarely buys factory-fresh weapons but rather recycles surplus from its standing army or those acquired during cross-border excursions into the Congo. The company's selling proposition was very attractive to arms dealers – mostly South African – servicing the military hardware needs of the many small countries in the region. Immediately the money appeared in ZDI's bank account, the shipment process would get under way. The arms would be transported to the military side of Harare International Airport. At the same time, an anonymous cargo plane would leave South Africa and land at Harare to pick up the shipment; next stop, the customer's designated point of delivery. (Does this sound familiar?)

A South African reporter discovered the first unresolved anomaly in this strange affair. He was shown a copy of a ZDI invoice for the sale of weapons. The total was 6.86 million rand (about one million US dollars); it was dated in February 2004 and addressed to Military Technical Services, a Bahamas-registered concern owned by Nick du Toit.[101] Clearly, du Toit was doing business as an arms dealer and ZDI was his major supplier. Could it have been that his coup partner had advised Simon Mann to buy the weapons from the Harare concern? If that was the case, why did the Zimbabwean military decide to stop the shipment going through and cause a big client to be imprisoned? The answer to that might relate to Zimbabwe's need to establish a reliable supply of oil; one pariah state cosying up to another. But the real mistake by the plotters was in directly linking the opening moves of the coup with the collection of the small arms. It was completely unnecessary; why didn't du Toit just add what they needed for Equatorial Guinea to his February order? There must have been somewhere on the continent they could safely stash it for a few weeks. The outcome of the plotters' opening gambit was to deliver themselves into the delicate hands of Mugabe and Obiang.

'Obiang Will Eat My Testicles'

Who was promoting this coup? Back in Spain, Severo Moto's 'Government-in-Exile' was issuing denials. Mr Moto had not even left Spain and the CIA, MI6 and Spain's CNI all denied they were in the loop. The exiled politician used the opportunity to have a rant about *el Jefe*: Obiang is an 'authentic cannibal', he said, 'who systematically eats his political rivals'.

A while back he paid millions to those they call marabou [sorcerers] to tell him if his power base was safe. They told him that to keep his grip on power he had to kill people close to him... Obiang wants me to go back to Guinea and [wants to] eat my testicles: that's clear... Obiang is a real demon among an extraordinarily peaceful population. He has just devoured a police commissioner. I say 'devoured' as this commissioner was buried without his testicles and brain. We are in the hands of a cannibal.[102]

A spokesman for Moto's government-in-exile added that his administration wanted to see a peaceful election and an end to the excesses of the Obiang regime. 'We are seeking an end to the assassinations, humiliations, arrests and the torture carried out by Obiang Nguema's regime and we are calling for an electoral campaign without violence.'

Meanwhile, it had been established that the Boeing 727 was owned by Logo Logistics, a company registered in the British Virgin Islands. Unlike du Toit, Charles Burrow, a Logo senior executive, was sticking to the cover story; the alleged mercenaries were security guards *en route* to mining operations in the Congo. It was all a dreadful misunderstanding. Logo Logistics is owned by Simon Mann, who was now down two expensive aircraft, the B-727 to Mugabe and his personal Aerostar executive jet as payment-in-kind to his own lawyers. The first thing Mann's legal team did was to allege that he had been tortured to extract a confession. Du Toit made the same allegation in Equatorial Guinea.

Just as we are trying to decide between 'dreadful misunderstanding', incompetence and a CIA/MI6 plot to oust *el Jefe* and his family, along comes yet another twist. It is not difficult to wade through all the denials and conclude that Severo Moto had *something* to do with the putsch. Both Nick du Toit and Simon Mann claimed that a major backer of the coup was a Lebanon-born businessman called Ely Calil. Calil made so much money from doing oil deals in Nigeria that he can afford to live in a £12 million house in London's Royal Borough of Kensington and Chelsea. The social circle in which he mixes in Britain is as colourful as his suspect chums in Africa. He had been an 'adviser' to serial novelist and convicted liar Jeffrey 'Lord' Archer and was even known to do lunch with ex-MP Peter Mandelson, Prime Minister Tony Blair's best friend. Being sacked from the British Cabinet twice has not prevented Mandelson from becoming the European Union's Trade Commissioner. And Ely Calil is also a friend and supporter of Severo Moto, considering him to be the only option as a replacement for Obiang.

According to a London newspaper, Calil agreed to pay Simon Mann five million dollars to stage the coup (hopefully not in advance).[103] So who was really promoting the putsch? The people who paid du Toit ten million dollars? Or Calil, who paid Mann five million dollars? Or was it all of them? Or maybe it was someone completely different? In any case, all of them started denying everything for the time being.

Within weeks documents were leaked concerning the establishment of a joint-venture company called 'Triple Option 610 cc EG SA'. The agreement to form Triple Option was signed on 15 December 2003 by Nick du Toit and Armengol Ondo Nguema, President Obiang's brother and former Minister of Security. Armengol is also the owner and director of *Sociedad Nacional de Vigilancia* (Sonavi), a company that has a total monopoly on private security services within Equatorial Guinea. The other signatories were presidential adviser António-Javier Nguema Chemo and Agustín Masoko Abegue, *el Jefe's* Chief of Protocol.

We have a copy of the contract and it is for the supply and maintenance of a Russian Antonov transport aircraft. But why did it concern the Chief of Protocol? A further contract between du Toit and Simon Mann's company Logo Logistics for the two-million-dollar 'provision of services' suggested that the real coup leader in terms of planning and execution was the South African, not the Brit.

The mercenaries apprehended at Harare Airport were on trial for a variety of alleged offences; Mann pleaded guilty to conspiring to buy arms without an end-user certificate. From his prison cell he wrote an impassioned plea for help:

> Our situation is not good and it is very urgent. They [the lawyers] get no reply from Smelly and Scratcher [who] asked them to ring back after the Grand Prix race was over! This is not going well...

'Smelly' is thought to be Ely Calil and 'Scratcher' the South African resident, millionaire son of former British Prime Minister Margaret Thatcher. Mann's letter continued:

> I must say once again: what will get us out is major clout. We need heavy influence of the sort that Smelly, Scratcher, David Hart [have] and it needs to be used heavily and now. Once we get into a real trial scenario we are f****d.

(The asterisks are thought to be the work of Simon Mann's wife. David Hart was a political adviser to Margaret Thatcher during the 1980s.)

> This is a situation that calls for everyone to act in concert. It may be that getting us out comes down to a large splodge of wonga [cash]! Of course investors did not think this would happen. Did I? Do they think they can be part of something like this with only upside potential – no hardship or risk of this going wrong? Anyone and everyone in this is in it – good times or bad. Now its bad times and everyone has to F-ing well pull their full weight. Anyway... was expecting project funds inwards to Logo from Scratcher (200).

Project funds from Sir Mark Thatcher? We wonder what project that could be. So did the government of Equatorial Guinea, which tried to get Thatcher extradited from South Africa. It failed because Pretoria wanted first shot at him for breaking their stringent anti-mercenary laws. Mummy tried to fix it for her boy, and people close to Lady Thatcher made calls to the office of President Thabo Mbeki. The response they got was far from encouraging: 'This is a judicial matter, not a political one.' In the end a plea bargain was done; Thatcher *fils* pleaded guilty to being confused about the exact role to be played by the $285,000 helicopter he bought for the plotters in return for a five-year suspended prison sentence and a fine of 500,000 dollars. (The 727 pilot Neil Steyl rather spoiled the fun by telling the world's media that Thatcher knew damn well he was backing a coup in Equatorial Guinea.) South Africa ignored Obiang's extradition request and allowed Sir Mark to leave the country; he was last spotted hiding behind the curtains of his mother's house in London's Belgravia. Simon Mann's lawyers got his sentence negotiated down from seven to four years and most of the mercenary soldiers are back home after having served terms of only a few months. Nick du Toit's prospects look far grimmer, having been given a 34-year sentence that was not suspended.

In the meantime, *el Jefe* turned his attentions to the UK and is attempting to get the supposed coup plotters extradited from there. When it was revealed that MI6 knew about the plot all along but forgot to tell him, he made a formal complaint to Foreign Secretary Jack Straw. Straw might have been sympathetic because it seems that MI6 hadn't told him either; he'd earlier announced that Britain knew nothing about the planned coup.

It was back to business in Equatorial Guinea itself, where President Teodoro Obiang Nguema Mbasogo was tidying up after his *second coup d'état* of 2004. This one took place on the offshore island of Corisco, where five rebels were killed and the ones captured soon confessed to being the reconnaissance party for a group of Angolan and Rwandan mercenaries. They were, it was claimed, all being paid by exiled political opponent Adolfo Obiang Biko.

In September 2002 President Obiang was in Washington DC, where businessmen and investors gave 'a lunch in his honour'. (A noble idea, while his country's children continued to die from intestinal worms and malnutrition.) In his speech, *el Jefe* praised George Bush and promised to fight terrorism and organised crime. Without a hint of irony Bush had just restored diplomatic relations with the primary instigator of terrorism and organised crime in Equatorial Guinea.

Ken Connor: The Mercenary Fink

A guy I knew very well when I was serving in the SAS decided to leave and seek his fortune selling his services to the highest bidder. In short, he decided to become a mercenary. Back then, it could be a very lucrative way of earning a living but there was a down-side. The government frowned on it as an occupation and the police were in the habit of arresting and charging anybody who had aspirations in this direction. As a consequence, recruiting for the various jobs on offer was done very discreetly and purely by word of mouth to a very trusted small circle of acquaintances.

In an age when the more flamboyant leaders had names that always began with 'Mad Dog' or 'Mad Mike' this guy went under a more mundane pseudonym which was something like 'Parky'. Also, unlike a lot of the other, more flaky, characters, he had seen a great deal of active service soldiering and had a very calm demeanour when he was under stress. He was the epitome of what would make the perfect soldier of fortune, well trained, calm and undemanding. He got involved in a couple of covert escapades in Africa and the Indian Ocean where his role was to go in first, carry out the required reconnaissance and then melt away into the background before the 'Dogs of War' appeared on the scene and caused chaos and a great deal of unpleasant publicity. For this he was very well paid and escaped the resultant backlash from the authorities.

But the atmosphere in the UK was already changing. There was much publicity and calls to prosecute the mercenaries who were supposedly exploiting the newly independent democracies. The fact that there was too much work for the guys available seemed to escape the powers that be. Anyway, they were already encouraging men who had left the regiment to work in Dhofar with the local tribesmen and fight the terrorists there. Perhaps this freelancing was impacting on the ability to recruit for that war. Whatever the reason, 'Inspector Knacker' of Special Branch set up a covert helpline for trusted people; those in the know could inform on the recruiters.

Having appealed to Parky's sense of patriotism, they were pleasantly surprised to receive a call from him very shortly afterwards. He detailed the latest scheme that he was involved in, including names, destination etc. This proved to be the start of a lucrative partnership between Parky and the Plod (the police) who had added him to the informer payroll. For the next few months Parky was arrested numerous times, along with diverse and numerous wanna-be Dogs of War at the Post House Hotel at Heathrow Airport. For some reason this was the favoured jumping-off point for various regime-changing gangs. After a night in the cells, Parky would be released without charge due to a lack of evidence. The rest of the group would be held incommunicado until the details of the intended coup had been relayed to the authorities in whichever Third World country was the target. Parky's complicity in the discovery of these plots was never suspected, such was his reputation for integrity, while the stock of the security services rose ever higher in Whitehall.

The situation could have continued indefinitely if Knacker had not made the fundamental mistake of attempting to con Parky. He received a call to provide services to another fledgling democracy. He relayed the details to Plod to check that what he was being asked to do was in the interests of Her Britannic Majesty's Government. Having being warned off that he should not touch the job with a barge pole, he was gobsmacked to discover a few weeks later to be asked to do the same job through another London-based company. This was repeated again several months later. Plod was passing Parky's jobs on to rival companies. The only difference that he could see was that these other companies were run by pillars of society, ex-Household Division, public-school types. Realising that the only weapon he had was to go public, and this was something he could not do without being branded a fink, Parky retired from the field a bitter and broken man.

Private Military Cock-ups (PMCs)

The major challenge for a non-professional coup leader is finding the team of ex-soldiers who will turn your dreams of power and glory into reality. Who do you speak to first? Get it wrong and you are in the black hole becoming acquainted with some nasty instruments of torture. Even if you do speak to someone who doesn't immediately grass on you, will they be able to deliver the goods? We hope that the following thoughts will help you in your quest and open your eyes to some of the more obvious pitfalls.

Your first port of call might be to a Private Military Company (PMC).

These businesses are often represented by a well-known and respected person, usually with an impeccable military résumé. When you consult them, they will draw up a proposal outlining what they can bring to the table. But how can you be certain that they can deliver what they are asking you to pay for?

Don't be misled if the people you are negotiating with are part of and vouched for by the Establishment. Equally, don't be over-impressed by an ancestry going back to the Dark Ages. Most of them are on the look-out for a quick buck and will take you to the cleaners as soon as look at you. Many of the directors and front men are people with a long history in the armed forces. Again, ask yourself, if someone has had a long and supposedly distinguished military career and has retired on full pay, why is he so keen to help you?

The answer will always come back to money and a feeling of things unaccomplished. These guys who were at the pinnacle of the military echelon have often never seen a shot fired in anger or, if they have, were so far away from the action that they could not hear the crack of the rounds. They have conformed to the strictures of working for the government much the same as a civil servant going to work in the nation's capital. They have had to do the bidding of ministers while at the same time envying the freedom of the guys at the sharp end, the ones doing the dirty work. Now, perhaps your regime-change project is their last fling; but you are paying for it and you might pay for it with your neck. They will daydream and fly first-class around the globe at your expense, and plan to put into practice all of the fantasies of their youth. Look very carefully at their proposals and check where the planners will be when the dirty deeds start. If they are not going to be where the action is thickest, then move on to dial the next number on your list.

In particular, cast your eyes carefully over the list of equipment you will be asked to pay for. When one looks back over many regime-change operations, it is surprising how many called for pieces of military hardware which were totally unsuitable for the job. Another surprise is how much those same pieces of hardware cost. The world is awash with weaponry and if you want to buy an AK-47 you can get them anywhere for less than the price of a carton of cigarettes, but when you check your invoices they are being sold to you at thousands of dollars each. Check also whether the hardware will be new or used. A favourite ploy is to gloss over the detail but you will often find that you are paying for new and getting second-hand. Ask yourself, if these PMC chaps can't source cheap guns in today's world, are they really the guys you should be dealing with to get rid of your brother-in-law?

The final thing to be very cautious about is the quality of the personnel the PMC will supply to do the job. These companies do not keep thousands, hundreds or even tens of people on their books eating into the profits. When they have a job then they go into the marketplace and recruit anyone who may be available. The problem for you is that the marketplace is affected by supply and demand. When there is a high demand then prices will be high, when there is low demand then prices are consequently lower. Another problem you will face is the quality of some of these 'operators'. The best guys will always be in work while the less able are always available on Monday. When the labour market is affected by freak conditions like the security situation in Iraq then there will be a huge manpower shortage. As anyone who has worked in Iraq will verify, the security industry there is employing people who can barely walk, talk and carry an M-16 at the same time – and paying top US taxpayers' dollar for the privilege.

Here is another tip to help you. You might be interested to know the ratio between how much the PMC wants to charge you and how much they will pay the troops. They will usually work on a ratio of three to one for a short-term task and two to one for longer-term commitments. Think about that for a moment. You are paying, say, a thousand bucks a day each for a hundred men. To help you with the arithmetic that will be a total of 100,000 dollars *every day*. The PMC will be paying out 30,000 dollars a day; the rest they will keep for the privilege of ripping off a load of guys who are desperate to earn a crust. What you will get is a gang of discontented, untrained and uncommitted individuals who will take every opportunity to turn another dishonest buck.

After all of that, where does it leave you? If you really must go ahead, do it yourself. You can very easily source your own hardware. If you need good blokes, ask around in the right bars in the right cities; cut out the middle-man. If anyone is going to profit from your adventure it should, at least, be the guys taking the greatest risk. They are the men who are going to be at the sharp end, along with you and your confederates and your family. The PMCs have ripped off enough people already and they hardly need your money to fund a lifestyle only they believe they deserve.

Ken Connor: Not Seeing the Wood for the Trees

I was once asked to get involved in an outsourced project of this sort in a West African state that had better remain nameless. The financing for the coup was going to be raised by exploiting the country's natural resources. The first of these was the hardwood forests of the interior. The plan called for the felling of all the trees and the sale of the timber products on the world markets. This would then fund the second phase of the operation. The only problem was that the timber would have to be extracted using armed guards because of the threat from government security forces. The cost of the operation meant there would not be a great deal of profit left to finance phase two – the extraction and sale of the country's diamond assets. These again would be sold internationally and, again because of the cost of protecting the operation, the profits would not be big enough to finance phase three of the project. Phase three? Oh, that was the overthrow of the established government. What I found interesting about the whole scheme was that, at the first sniff, it was exceedingly easy to find people who, at a price, could sell hardwood and diamonds. It was not so easy to find former soldiers with the necessary attributes and skills, and the courage to carry out the dangerous parts. They, however, were the ones who were expected to work for the least money and take the most risk.

Chapter 10
Where Next? Who Next?

Spreading 'Liberty and Democracy'

Coups d'état were relatively rare events until the post-World War II era. Then two things happened that stimulated their rise as a political phenomenon.

The first was the advent of the Cold War and the battle between the United States of America and the Union of Soviet Socialist Republics for the affiliation and affection of the rest of the world. The extent to which the USSR was a genuine threat to America's interests in the Third World is now widely questioned. An examination of our database of coups shows extensive and persistent intervention by the United States in the internal affairs of other countries. By comparison, Moscow's boot-print is rarely seen, Afghanistan being the most notable, and perhaps terminal, exception.

In a precursor to George Bush's 'Axis of Evil', President Ronald Reagan called the Soviet Union the 'Evil Empire'. Although the neo-conservatives have claimed victory for America in the Cold War, all the evidence suggests that the Soviet Bloc's disastrous command economy imploded of its own accord. So what was the USA doing in the Third World? Mostly it was protecting its own interests, not against Russia, but against the client countries deciding that they wanted a better deal, or that they just wanted to do things differently. From that point of view, questions have to be asked about the effectiveness of coup-sponsorship as an instrument of foreign policy.

Stephen Hosmer, a researcher for the Rand Corporation think-tank studied the whole business of US intervention in a lengthy paper published in 2001.[104] In looking specifically at support for *coups d'état*, he outlined the following conditions for a successful outcome.

- US sponsorship would be enough to tip the balance in favour of victory for the plotter.

- The post-coup government would be more pro-US than the incumbent regime.

- If the coup should fail, the threat of future attempts must enable the US to maintain a sustained controlling influence over the enemy government.

- Should the US military actually become involved in fighting enemy forces, this should only be done to divert the enemy from the insurgent forces.

You can, of course, substitute the name of any country for 'US' in the above and the criteria will still apply.

Interestingly, though, Hosmer questions the effectiveness of the policy of sponsoring coups. Referring to America's Cold War policy of intervention whenever a government looked likely to snuggle up to the Soviets (or, more probably, to nationalise the banana industry) he states, 'With a few notable exceptions, such US attempts to remove undesirable leaders by coup or rebellion have failed.'[105] What he omits to do is consider why that might be the case.

We assume that the 'few notable exceptions' include Iran 1953 (Chapter 3) and Chile 1973 (Chapter 6). In both cases these were veto coups which used armed force to overthrow fairly elected governments, quite contrary to declared US foreign policy of spreading 'freedom and democracy' throughout the world. For veto coups to stick, they have to be followed by autocratic regimes, quite often *brutal* autocratic regimes that are resistant to counter-coup and foreign pressure. The Shah of Iran's rule lasted for twenty-six years, Pinochet's for seventeen. Chile did eventually become a European-style liberal democracy, but Iran became a card-carrying member of George W. Bush's 'Axis of Evil', an anti-American Islamic theocracy with less-than-free elections.

Will the United States continue to sponsor coups in the developing world? We believe that it will, especially now that a newly re-elected president continues to declare America the 'leader' and 'policeman' of the free world. The expensive mess of Iraq will encourage a re-evaluation of the *coup d'état* as a device for regime change.

The second global phenomenon of the post-World War era was the withdrawal from empire of the old colonial powers; Britain, France, Spain and Portugal. This had its biggest impact in Africa. Time after time, flags would be saluted, new anthems played, and elections held… only to be followed by the first military coup.

The map of Africa shows borders that look suspiciously as though they were drawn using a ruler in government foreign-affairs departments in London, Lisbon, Rome or Madrid. The administrative convenience of such empire-building almost always went contrary to any borders determined by tribal allegiances, ethnicity and religion. But after the imperial masters were gone it was realised that a new flag and a new anthem does not make a new nation. Nigeria, for example, is two, maybe three, countries pretending to be one. Protestations of patriotism sound empty against the sound of small-arms fire. We have no easy answer to this problem.

Putsch Prognosis

We have discussed at length the motives of plotters throughout the world, but is it possible to summarise all the factors that influence the susceptibility of a country to sustained military involvement in its political life? None of these considerations is any guarantee that your coup will be a resounding, popular success acclaimed by the UN Security Council. It does, however, set the stage for an effective coup; indeed, maybe for a whole string of them.

Some of the precursors may seem a little arbitrary. For example, why do so many coups seem to occur between the Tropic of Cancer and the Tropic of Capricorn? That could be no more than an indication that those were the countries colonised by England, France, Spain and Portugal during the fifteenth to nineteenth centuries. On the other hand, there is nothing arbitrary about the presence of oil reserves and the way in which that strategic resource will lubricate the wheels of military intervention in politics.

Here, then, is a ten-point checklist: the more times 'yes' is circled, the more likely is a country to experience a coup, counter-coup or attempts at both.

Name of Country:

1	Former colony or overseas possession?	Yes	No
2	Lies in tropical latitudes?	Yes	No
3	Religious, ethnic and/or tribal divisions?	Yes	No
4	Substantial natural resources, especially oil?	Yes	No
5	Endemic corruption and nepotism?	Yes	No
6	Strategically located?	Yes	No
7	Long-term despotic regime?	Yes	No

8   Army staff officers trained overseas?   Yes No
9   Finance available for mercenaries?   Yes No
10   Had a *coup d'état* previously?   Yes No

and this is what it might look like when completed for Equatorial Guinea:

Name of Country: **EQUATORIAL GUINEA**		
1	Former colony or overseas possession?	(Yes) No
2	Lies in tropical latitudes?	(Yes) No
3	Religious, ethnic and/or tribal divisions?	(Yes) No
4	Substantial natural resources, especially oil?	(Yes) No
5	Endemic corruption and nepotism?	(Yes) No
6	Strategically located?	Yes (No)
7	Long-term despotic régime?	(Yes) No
8	Army staff officers trained overseas?	(Yes) No
9	Finance available for mercenaries?	(Yes) No
10	Had a coup d'état previously?	(Yes) No

9/10

From this it can be seen that Equatorial Guinea is a coup waiting to happen. In fact, we would venture to suggest that a successful coup *ought* to happen in Equatorial Guinea. To hijack the words of Brigadier David Richards, we are not the sort of people who would wish anyone dead, but in the case of Teodoro Obiang Nguema Mbasogo we are prepared to make an exception. Even before oil became a factor he confused honest and fair governance with murder, brutality and torture. And when the oil did start to flow, he systematically robbed those of his people who hadn't been able to make their escape. But overthrowing *el Jefe* is going to demand better coup leadership than you will get from the likes of Simon Mann and Nick du Toit.

Equatorial Guinea has a corrupt electoral system and so does Zimbabwe; there the democratic path seems closed too. It is possible that there will be genuine change when Robert Mugabe dies, but in the meantime all the pressure in the world from the UN, the Commonwealth of Nations and the International Cricket Council is unlikely to dislodge him. A coup would be dependent on the growth of substantial disloyalty in the Zimbabwean armed forces, but Mugabe has always made a point of keeping the military sweet. His regime presides over a wrecked economy and has inflicted awful deprivation on its people. As the old guard dies off, the chances that some of the younger military leaders will take the initiative and decide that Zimbabwe should join the twenty-first century will increase markedly. As in Equatorial Guinea, its citizens deserve better.

What is remarkable about the Democratic People's Republic of Korea is that it hasn't had some kind of uprising already. There is, however, tremendous potential for South Korea to sponsor a *coup d'état* in the North. A promise of a better life – any kind of life – and some immediate cash inducements to military leaders should do the trick, but the problem lies in getting at the people who can and will lead an armed overthrow of Kim Jong-il. The need to do this without sparking off an all-out war must also to be taken into consideration.

Iran was the third country in George W. Bush's 'Axis of Evil' and for a time it has looked as though that would be a candidate for invasion straight after Iraq. During her 'getting to know you' tour of Europe US Secretary of State Condoleezza Rice stated that military action against Iran was not on the agenda 'at this moment in time'; in other words, it hadn't been ruled out. The European Union has made some progress in getting Tehran to rein in its nuclear programme and, in the light of the disaster in Iraq, the White House is now bound to think twice about undertaking such an armed occupation again. Those newly furbished air bases in Iraq are there for a reason, the launch-points for 'surgical' strikes using 'precision' weapons. However it is done, usurping a theocracy like Iran will be an even more bloody affair.

We predict that, for some time, Africa will remain the coup continent of the world, especially now that Latin America and The Gulf have settled down somewhat. But look out for coup reports from some of the nasty regimes that have sprung up in the aftermath of the fall of the Soviet empire. Byelorussia and Kazakhstan (and anywhere else ending in 'stan') are first-division candidates for coups.

Finally, we need to add any unsuspecting country suddenly discovering that it has strategic reserves of oil…

Appendix A:

Military *Coups D'état* By Country

'BT' = Breakthrough, 'Gdn' = Guardian, 'Veto' = Veto
Entries in bold have been described in the chapters indicated.
Names under 'Notes' are coup leaders unless otherwise indicated.

Country	Year	Type	Sponsor	Chap	Notes
Abu Dhabi	**1966**	**Gdn**	**UK**	**8**	**Sheikh Zayed replaces brother. [UAE]**
Afghanistan	1973	BT			Monarchy overthrown.
Afghanistan	1979	Veto	USSR		Russian-backed coup.
Albania	**1950**	**BT?**	**US, UK**	**3**	**CIA, MI6 backed military intervention.**
Algeria	**1961**	**Veto**		**3**	**"The Generals' Putsch"**
Algeria	**1991**	**Veto**		**3**	**Military moves the stop Islamic take-over in polls.**
Angola	1975	BT?	US, Cuba		
Argentina	**1943**	**Gdn**		**1**	**Military coup**
Argentina	**1945**	**Gdn**		**1**	**Military coup supported by Peron**
Argentina	**1955**	**Gdn**		**1**	**Juan Peron overthrown.**
Argentina	**1976**	**Veto**		**1**	**Evita Peron overthrown.**
Argentina	1987	Gdn			Coup attempt against Raul Alfonsin.
Benin	1963	Gdn			Gen. Christophe Soglo deposes Hubert Maga.
Benin	1967	Gdn			Group of young army officers depose Soglo (Dec)
Benin	1969	Gdn			In December the army takes power again.
Benin	1972	Gdn			Another army coup installs Lt Col Mathieu Kérékou.
Benin	1977	Gdn			50 Europeans led by Bob Denard attempt coup.
Benin	1988	Gdn			Military attempt to seize power again and fail.
Benin	1991	Gdn			May: failed coup attempt.
Benin	1992	Gdn			July 4: gov quells mutiny led by fr. member Pres. Guard.
Bolivia	1970	1	Gdn		Coup

Bolivia	1970	2	Gdn			Leftist counter-coup.
Bolivia	1980		Gdn			"Cocaine coup" government ruled until 1982.
Brazil	1964		Gdn			Gen Vernon Walters involved.
Burkina Faso	1987		Gdn			Blaise Compaoré
Burma	1988		Veto			Brig-Gen Sein Lwin imposes martial law.
Burma	2004		Gdn			Burmese junta sacks Prime Minister Khin Nyunt.
Burundi	1996		Gdn?			
Cambodia	1997		Gdn?			
Central African Empire	1982		Gdn?			
Central African Republic	2002		Gdn			
Chad	1990		Gdn			Idriss Déby
Chechenya	1994		Veto?	Russia		Russian-sponsored coup (failed).
Chile	**1970**		**Veto**	**US**	**6**	**Failed attempt 22 October.**
Chile	**1973**		**Veto**	**US**	**6**	
China	**1911**		**BT**		**1**	**"The Wuchang Uprising"**
Comoros	**1975**		**Gdn**	**France?**	**7**	**President Abdallah over-thrown.**
Comoros	**1978**		**Gdn**		**7**	**Teenage coup: Ali Saleh killed by Bob Denard**
Comoros	**1989**		**Gdn**		**7**	**Pres Ahmed Abdallah assas-sinated in a coup.**
Comoros	**1995**	**1**	**Gdn**		**7**	**Bob Denard leads another coup.**
Comoros	**1995**	**2**	**Gdn**	**France**	**7**	**French-backed count-er-coup.**
Comoros	**1999**		**Gdn**		**7**	**Col Azali Assoumani, army chief of staff, again.**
Comoros	**2000**		**Gdn**		**7**	**Coup-attempt foiled.**
Côte d'Ivoire	1999		Gdn			Gen. Robert Guei ousts Pres. Henri Konan Bedie.
Côte d'Ivoire	2002		Gdn			
Cuba	**1959**		**BT**	**USSR?**	**1**	**Castro overthrows Batista**
Cuba	1961		BT	US		"Bay of Pigs": Falied to stimu-late uprising.
Cyprus	1974		Gdn?			

Czechoslovakia	1948		BT?		
Dom. Republic	1962		Gdn		Overthrow of Juan Emilio Bosch Gaviño.
DR Congo	2004	1	Gdn		
DR Congo	2004	2	Gdn		
Ecuador	1808		Veto?		Spain falls to Napoleon.
Ecuador	1925		Gdn		
Ecuador	1931		Gdn		
Ecuador	1944		Gdn		
Ecuador	1947		Gdn		
Ecuador	**1963**		**Gdn**	**US**	**2**	**Small coup in Ecuador, not many dead.**
Ecuador	1972		Gdn		
Ecuador	1976		Gdn		
Ecuador	**2000**		**Gdn**		**2**	**"Green" coup of Gutiérrez and Lluco.**
Egypt	**1953**		**BT**		**1**	**King Farouk overthrown by Nasser.**
Eq. Guinea	**1972**		**Gdn**		**3, 9**	**Freddie Forsyth's coup: Dogs of War**
Eq. Guinea	**1979**		**Gdn**		**9**	**Teodoro Obiang Nguema Mbasogo**
Eq. Guinea	**1997**		**Gdn**	**Russia?**	**9**	**Severo Moto expelled.**
Eq. Guinea	**2002**		**Gdn**		**9**	**March attempt to o/t Mbasogo.**
Eq. Guinea	**2003**	**1**	**Gdn**		**9**	**October ditto.**
Eq. Guinea	**2003**	**2**	**Gdn**		**9**	**December ditto.**
Eq. Guinea	**2004**	**1**	**Gdn**	**Spain?**	**3, 9**	**Simon Mann's coup. Not a shot fired!**
Eq. Guinea	**2004**	**2**	**Gdn**		**9**	**July. Fake coup?**
Ethiopia	1974		BT		Monarchy overthrown.
Fiji	**1987**	**1**	**Veto**	**US**	**7**	**Rabuka 1 (Vernon Walters involved)**
Fiji	**1987**	**2**	**Veto**	**US?**	**7**	**Rabuka 2**
Fiji	**2000**		**Veto**		**7**	**Civilian coup of George Speight.**
Fiji	**2006**		**Gdn**		**7**	**Military coup of Commodore Frank Bainimarama**
France	**1799**		**BT**		**1**	**"Coup of 18 Brumaire" Bloodless**

Gambia, The	1981	Gdn		Coup attempt by leftist soldiers. SAS interdiction.
Gambia, The	1994	Gdn		Yahya Jammeh, Chairman of the Junta.
Gambia, The	2014	Gdn		Ex-pat plotters attempt overthrow of Jammeh.
Georgia	2004	Gdn		Bloodless
Germany	1923	Gdn?		"The Beer Hall Putsch"
Germany	**1944**	**Gdn**	**1**	**"The July Putsch" Attempt to assassinate Hitler.**
Ghana	1966	Gdn?		
Ghana	1972	Gdn		Bloodless
Ghana	1975	Gdn?		
Ghana	1981	Gdn?		
Ghana	2004	Gdn		Army coup plotters arrested.
Greece	1935	Gdn		
Greece	1967	Gdn?		
Greece	1973	Gdn?		Monarchy overthrown.
Grenada	1979	Gdn?		
Grenada	1983	Gdn?		
Guatemala	1954	Gdn	US	Operation BPSUCCESS.
Guinea	1984	Gdn		Lansana Conté
Guinea-Bissau	1980	Gdn		
Guinea-Bissau	2003	Gdn?		Bloodless
Guinea-Bissau	2004	Gdn		Army coup plotters kill General and Lt-Col.
Haiti	1991	Gdn		First coup attempt against Aristide.
Haiti	2001	Gdn		Coup attempt by Phillipe against Aristide.
Haiti	2004	Gdn		Successful coup against Aristide.
Honduras	1963	Gdn?		
Indonesia	1957	Gdn?	US	Colonels' Revolt (1957–1958)
Indonesia	1965	Gdn?		
Iran	**1953**	**Veto**	**UK/US** **3**	**Elected government replaced by Shah.**
Iraq	**1958**	**BT**	**8**	**Monarchy overthrown by Qasim.**

Iraq	1959		Gdn	US	8	CIA attempts to assassinate Qasim.
Iraq	1963	1	Gdn	US	8	Coup: Ba'ath Party takes over Iraq.
Iraq	1963	2	Gdn		8	Counter-coup: Ba'athists ejected.
Iraq	1968		Gdn	US	8	Coup finally establishes rule of the Ba'ath Party
Japan	1932		Gdn?			"The May 15th Incident"
Japan	1936		Gdn			"The February 26th Incident"
Kenya	1982		Gdn		6	Attempted coup by Odinga. Stopped at docks by BMcK.
Korea (South)	1961		Gdn?			
Korea (South)	1979	1	Gdn			26 Oct: KCIA assassinates Pres Kim Jea Kyu.
Korea (South)	1979	2	Gdn			Coup d'état of December 12th
Laos	1961		Gdn?			
Laos	1964		Gdn?			
Laos	1975		BT			Monarchy overthrown.
Lesotho	1998		Gdn			"Virtual coup"?
Libya	1969		BT			Colonel Qadhafi overthrows monarchy
Libya	1982		Veto?	US		Attempt to spark anti-Qadhafi coup.
Madagascar	1972		Gdn?			
Mauritania	1984		Gdn			Maaouya Ould Sid'Ahmed Taya
Mauritania	2003		Gdn			Army attempt to overthrow Taya.
Mauritania	2004		Gdn			Same army group as 2003.
Mauritania	2008		Gdn			Mohamed Ould Abdel Aziz overthrows Sidi Ould Cheikh Abdallahi.
Morocco	1971		BT			10 July army attempt to overthrow Hassan II
Nepal	2005		Veto			King uses army to overthrow elected government.
Niger	1996		Gdn?			Col. Mainassara wins power from Pres. Ousmane.
Nigeria	1966	1	Gdn			"Igbo" Coup January

Nigeria	1966 2	Gdn			Counter-coup July. Officers shot by NCOs.
Nigeria	1975	Gdn			Murtala Mohammed coup. (Sandhurst graduate.)
Nigeria	1976	Gdn			Col. B. Dimka's failed military coup.
Nigeria	1983	Gdn			Junta called Supreme Military Council set up
Nigeria	1985 1	Gdn			Maj Gen Ibrahim Babangida ousts Maj Gen Buhari.
Nigeria	1985 2	Gdn			Coup attempt against Maj Gen Ibrahim Babangida.
Nigeria	1990	Gdn			Maj Gideon Orkar overthrows Gen Ibrahim Babangida
Nigeria	1993	Gdn			Gen Sani Abacha takes power after elections cancelled
Nigeria	2004	Gdn			Coup plot investigated?
Oman	**1970**	**Gdn**	**UK**	**8**	**Sultan replaced by son, Sheikh Qabus.**
Pakistan	1977	Veto?			
Pakistan	1999	Gdn			Bloodless
Panama	1968	Gdn?			
Panama	1969	Gdn?			
Panama	1988	Gdn?	US		Failed US-sponsored coup against Noriega.
Panama	1989	Gdn			Bloodless coup by Maj Moises Giroldi.
Paraguay	1989	Gdn?			
Peru	1992	Gdn			Alberto Fujimori launches a self-coup in Peru
Philippines	2003	Gdn			
Poland	1926	Gdn?			Coup of Jozef Pilsudski
Portugal	1910	BT			Monarchy overthrown.
Portugal	**1974**	**BT**		**Intro**	**"The Carnation Revolution"**
Qatar	1995	Gdn			
Qatar	1996	Gdn			
Russia	1917 1	Veto?			"The February Revolution"
Russia	1917 2	BT			"The October Revolution"
Russia	1991	Gdn?			Failed coup attempt in the Soviet Union

Samoa (Western)	1887	Veto?			German residents stage a coup.
São Tomé e Príncipe	2003	Gdn			
Seychelles	**1977**	**Veto**		**7**	**4-5 June: Rene overthrows Mancham.**
Seychelles	**1978**	**Veto**		**7**	**April: Mancham attempts to overthrow Rene.**
Seychelles	**1979**	**Veto**	**RSA. Fr?**	**7**	**"Mad Mike" Hoare's 1st coup attempt.**
Seychelles	**1981**	**Veto**	**US**	**7**	**"Mad Mike" Hoare's 2nd coup attempt. (25 Nov.)**
Seychelles	**1982**	**Gdn**		**7**	**August SPDF mutiny put down by Tanzanian soldiers.**
Seychelles	**1986**	**Veto**	**US, UK**	**7**	**Op Distant Lash. Def Min Ogilvy Berlouis implicated.**
Seychelles	**1987**	**Veto**		**7**	**Coup attempt thwarted in Britain.**
Sierra Leone	**1992**	**Gdn**		**1**	
Sierra Leone	**1996**	**Gdn**		**2**	
Somalia	1969	Gdn?			
Spain	1936	Veto			Army seizes control of parts of Spain.
Spain	1981	Gdn			Failed coup led by Antonio Tejero
Sudan	**1964**	**Gdn?**		**6**	
Sudan	**1968**	**Gdn?**		**6**	
Sudan	1989	Gdn			Omar Hassan Ahmad al-Bashir
Sudan	2004	Gdn			24/9 Islamist coup plot foiled.
Syria	1961	Gdn			Following 28 Sep. coup, Syria splits from Egypt (UAR).
Syria	1963	Gdn			
Thailand	1947	Gdn?			
Thailand	1957	Gdn?			
Thailand	1970	Gdn?			
Thailand	2006	Veto			Military overthrow of civilian elected government
Thailand	2014	Veto			Prayuth Chan-ocha overthrows Niwatthamrong Boonsongpaisan.

Togo	1967	Gdn			Gnassingbé Eyadéma
Togo	2004	Gdn			11 soldiers held Benin 'wanted to overthrow Eyadema'.
Togo	2005	Gdn			Eyadema dies, his son has army make him head of state.
Tunisia	1987	Gdn			Zine El Abidine Ben Ali
Turkey	1922	BT			Monarchy abolished.
Turkey	**1960**	**Gdn**		**1**	
Turkey	**1971**	**Gdn**		**1**	
Turkey	**1980**	**Gdn**		**1**	
Turkey	**2016**	**Gdn**		**Intro**	**Coup attempt against Erdoğan government**
Uganda	**1971**	**Gdn**	**UK**	**6**	**Idi Amin put into power by the British**
Uganda	**1979**	**Gdn**	**UK**	**6**	**Idi Amin removed from power by the British**
Uruguay	1973	Gdn			President dissolves Parliament and heads coup
Vanuatu	**1980**	**Gdn?**		**7**	**Coup backed by Robert Jan Doorn?**
Vanuatu	**1997**	**Gdn?**		**7**	**Military coup in New Hebrides.**
Venezuela	**1998**	**Veto**	**US**	**2**	**Veto coup planned to block Chavez elctn.**
Venezuela	**2002**	**Veto**	**US**	**2**	**Failed coup to overthrow Hugo Chávez**
Venezuela	**2004**	**Veto**	**US**	**2**	**Colombian 'terrorists' arrested.**
Vietnam	1947	Gdn?			
Vietnam	1964	Gdn			Coup overthrowing Duong Van Minh
Yemen	1955	Gdn?			
Yemen	1967	Gdn?			
Yemen	1977	Gdn?			
Yemen	1978	Gdn?			
Yemen	2015	Veto?	Iran?		Mohammed Ali al-Houthi overthrows Abd Rabbuh Mansur Hadi.

Appendix B:
Military *Coups D'état* By Date

'BT' = Breakthrough, 'Gdn' = Guardian, 'Veto' = Veto
Entries in bold have been described in the chapters indicated.

Year		Country	Type	Sponsor	Chapter
1799		**France**	**BT**		**1**
1808		Ecuador	Veto?		
1887		Samoa (Western)	Veto?		
1910		Portugal	BT		
1911		**China**	**BT**		**1**
1917	1	Russia	Veto?		
1917	2	Russia	BT		
1922		Turkey	BT		
1923		Germany	Gdn?		
1925		Ecuador	Gdn		
1926		Poland	Gdn?		
1931		Ecuador	Gdn		
1932		Japan	Gdn?		
1935		Greece	Gdn		
1936		Japan	Gdn		
1936		Spain	Veto		
1943		**Argentina**	**Gdn**		**1**
1944		Ecuador	Gdn		
1944		**Germany**	**Gdn**		**1**
1945		**Argentina**	**Gdn**		**1**
1947		Ecuador	Gdn		
1947		Thailand	Gdn?		
1947		Vietnam	Gdn?		
1948		Czechoslovakia	BT?		

Year		Country	Type	Sponsor	Chapter
1950		**Albania**	**BT?**	US, UK	3
1953		**Egypt**	**BT**		1
1953		**Iran**	**Veto**	UK/US	3
1954		Guatemala	Gdn	US	
1955		**Argentina**	**Gdn**		1
1955		Yemen	Gdn?		
1957		Indonesia	Gdn?	US	
1957		Thailand	Gdn?		
1958		**Iraq**	**BT**		8
1959		**Cuba**	**BT**	USSR?	1
1959		**Iraq**	**Gdn**	US	8
1960		**Turkey**	**Gdn**		1
1961		**Algeria**	**Veto**		3
1961		Cuba	BT	US	
1961		Korea (South)	Gdn?		
1961		Laos	Gdn?		
1961		Syria	Gdn		
1962		Dominican Republic	Gdn		
1963		Benin	Gdn		
1963		**Ecuador**	**Gdn**	US	2
1963		Honduras	Gdn?		
1963	1	**Iraq**	**Gdn**	US	8
1963	2	**Iraq**	**Gdn**		8
1963		Syria	Gdn		
1964		Brazil	Gdn		
1964		Laos	Gdn?		
1964		**Sudan**	**Gdn?**		6
1964		Vietnam	Gdn		
1965		Indonesia	Gdn?		
1966		**Abu Dhabi**	**Gdn**	UK	8
1966		Ghana	Gdn?		
1966	1	Nigeria	Gdn		
1966	2	Nigeria	Gdn		
1967		Benin	Gdn		
1967		Greece	Gdn?		
1967		Togo	Gdn		
1967		Yemen	Gdn?		
1968		**Iraq**	**Gdn**	US	8

Year		Country	Type	Sponsor	Chapter
1968		Panama	Gdn?		
1968		**Sudan**	**Gdn?**		6
1969		Benin	Gdn		
1969		Libya	BT		
1969		Panama	Gdn?		
1969		Somalia	Gdn?		
1970	1	Bolivia	Gdn		
1970	2	Bolivia	Gdn		
1970		**Chile**	**Veto**	**US**	6
1970		**Oman**	**Gdn**	**UK**	8
1970		Thailand	Gdn?		
1971		Morocco	BT		
1971		**Turkey**	**Gdn**		1
1971		**Uganda**	**Gdn**	**UK**	6
1972		Benin	Gdn		
1972		Ecuador	Gdn		
1972		**Equatorial Guinea**	**Gdn**		3, 9
1972		Ghana	Gdn		
1972		Madagascar	Gdn?		
1973		Afghanistan	BT		
1973		**Chile**	**Veto**	**US**	6
1973		Greece	Gdn?		
1973		Uruguay	Gdn		
1974		Cyprus	Gdn?		
1974		Ethiopia	BT		
1974		**Portugal**	**BT**		Intro
1975		Angola	BT?	US, Cuba	
1975		**Comoros**	**Gdn**	**France?**	7
1975		Ghana	Gdn?		
1975		Laos	BT		
1975		Nigeria	Gdn		
1976		**Argentina**	**Veto**		1
1976		Ecuador	Gdn		
1976		Nigeria	Gdn		
1977		Benin	Gdn		
1977		Pakistan	Veto?		
1977		**Seychelles**	**Veto**		7
1977		Yemen	Gdn?		

Year		Country	Type	Sponsor	Chapter
1978		Comoros	Gdn		7
1978		Seychelles	Veto		7
1978		Yemen	Gdn?		
1979		Afghanistan	Veto	USSR	
1979		Equatorial Guinea	Gdn		9
1979		Grenada	Gdn?		
1979	1	Korea (South)	Gdn		
1979	2	Korea (South)	Gdn		
1979		Seychelles	Veto	RSA/Fr?	7
1979		Uganda	Gdn	UK	6
1980		Bolivia	Gdn		
1980		Guinea-Bissau	Gdn		
1980		Turkey	Gdn		1
1980		Vanuatu	Gdn?		7
1981		Gambia, The	Gdn		
1981		Ghana	Gdn?		
1981		Seychelles	Veto	US	7
1981		Spain	Gdn		
1982		Central African Empire	Gdn?		
1982		Kenya	Gdn		6
1982		Libya	Veto?	US	
1982		Seychelles	Gdn		7
1983		Grenada	Gdn?		
1983		Nigeria	Gdn		
1984		Guinea	Gdn		
1984		Mauritania	Gdn		
1985	1	Nigeria	Gdn		
1985	2	Nigeria	Gdn		
1986		Seychelles	Veto	US, UK	7
1987		Argentina	Gdn		
1987		Burkina Faso	Gdn		
1987	1	Fiji	Veto	US	7
1987	2	Fiji	Veto	US?	7
1987		Seychelles	Veto		7
1987		Tunisia	Gdn		
1988		Benin	Gdn		
1988		Burma	Veto		
1988		Panama	Gdn?	US	

Year		Country	Type	Sponsor	Chapter
1989		**Comoros**	**Gdn**		7
1989		Panama	Gdn		
1989		Paraguay	Gdn?		
1989		Sudan	Gdn		
1990		Chad	Gdn		
1990		Nigeria	Gdn		
1991		**Algeria**	**Veto**		3
1991		Benin	Gdn		
1991		Haiti	Gdn		
1991		Russia	Gdn?		
1992		Benin	Gdn		
1992		Peru	Gdn		
1992		**Sierra Leone**	**Gdn**		1
1993		Nigeria	Gdn		
1994		Chechenya	Veto?	Russia	
1994	**Intro**	**Gambia, The**	**Gdn**		
1995	**1**	**Comoros**	**Gdn**		7
1995	**2**	**Comoros**	**Gdn**	**France**	7
1995		Qatar	Gdn		
1996		Burundi	Gdn?		
1996		Niger	Gdn?		
1996		Qatar	Gdn		
1996		**Sierra Leone**	**Gdn**		2
1997		Cambodia	Gdn?		
1997		**Equatorial Guinea**	**Gdn**	**Russia?**	9
1997		**Vanuatu**	**Gdn?**		7
1998		Lesotho	Gdn		
1998		**Venezuela**	**Veto**	**US**	2
1999		**Comoros**	**Gdn**		7
1999		Côte d'Ivoire	Gdn		
1999		Pakistan	Gdn		
2000		**Comoros**	**Gdn**		7
2000		**Ecuador**	**Gdn**		2
2000		**Fiji**	**Veto**		7
2001		Haiti	Gdn		
2002		Central African Republic	Gdn		
2002		Côte d'Ivoire	Gdn		

Year		Country	Type	Sponsor	Chapter
2002		Equatorial Guinea	Gdn		9
2002		Venezuela	Veto	US	2
2003	1	Equatorial Guinea	Gdn		9
2003	2	Equatorial Guinea	Gdn		9
2003		Guinea-Bissau	Gdn?		
2003		Mauritania	Gdn		
2003		Philippines	Gdn		
2003		São Tomé e Príncipe	Gdn		
2004		Burma	Gdn		
2004	1	DR Congo	Gdn		
2004	2	DR Congo	Gdn		
2004	1	Equatorial Guinea	Gdn	Spain?	3, 9
2004	2	Equatorial Guinea	Gdn		9
2004		Georgia	Gdn		
2004		Ghana	Gdn		
2004		Guinea-Bissau	Gdn		
2004		Haiti	Gdn		
2004		Mauritania	Gdn		
2004		Nigeria	Gdn		
2004		Sudan	Gdn		
2004		Togo	Gdn		
2004		Venezuela	Veto	US	2
2005		Togo	Gdn		
2005		Nepal	Veto		
2006		Thailand	Veto		
2006		Fiji	Gdn		
2008		Mauritania	Gdn		
2014		Thailand	Veto		
2015		Yemen	Veto		
2016		Turkey	Gdn		Intro.
2014		The Gambia	Gdn		Intro.

Notes

1   Michael Moore: *Stupid White Men... and Other Sorry Excuses for the State of the Nation!* Penguin Books, London, 2001, 2002.

2   William C. Kimberling, Deputy Director, Federal Election Commission Office of Election Administration: *The Electoral College* 2003 at http://www.fec.gov/pdf/eleccoll.pdf.

3   Jessica Cutler: 'Senator Sacked Me Over Tales of Congress', the *Guardian* (London), 2 June 2004.

4   *Merriam-Webster Collegiate Dictionary.*

5   Edward Luttwak: *Coup d'Etat: A Practical Handbook*, Allen Lane The Penguin Press, London, 1968, 1980.

6   John Tirman: *Spoils of War: The Human Cost of America's Arms Trade*, Free Press, New York, 1997.

7   For more information about this grim period of Argentine history, visit the Vanished Gallery at http://www.yendor.com/vanished/.

8   Edward Luttwak.

9   Eddie Dean and Stan Ritova: *Rabuka: No Other Way*, The Marketing Team International Ltd, Fiji, 1988.

10   Will Scully: *Once a Pilgrim*, Headline, London, 1998.

11   Project Underground. Drillbits & Tailings: June 7, 1998. URL: www.moles.org/ProjectUnderground/drillbits/980607/98060704.html.

12   Nowa Omoigui: *The Orkar Failed Coup of April 22, 1990*, 21 Jun 2002. (Quoted in.) URL: www.waado.org/NigerDelta/Nigeria_Facts/MilitaryRule/Omoigui/OrkarCoup1990-PartOne.html.

13   Marta Harnecker: *Interview with Hugo Chávez* (trans. Alejandro Palavecino and Susan Nerberg), October 2002. ZNet URL: http://www.zmag.org/venezuela_watch.cfm.

14   Philip Agee: *Inside the Company: CIA Diary*, Bantam Books, New York, 1975. (Now difficult to get hold of; try a library.)

15   William Blum: *Killing Hope*, Common Courage Press, Monroe, Maine, 1995, 2004.

16 William Blum.

17 Narco News. URL: www.narconews.com/Issue31/article850.html.

18 US Department of State: *Ecuador Country Report on Human Rights Practices for 1998*. Released by the Bureau of Democracy, Human Rights, and Labor, February 26, 1999. URL: www.state.gov/www/global/human_rights/1998_hrp_report/ecuador.html.

19 The National Security Archive at George Washington University, Washington DC: http://www.gwu.edu/~nsarchiv/.

20 CIA: *'Zendebad, Shah!'*: The Central Intelligence Agency and the Fall of Iranian Prime Minister Mohammed Mossadeq, August 1953, Top Secret Draft History, History Staff, Central Intelligence Agency, June 1998. National Security Archive: http://www.gwu.edu/~nsarchiv/NSAEBB/NSAEBB126/iran980600.pdf.

21 Kim Philby: *My Silent War*, MacGibbon & Kee, London, 1968, Grove Press, New York, 1968.

22 Dr Donald Wilber: *CIA Clandestine Service History, Overthrow of Premier Mossadeq of Iran, November 1952–August 1953*, March 1954. http://www.gwu.edu/~nsarchiv/NSAEBB/NSAEBB28/index.html#documents

23 Kim Philby.

24 Dean Acheson: *Present at the Creation: My Years in the State Department*, W. W. Norton & Company, New York, 1969, 1987.

25 Dr Donald Wilber: Appendix A, p. 7.

26 C. M. Woodhouse: *Something Ventured*, Granada, London, 1982.

27 Dr Donald Wilber: http://www.gwu.edu/~nsarchiv/NSAEBB/NSAEBB28/index.html#documents.

28 Dr Donald Wilber.

29 Dr Donald Wilber.

30 CIA: *'Zendebad, Shah!'*: The Central Intelligence Agency and the Fall of Iranian Prime Minister Mohammed Mossadeq.

31 The Zahedi family photograph album can be found at http://homepage.mac.com/zahedi/FAMILY/PhotoAlbum3.html.

32 Anthony Clayton: *The Wars of French Decolonization*, Longman, London, 1994, 1998.

33 Directed by Gillo Pontecorvo, the 1967 film *The Battle of Algiers* is a remarkable documentary-style insight into what was happening in the city in the late-1950s. It is still available today on VHS and DVD formats.

34 Alistair Horne: *A Savage War of Peace*, Macmillan, London, 1977, 1987.

35 Alistair Horne.

36 Frederick Forsyth: *The Day of the Jackal*, G. K. Hall, London, 1971, 1974.

37 Frederick Forsyth: *The Dogs of War*, Arrow, London, 1974, 1996.

38 'Rupert': Slightly derogatory term among the ranks for a British Army officer.

39 Lt-Col Charles J. Dunlap Jr: *The Origins of the American Military Coup of 2012, Parameters*, Winter 1992–93, pp. 2–20, http://carlisle-www.army.mil/usawc/Parameters/1992/dunlap.htm

40 Ross Anderson: *A5 – The GSM Encryption Algorithm*, 17 June 1994. Newsgroup post: www.chem.leeds.ac.uk/ICAMS/people/jon/a5.html.

41 Ross Anderson.

42 Judy Siegel-Itzkovich and Damian Carrington: 'GSM phone encryption "can be cracked"', *New Scientist*, 4 September 2003.

43 Simon Singh: *The Code Book*, Fourth Estate, London, 2000.

44 CIA *Operating Guidance Cable on Coup Plotting*, 16 October 1970. National Security Archive: www.gwu.edu/~nsarchiv/NSAEBB/NSAEBB8/ch05-01.htm.

45 CIA *Report on Chilean Task Force Activities*, 18 November 1970. National Security Archive: www.gwu.edu/~nsarchiv/NSAEBB/NSAEBB8/ch01-01.htm.

46 Declassified cable from CIA station, Santiago to CIA Headquarters, 18 October 1970. National Security Archive: www.gwu.edu/~nsarchiv/NSAEBB/NSAEBB8/ch27-01.htm.

47 Declassified cable from CIA Headquarters to CIA station, Santiago, 18 October 1970. National Security Archive: www.gwu.edu/~nsarchiv/NSAEBB/NSAEBB8/ch29-01.htm.

48 The National Security Archive at George Washington University: www.gwu.edu/~nsarchiv/.

49 Patrick Ryan: *Department of Defense, US Military Group, Chile, Situation Report #2*, 1 October 1973. National Security Archive, URL: http://www.gwu.edu/~nsarchiv/NSAEBB/NSAEBB8/ch21-01.htm.

50 Patricia Verdugo: *Interferencia Secreta*, Sudamericana, October 1998.

51 Patrick Ryan.

52 Hernan C. Quezada: *The Carlos Prats Case: an Historic Trial*, *Memoria y Justicia* web-site. URL: www.memoriayjusticia.cl/english/en_focus-carlosprats.htm.

53 Patrick Ryan.

54 Jonathan Franklin: 'Chile identifies 35,000 victims of Pinochet', the *Guardian*, London, 15 November 2004.

55 Robert Scherrer: *FBI Report on Operation Condor*, 28 September 1976. URL: www.gwu.edu/~nsarchiv/NSAEBB/NSAEBB8/ch23-01.htm.

56 C. M. Woodhouse.

57 *Private Eye* Magazine, London, 27 April 1979.

58 Richard Dowden: 'Revealed: how Israel helped Amin to take power', *The Independent*, London, 17 August 2003. Although Dowden may have been first to quote the Slater cable, he was over twenty years late with his 'revelation' about Israeli involvement in the coup. That, along with MI6's very active role, was first published by Jonathan Bloch and Patrick Fitzgerald in their 1983 book.

59 Chapman Pincher: *The Truth About Dirty Tricks*, Sidgwick & Jackson, London, 1991.

60 Jonathan Bloch and Patrick Fitzgerald: *British Intelligence and Covert Action*, Brandon Books, London, 1983.

61 BBC Radio 4 p.m. Programme Friday, 15 August, 2003.

62 Richard Tomlinson: *The Big Breach: From Top Secret to Maximum Security*, Cutting Edge Books, London, 2001. Chapter 4 of Tomlinson's account of his career as an SIS officer includes a colourful account of his time at Fort Monkton.

63 Eric Margolis: 'The Dogs of War', *The Toronto Sun*, 10 October 1995.

64 Eric Micheletti: *French Special Forces*, Histoire & Collections, Paris, 1999.

65 David Lea: *Melanesian Land Tenure in a Contemporary and Philosophical Context*, University Press of America, 1997.

66 Rob Kay: *Fiji Guide: The Book*. Available on-line. URL: www.fijiguide.com/Book/.

67 Ahmed Ali: *Fiji*: 'The politics of a plural society', in Ahmed Ali and Ron Crocombe (eds), *Politics of Melanesia*. Suva: Institute of Pacific Studies, University of the South Pacific, 1982.

68 Eddie Dean with Stan Ritova.

69 Eddie Dean with Stan Ritova.

70 Eddie Dean with Stan Ritova.

71 Eddie Dean with Stan Ritova.

72 Eddie Dean with Stan Ritova.

73 Glenn Alcalay: 'The not-so-pacific Pacific', *Cultural Survival Quarterly*, Issue 11.3, September 1987.

74 Glenn Alcalay.

75 Eddie Dean with Stan Ritova.

76 Ken Connor: *Ghost Force: The Secret History of the SAS*, Weidenfeld & Nicholson, London, 1998.

77 Wilfred Thesiger: *Arabian Sands*, Penguin Books, London, 1984.

78 Ken Connor.

79 Jonathan Bloch and Patrick Fitzgerald.

80 William Blum.

81 Richard Sale: *Saddam key in early CIA plot*, report filed by UPI Intelligence Correspondent, published 4/10/2003. URL: www.upi.com/view.cfm?StoryID=20030410-070214-6557r.

82 Adel Darwish and Gregory Alexander: *Unholy Babylon: The Secret History of Saddam's War*, Diane Publishing Co., New York, 1991.

83 Richard Sale.

84 Adel Darwish and Gregory Alexander.

85 Bob Woodward: *Plan of Attack*, Simon & Schuster, New York and London, 2004.

86 Frederick Forsyth: *The Dogs of War*. Still in print, this has been described as a 'textbook for *coups d'état*', but keep in mind that the real-life original version failed.

87 Frederick Forsyth: *The Biafra Story: Making of an African Legend*, Penguin, London, 1969, Pen & Sword Books / Leo Cooper, London, 2001.

88 Frederick Forsyth: *The Day of the Jackal*.

89 Anthony Divall also played a hand in the Uganda 1971 coup. See Chapter 6.

90 Frederick Forsyth: *The Dogs of War*.

91 US Department of State: *Background Note: Equatorial Guinea*, 10 June 2004. URL: www.state.gov/r/pa/ei/bgn/7221.htm.

92 Amnesty International: *Equatorial Guinea: Further information – Fear of torture /possible prisoners of conscience and new concern: death penalty*, 7 June 2002. URL: http://web.amnesty.org/library/index/ENGAFR240082002.

93 Amnesty International: *Equatorial Guinea: Further Information on Torture/Health concern/Fear for Safety*, 23 March 2004. URL: http://web.amnesty.org/library/index/ENGAFR240052004.

94 US Department of State: *Background Note: Equatorial Guinea*, 10 June 2004. URL: www.state.gov/r/pa/ei/bgn/7221.htm.

95 Joaquín Alogo: *Mis relaciones políticas con el Presidente Obiang Nguema Mbasogo* (My Political Relations with President Obiang Nguema Mbasogo). Afrol.com, 1997. URL: http://www.afrol.com/html/es/Paises/Guinea_Ecuatorial/documentos/alogo.htm.

96 United States Senate Permanent Subcommittee on Investigations. Minority Report on *Money Laundering and Foreign Corruption: Enforcement and Effectiveness of The Patriot Act (Case Study Involving Riggs Bank)*. 15 July 2004. URL: http://www.senate.gov/~gov_affairs/022801_psi_case_contents.htm.

97 United States Senate Permanent Subcommittee on Investigations. Minority Report on *Money Laundering and Foreign Corruption: Enforcement and Effectiveness of The Patriot Act (Case Study Involving Riggs Bank)*. 15 July 2004. URL: http://www.senate.gov/~gov_affairs/022801_psi_case_contents.htm.

98 Santos Pascal Bikomo: The Guinea Connection. Afrol.com, 24 July 1997. URL: http://www.afrol.com/html/Countries/Equatorial_Guinea/documents/guinea_connection.htm (English translation). URL: http://www.afrol.com/html/es/Paises/Guinea_Ecuatorial/documentos/guinea_conexion_97.htm (Spanish original). Bikomo was formerly Equatorial Guinea's Minister of Information.

99 United States Senate Permanent Subcommittee on Investigations. Minority Report on *Money Laundering and Foreign Corruption: Enforcement and Effectiveness of The Patriot Act (Case Study Involving Riggs Bank)*. 15 July 2004. URL: http://www.senate.gov/~gov_affairs/022801_psi_case_contents.htm.

100 Organisation for Economic Co-operation and Development: *Financial Action Task Force on Money Laundering*. URL: http://www1.oecd.org/fatf/NCCT_en.htm#List.

101 Brendan Seery: 'Gun-running that Zim wants to keep secret?' *The Star* (South Africa), 8 May 2004.

102 Interview with Spanish radio station *Onda Cero*, 9 March 2004.

103 Antony Barnett and Patrick Smith: 'Did African coup begin in Chelsea?', *The Observer*, 14 March 2004.

104 Stephen T. Hosmer: *Operations Against Enemy Leaders*, Rand Corporation, 2001. Available free at: www.rand.org/publications/MR/MR1385/.

105 Stephen T. Hosmer.

106 Details of this plot can be found in a Secret Intelligence Service (MI6) report available at: www.mathaba.net/data/sis/transcript.shtml.

107 Désiré Bouterse was later convicted in The Netherlands on drugs-related charges.

Index

221